Salesforce® Service Cloud® FOR DUMMIES®

A Wiley Brand

by Jon Paz and TJ Kelley

FOR DUMMIES®

A Wiley Brand

Salesforce® Service Cloud® For Dummies®

Published by: **John Wiley & Sons, Inc.,** 111 River Street, Hoboken, NJ 07030-5774, www.wiley.com

Copyright © 2015 by John Wiley & Sons, Inc., Hoboken, New Jersey

Published simultaneously in Canada

For general information on our other products and services, please contact our Customer Care Department within the U.S. at 877-762-2974, outside the U.S. at 317-572-3993, or fax 317-572-4002. For technical support, please visit www.wiley.com/techsupport.

Wiley publishes in a variety of print and electronic formats and by print-on-demand. Some material included with standard print versions of this book may not be included in e-books or in print-on-demand. If this book refers to media such as a CD or DVD that is not included in the version you purchased, you may download this material at http://booksupport.wiley.com. For more information about Wiley products, visit www.wiley.com.

Library of Congress Control Number: 20149557811

ISBN 978-1-119-01068-5 (pbk); ISBN 978-1-119-01069-2 (ebk); ISBN 978-1-119-01070-8 (ebk)

Manufactured in the United States of America

10 9 8 7 6 5 4 3 2 1

Contents at a Glance

Introduction 1

Part I: Getting Started with Salesforce Service Cloud...... 5
Chapter 1: Solving Business Challenges with Service Cloud...7
Chapter 2: Navigating Service Cloud...15
Chapter 3: Personalizing Service Cloud...35

Part II: Handling Customer Issues 49
Chapter 4: Creating and Managing Cases...51
Chapter 5: Solving Cases Efficiently 69
Chapter 6: Collaborating on Cases 95

Part III: Improving Your Service Organization's Effectiveness 111
Chapter 7: Capturing Cases in a Multi-Channel World...113
Chapter 8: Managing a Contact Center with Service Cloud Console 131
Chapter 9: Implementing the Service Cloud Console...139

Part IV: Leveraging Your Organizational Knowledge ... 151
Chapter 10: Planning Your Knowledge Implementation..153
Chapter 11: Setting Up Salesforce Knowledge 163
Chapter 12: Managing and Categorizing Articles...181

Part V: Recognizing When It Takes a Community 203
Chapter 13: Understanding Communities...205
Chapter 14: Creating a Community 215
Chapter 15: Optimizing Your Community 231

Part VI: Measuring Contact Center Performance......... 253
Chapter 16: Understanding Key Salesforce Contact Center Reports....................................255
Chapter 17: Customizing Reports 263
Chapter 18: Building Contact Center Dashboards..271

Part VII: Designing Your Service Solution with Force.com 287

Chapter 19: Understanding the Configuration for Your Business 289
Chapter 20: Customizing Service Cloud with Force.com 305
Chapter 21: Extending beyond Service Cloud 325

Part VIII: The Part of Tens 333

Chapter 22: Ten Questions to Ask Before Implementing Knowledge 335
Chapter 23: Ten Bad Habits to Leave with Your Legacy System 341

Index 347

Table of Contents

Introduction *1*

About This Book 1
Foolish Assumptions 2
Icons Used in This Book 2
Beyond the Book 3
Where to Go from Here 3

Part I: Getting Started with Salesforce Service Cloud 5

Chapter 1: Solving Business Challenges with Service Cloud 7

Keeping Your Customers Happy 8
Measuring the Health of Your Business 9
Establishing a Single Source of Truth 10
Collaborating with Your Coworkers 10
Getting the Data You Need When and Where You Need It 11
Building Brand Loyalists 11
Reducing customer frustration 12
Giving your customers options 12
Creating connections with your customers 12
Improving the quality of agent interactions 13
Expediting the service process 13

Chapter 2: Navigating Service Cloud 15

Choosing the Right Edition of Service Cloud for Your Business 15
Logging In to Service Cloud 16
Open sesame: Setting up a password 16
I call do-over!: Resetting your password 17
Logging in and authenticating 18
Navigating the Home Page 19
Using the sidebar and custom links 20
Using the Chatter feed 24
Managing My Tasks and Calendar 25
Visualizing analytics with Dashboard snapshots 27
Getting Started with Records 28
Creating new records 28
Editing or deleting records 30
Getting the most out of the Detail page 32
Finding the Help and Setup Menu 33

Chapter 3: Personalizing Service Cloud..........................35

Understanding the My Settings Page 35
Updating Your Personal Information 37
Modifying your user record...38
Changing your password 38
Creating personal groups 39
Changing your display..40
Granting others login access...42
Using Calendar sharing 43
Reminding and alerting yourself......................................44
Customizing your email settings......................................45
Working with Salesforce Remotely and Offline.........................46
Changing Chatter Preferences 46

Part II: Handling Customer Issues................................ 49

Chapter 4: Creating and Managing Cases........................51

Opening Cases for Customers...52
Understanding the case record..53
Identifying and qualifying your customers............................56
Managing Your Cases...57
Capturing case details...57
Researching and resolving the issue..................................59
Communicating the solution 60
Ensuring consistency with email templates............................61
Closing a Case 65

Chapter 5: Solving Cases Efficiently..........................69

Managing Cases with Views and Queues..................................69
Creating a view...70
Managing your organization's views...................................75
Creating a case queue 78
Using Automation to Your Advantage 79
Assigning cases within your organization.............................80
Creating assignment rules 80
Setting up automatic responses for your organization 82
Defining auto-response rules...83
Researching the Issue 84
Investigating Content 85
Solving cases with suggested solutions...............................89
Using Knowledge..91

Chapter 6: Collaborating on Cases 95

Getting Assistance with Case Teams 96
    Defining case team roles and access 96
    Setting up case teams 97
    Using predefined case teams 98
    Adding team members to your case 99
Escalating a Case 100
    Reassigning a case 101
    Creating escalation rules by criteria 102
    Setting up escalation actions 103
Leveraging Chatter on Cases 105
    Tapping into internal knowledge 106
    Communicating with customers and partners 109

Part III: Improving Your Service Organization's Effectiveness *111*

Chapter 7: Capturing Cases in a Multi-Channel World 113

Offering Multiple Service Channels 114
Setting Up Web-to-Case 114
    Recognizing the limitations of Web-to-Case 115
    Preparing to enable Web-to-Case 116
    Enabling Web-to-Case 116
Implementing Email-to-Case 117
Discovering Computer Telephony Integration 120
Implementing Live Agent Chat 121
    Enabling Live Agent 121
    Adding Live Agent Users 122
    Granting Live Agent users the right permissions 122
    Adding Live Agent skills 124
    Assigning Live Agent configurations 124
    Creating Live Agent chat buttons and deployments 125
    Setting up live chat transcripts and visitors 127
    Planning a pre-chat form 129
    Reporting on Live Agent sessions 129
Discovering Social Channels 130

Chapter 8: Managing a Contact Center with Service Cloud Console 131

Using the Service Cloud Console 132
Saving Time with Keyboard Shortcuts 134
Getting Familiar with Service Cloud Console Terms 136
Preparing Your Strategy for the Console 137

Chapter 9: Implementing the Service Cloud Console **139**

Understanding the Service Cloud Console...140
Enabling the Highlights Panel 141
Adding an App for the Service Cloud Console......................................142
Building Interaction Logs 144
Enabling interaction logs for the console.....................................144
Customizing and assigning interaction logs................................145
Choosing a List Display for the Console..147
Selecting Users to Work in the Console...149

Part IV: Leveraging Your Organizational Knowledge.... 151

Chapter 10: Planning Your Knowledge Implementation **153**

Understanding Basic Knowledge Terminology......................................154
Categorizing and Adding Article Types 156
Displaying Articles and Layouts 158
Thinking about Approval Processes 159
Designating Article Access and Permissions 159

Chapter 11: Setting Up Salesforce Knowledge **163**

Segmenting Knowledge with Article Types...164
Building article types 165
Identifying article type properties and fields.............................166
Modifying article-type layouts and templates............................168
Designating article access 171
Turning on Salesforce Knowledge..172
Enabling Knowledge 172
Opening up Knowledge access to users and public groups.........173
Using Cases with the Knowledge Base 177
Suggesting articles on new cases...177
Enabling article submission upon case closure...........................178
Attaching articles to a case 179

Chapter 12: Managing and Categorizing Articles **181**

Managing Articles...182
Creating a draft article 184
Assigning articles and sending them for approval......................186
Publishing articles 187
Searching for articles 188
Updating and archiving articles...190
Categorizing Articles into Data Categories 193
Planning your category groups and hierarchy 194
Setting up data categories 194
Editing default data category visibility settings 197

Automating Article Management..199
    Setting up an approval process for article
        review and publication...200
    Creating workflow rules to manage articles....................202

Part V: Recognizing When It Takes a Community........ 203

Chapter 13: Understanding Communities.........................205
Distinguishing Use Cases for Community Types....................205
    Determining your community type 207
    Exploring customer communities...................................207
    Understanding partner communities 208
Comparing Communities with s 209
    Identifying what has carried over from Portals..............209
    Getting familiar with what's new in Communities..........210
Glimpsing a Customer Community for New Members 212

Chapter 14: Creating a Community 215
Planning Your Community 215
Setting Up Communities 216
    Enabling Salesforce Communities in your organization...............216
    Selecting a domain name for your community 217
Creating Your Community..218
    Turning on the Global Header for Communities............219
    Understanding Communities statuses 221
Adding Members to Your Community......................................222
    Adding members using profiles 222
    Adding members with permission sets...........................223
    Creating partner and customer users 225
Adding Tabs to Your Community...226
    Displaying tabs in your community................................226
    Choosing a landing tab for your community members 227
    Enabling cases in your community.................................229
Previewing Your Community 229

Chapter 15: Optimizing Your Community 231
Customizing and Branding Your Communities 231
    Customizing your community's look and feel...............232
    Enhancing the login page for your community...............235
    Selecting email templates and settings for your community.......238
Publishing and Governing Your Communities........................240
    Publishing your community and welcoming members 240
    Selecting a Community Manager 241
    Leveraging the Community Engagement Console...........242

Utilizing Communities analytics 244
Moderating your community... 246
Educating your users about communities.......................... 247
Integrating your community.. 249

Part VI: Measuring Contact Center Performance 253

Chapter 16: Understanding Key Salesforce Contact Center Reports 255

Navigating the Reports Home Page..................................... 255
Leveraging Common Support Reports.................................. 257
Agent Case Load by Type 257
Average Age of Open Cases 258
Average Case Age by Agent (Closed) 260
Popular Knowledge Articles 261
Top Articles Associated with Cases 261

Chapter 17: Customizing Reports............................... 263

Building a Report from Scratch 263
Modifying Existing Reports 266
Sifting through Reports... 267
Using the Drill Down feature 267
Setting your report options 268
Clearing filters 268
Showing and Hiding Details... 268

Chapter 18: Building Contact Center Dashboards 271

Planning for Dashboards 271
Understanding how source reports feed components ... 272
Discovering the component options 272
Planning a purpose for each component....................... 274
Creating a Dashboard for Your Contact Center 275
Editing dashboard properties 278
Creating a component 279
Modifying the layout... 282
Organizing Your Dashboards... 283
Building dashboard folders 283
Defining dashboard access.. 283

Part VII: Designing Your Service Solution with Force.com 287

Chapter 19: Understanding the Configuration for Your Business . . . 289

Looking at Administration Setup 290
    Planning configuration for success 290
Viewing Your Company Profile 291
    Updating your company information 291
    Setting your organization's business hours and holidays 292
Building the Role Hierarchy 294
Defining Your Sharing Model 296
    Setting organization-wide defaults 296
    Creating groups 297
    Allowing further access with sharing rules 298
Creating and Managing Profiles 299
    Reviewing standard Service Cloud profiles 299
    Creating custom profiles 300
Setting Up Users in Your Organization 302
Reviewing Other Security Controls 303
    Defining field-level security 303

Chapter 20: Customizing Service Cloud with Force.com 305

Building and Editing Fields 306
    Creating new fields 307
    Updating existing fields 308
Customizing Page Layouts 309
    Modifying a page layout 309
    Assigning layouts to profiles 311
Managing Multiple Case-Management Processes 312
Leveraging Record Types 313
    Creating record types 314
    Viewing and editing record types 315
    Defining record-type access 316
    Choosing a record type when creating New records 316
Workflow and Validation Rules 317
    Understanding when to use workflow and validation rules 318
    Creating a workflow rule 318
    Creating a validation rule 321

Chapter 21: Extending beyond Service Cloud 325

Defining the AppExchange Platform 326
    Accessing the AppExchange 326
    Browsing the AppExchange 326
    Preparing to install AppExchange apps 329

Deploying Apps for Your Company...329
Testing your AppExchange apps 331

Part VIII: The Part of Tens.................................. 333

Chapter 22: Ten Questions to Ask Before Implementing
Knowledge...335

How Much Control Does Your Organization Need over
the Article Lifecycle? 336
Would Your Organization Like to Present Articles to Agents
in Various Formats?..336
Does Your Organization Need to Target Particular Audiences
with Certain Types of Articles?..336
Will Your Organization Need to Access Detailed Reports
and Metrics about Support Articles?...337
Does Your Organization Leverage Multiple Channels for Support? 337
Do Your Agents Need to Be Able to Rate Articles? 337
Should Your Agents Be Able to Find, Create, and Send Articles? 338
Do Your Agents Need to Collaborate on Support Articles
Using Chatter? 338
Do Your Agents Need Robust Search Functionality
to Locate Articles? 338
Do Your Agents Use the Service Console View?....................................339

Chapter 23: Ten Bad Habits to Leave with
Your Legacy System..341

Using Microsoft Outlook Folders for Everything...................................342
Reopening Cases...342
Recreating a Legacy System to Relieve Your Separation Anxiety.........342
Using Email Too Much 343
Data Quality: Do You Really Need All These Fields?..............................343
Users Don't Always Know Best 344
Don't Go Chasing Waterfall 344
It Doesn't End at Go-Live 345
Not Leveraging a Certified Administrator 345
Embracing the Change...346

Index... 347

Introduction

. . . .

*W*elcome to *Salesforce Service Cloud For Dummies,* a guide for long-time or new users of Service Cloud, a customer service application released by Salesforce that runs in the cloud. For our purposes, running in the cloud means that you get login credentials (a username and password) and use them to access your database from wherever you want. Think of it like Netflix or Gmail. No matter where you are, what time of day it is, or which device you choose to use, you can open your application and continue working from where you left off. The Service Cloud is one of the fastest-growing segments of Salesforce's business, helping customers worldwide address *their* customers' problems and needs in real-time, and this book sets out to cover it in an organized and succinct way.

About This Book

This book is for anyone looking to improve their customer service experience. Anyone can read this book, really, but it's intended for service reps, administrators, call center executives, or Salesforce enthusiasts who want an inside look at the features and capabilities of Service Cloud. It shows you how you can transform your customer care business with clicks not code, from anywhere, at anytime, in a matter of hours or days instead of months or years.

This book also takes an inside look at Communities and Salesforce Knowledge, two major and exciting new features that remain elusive to many.

Use this book to better support your customers, to collaborate with your teams, and to get the insights you need to improve your customer service business:

- ✔ **Faster support:** Collaborate with Chatter, streamline your view with the console, and serve your customers from anywhere with the mobile app.
- ✔ **Intelligent customer service:** Search your knowledge base for the answers your customers need.

✔ **Multichannel support:** Let your customers decide how they want to be supported. Chat with Live Agent, support customers on social media channels on any device, or give them the tools to help themselves with Communities.

✔ **Personalized service:** Use Service Cloud to get a complete view of your customer and always have their information at your fingertips.

Note: Not every portion of this book applies to your edition of Salesforce. Service Cloud has a number of editions, including Unlimited, Enterprise, and Professional, each with its own features and pricing. There are also certain topics we cover that require feature licenses, which come at a cost. We make sure to point these out where they appear.

Within this book, you may note that some web addresses break across two lines of text. If you're reading this book in print and want to visit one of these web pages, simply key in the web address exactly as it's noted in the text, pretending as though the line break doesn't exist. If you're reading this as an e-book, you've got it easy — just click the web address to be taken directly to the web page.

Foolish Assumptions

In writing this book, we made a few assumptions about you:

✔ You have a computer with internet access. (Don't laugh.)

✔ You're working in customer service and have customers or you at least want to join the field.

✔ You sell a product or service, or otherwise just possess a minimal level of business experience.

✔ You know that Salesforce is a database. If you didn't, now you do.

✔ You have access to an instance of Service Cloud to follow our (flawless) instruction.

Icons Used in This Book

As you read this book, you'll notice a number of icons used along the sides of the page. These icons are meant to serve as callouts for specific features, potential hiccups, or associated costs that you should be aware of. Here's what each icon means:

We use the Tip icon to notify you of best practices, shortcuts, and additional functionality that may be of interest to you. Anything marked with this icon helps you navigate, configure, and use Salesforce more effectively regardless of your role.

 Be sure to read each and every Warning icon as you move through the book. You'll find out about extra costs or irreversible decisions.

 The Technical Stuff icon jumps out at you when we feel the need to tell you something you likely don't care about. For those fellow geeks out there, please enjoy the Technical Stuff paragraphs.

 When you see the Remember icon, we're either reminding you of something important that we may have explained previously, or giving you a little nugget of knowledge to stick in your back pocket and save for later.

Beyond the Book

With *Salesforce Service Cloud For Dummies*, the fun doesn't stop at the turn of the final page. Check out these great resources for even more information:

- ✔ **Cheat Sheet:** What's that? You didn't remember everything you read? No problem! The online Cheat Sheet can help you get started with Service Cloud. You can find it at www.dummies.com/cheatsheet/ salesforceservicecloud.

- ✔ **Dummies.com online articles:** If you need a sampler or don't have time to wait for the book, you can check out our online articles about Service Cloud. We provide some quick-hit details on key information and functionality about Service Cloud. Check it out at www.dummies.com/extras/salesforceservicecloud.

Where to Go from Here

If you're completely new to Salesforce, flip the page and begin learning about the wide world of Service Cloud. If you're a beginning administrator and you have a deadline, you may want to jump ahead to Chapters 19, 20, and 21. If you're an experienced administrator researching Knowledge or Communities, jump to Chapter 13 or 15, respectively. If you're a customer support agent, turn to Chapters 4 and 5. If you're a manager, you can begin tracking and measuring your team's effectiveness in Chapter 16. No matter what you've come to *Salesforce Service Cloud For Dummies* to find or learn, we're sure you'll find what you're looking for.

Part I

Getting Started with Salesforce Service Cloud

getting started

with

salesforce

service cloud

In this part . . .

✔ See how Salesforce Service Cloud addresses and solves critical business challenges.

✔ Discover how easy it is to use and navigate through Salesforce.

✔ Personalize the system to make it your own and manage your business the way you want to.

✔ Understand important foundational Salesforce concepts and terminology to set you up for success.

Chapter 1

Solving Business Challenges with Service Cloud

In This Chapter

▶ Putting smiles on your customers' faces

▶ Gauging the health of your business

▶ Storing information in one place

▶ Working smoothly with your team

▶ Accessing data on the go

▶ Building customer loyalty

*W*hat keeps you up at night? Your profit margins? Your lack of visibility into what affects those profit margins? Is it that your employees don't address customers as well or as quickly as you'd like them to? And is that because they don't have access to the right information? Take a moment to think about your biggest concerns for your business. Odds are, Salesforce can help!

Salesforce is simpler than most customer relationship management (CRM) tools. By keeping things simple, Salesforce enables you to spend more time concentrating on your business challenges and less on troubleshooting the system. Understanding how to use and customize Salesforce, as well as properly aligning it to your business process, is the key to putting in place a powerful tool that will simplify your path to success.

In this chapter, we provide a high-level overview of native Salesforce features designed to address typical business challenges. We cover these common business problems and show you how to leverage Salesforce to ameliorate or even eliminate them.

Keeping Your Customers Happy

The customer is where everything starts. Customers are the lifeblood of any business. Without them, sales would be meaningless, service wouldn't exist, and there would be no one to market to. This concept may seem obvious, but research shows that customer service is one of the most commonly overlooked aspects in lost business. It's also one of the most influential aspects in bringing about repeat business and customer loyalty.

Customers expect excellent service. They want their issues resolved conveniently, painlessly, and as quickly as possible. One of the most effective barriers to providing excellent service is actually pretty simple to solve: In order to keep customers happy, you need to be able to readily access their information.

As a customer service representative, how much time have you wasted trying to identify a customer? Do you stumble and stall while trying to hunt for his previous support interactions? In this day and age, it's unacceptable not to have a 360-degree view of your customer (see the nearby sidebar). Without this critical ingredient, you're needlessly putting your organization at risk of losing a customer for good.

Salesforce Service Cloud helps businesses keep their customers happy by keeping their information in one central place. From one page, you can see a customer's personal information, as well as his recent interactions with your agents and the products he's purchased. Your agents have access to everything they need when they get that customer on the phone. Your customers will be pleased to have someone address their issue quickly without having to explain their backstory.

Even with the most customer-centric technology on earth, you can't truly create meaningful customer relationships without *people*. Your customer service representatives are vital to the success of any service organization. A holistic approach to customer service begins with your employees genuinely caring about and listening to your customers. Empathy and understanding — combined with the power of knowing who the customer is and the customer's history with your company — are gold.

Everyone on your team should be empowered to act on the deep understanding they have of your customers, as well as the desired customer experience. So, if Larry only contacts your business via email and never wants to receive phone calls, you can ensure that anyone servicing Larry will respect his wishes.

The 360-degree view

You may hear people refer to needing "a 360-degree view of the customer," but what does that mean? Generally speaking, when a customer interacts with your business, you must have a 360-degree view of the customer, or a way to draw from a rich repository of information pertaining to that customer. In other words, a 360-degree view of your customer allows you to see her personal information and, on the same page, view recent purchases, renewals, complaints, or phone conversations. This information is useful in multiple respects. Not only does it help to expedite the service process (thereby increasing customer loyalty and satisfaction), but it also saves you money, buys more time for your reps, shortens hold times, and facilitates upsell and cross-sell opportunities.

It is also worth mentioning that your customers may have customers themselves. Knowing the ultimate goals of your customer, who they sell to or provide services for, does wonders for your relationship with them, and the good news is that all this is possible with Salesforce.

With a 360-degree view, you can more effectively guide your approach to interaction with customers and service them in a much more personal and profound way. This does more than keep them happy — it creates loyalists for your brand.

Measuring the Health of Your Business

If you aren't gauging the health or progress of your business, trying to improve it won't get you far. The first step in improving your business is benchmarking: You need to know where you are before you can determine where you want to go.

Service Cloud allows you to quickly create and capture a multitude of data points that you deem most important to the success of your business. This, in turn, benefits all levels of your organization so that everyone from a first-tier support rep to the CEO can get real-time actionable information pertaining to the health of the organization. Service reps can check how many issues they've remediated this week, managers can drill into urgent escalations, and the CEO can view steady decreases in operational cost in response to her call-deflection strategy.

Service Cloud brings this all together by organizing only those data points you want to see into meaningful reports and comprehensible dashboards. Charts, graphs, and easy-to-use formulas are only the beginning of synthesizing an overwhelming volume of information into traceable and actionable data. Say goodbye to hours of grueling manual preparation in spreadsheets for those weekly meetings.

Establishing a Single Source of Truth

How many times have you had to look at different databases to find different kinds of information? You need to look up the customer in one system, log in to another system to get his address and order history, go to yet another system to enter new orders, and access yet another system that holds his warranty or service contract.

Of course, you can use all these legacy systems in conjunction with Service Cloud if you want to, but having a single source of truth solves a major business challenge for most businesses. You can quickly centralize your accounts, contacts, cases, entitlements for support, and interaction history or call logs in order to have a one-stop shop for all the information you need to effectively serve your customers.

Using Service Cloud, not only is all your customer's data updated and available, but this information is also accessible to other departments (only if you want it to be, of course, but sharing is caring). Breaking down silos in an organization is an effective tool to make sure that all sides of your business see the most up-to-date information about a customer. In this way, John in sales knows not to reach out and try to sell to the customer who just yelled at you about his broken product.

Collaborating with Your Coworkers

Collaboration is an often overlooked aspect of successful business. People are so caught up in the goings-on of their own teams and departments that they forget that any other team or department exists. *Silos* (independent teams with no visibility into other teams) impede productivity in organizations because they contribute to unnecessary duplicate effort and a lack of internal visibility, and they don't foster an open, collaborative work environment. Collaborating more often and more effectively with the right people in your organization can help you resolve customer support issues much more quickly.

Think about it: Doesn't that new guy always ask for historical knowledge or company policy updates that you can easily answer? Sometimes you find what he needs through email threads; other times you just exchange the information at the water cooler or at your cubicle.

Service Cloud allows you to collaborate with your team more effectively, with a feature called Chatter. Unlike email threads, Chatter consists of publicly viewable posts with news feeds that display different pieces of useful information. You can also be rewarded or reward others for collaborating, thus driving this behavior and increasing internal awareness of business issues that are most important to your company or department.

Another feature in Service Cloud that facilitates collaboration is the concept of Case Teams, which allow multiple agents to be added to a particular case so that a team can work together to service it. This is particularly useful in scenarios such as an agent taking a vacation, where the customers and cases he is responsible for aren't forgotten or left waiting.

Getting the Data You Need When and Where You Need It

Service Cloud provides the flexibility to make managing customer service inquiries easier for both agents and customers. Consumer bases are increasingly turning to technology to interact with brands and desire engagement with your brand more than ever before. You need to be able to engage with your customers on their terms.

Agents are happy when they have the necessary tools to be as successful as possible. This includes the ability to access customer information and provide world-class service even when they're not in the office. Empower your agents to succeed!

With Service Cloud, you can distribute your support centers throughout the world with chat-based support. Agents on the go can research answers to common problems and solve customer issues from their mobile devices. Your technicians out in the field can view customer addresses and report completed service on a tablet or smartphone. The opportunities are vast, and the increased speed and efficiency of service is quite noticeable.

Building Brand Loyalists

Every business has a base of loyal fans. These loyal fans, or *brand loyalists*, have the potential to become your evangelists — spreading the word about your product or service to their family and friends, and bringing more customers your way. Loyalists advocate on behalf of your brand (for free!) and stand up for you when times are tough. They also inspire others to love — or at least consider — your brand.

Every company wants and needs a loyal customer base. How to create brand loyalists can be a difficult question to answer, but there are some basic tools you can use with Service Cloud to help you get there.

Reducing customer frustration

Impeccable customer service is mandatory on the road to building customer loyalty. Do you ever get frustrated by interactive voice response (IVR) systems, those automated machines that interact with you via voice and keypad? How long do you hear the same loop of music while waiting on hold? Whether it's repeating information after call transfers, long hold times, or poorly designed IVR systems, listening to customer feedback and reducing customer frustration is critical in creating a brand that customers can rave about. Service Cloud can help by tracking customer feedback through surveys and adjusting how you engage with those customers accordingly.

Giving your customers options

Giving your customers the choice of how to access your customer service channels — be it through phone, a contact form on the web, chat, email, or social media — eliminates frustration. Some people prefer to wait on the phone for the next available service representative, but others want to chat with a live agent for immediate service. Using Service Cloud, customers can choose the way they want to interact with you. So, if a customer doesn't want to wait on hold, she can talk to a Live Agent on your website. Leave the choice up to the customer. Service Cloud allows you to engage with your customers on their terms.

Creating connections with your customers

Creating connections that make an impact is a powerful tool in building brand loyalists. It can be as small as knowing the customer's name and "remembering" her story when she calls. It can also take the form of reaching out to thank a customer over social media when she mentions your company. Service Cloud allows your reps to perform these functions and take the appropriate steps to building a loyal customer base.

Improving the quality of agent interactions

Agents in high-volume call centers need to be as productive as possible. They have to be able to focus more on their jobs and less on logistics or searching through clunky, disparate databases. Service Cloud has out-of-the-box features that focus on streamlining your call center and optimizing agent productivity. Here are just a few examples:

- The Service Cloud Console allows an agent to view and act on all his cases and related information at a glance.
- Service Cloud's computer telephony integration (CTI) can automatically present a pop-up displaying the customer's information to your agent before the agent picks up the phone.
- Case Teams allows for various agents to help service a particular case or customer.
- Centralized customer information allows for quick access to a great deal of information.
- Routing customer inquiries to agents based on skillset, language, or location saves immeasurable time in issue resolution.

These native Service Cloud components are timesaving tools that promote flexibility for your customer service organization and keep your employees and customers happier.

Expediting the service process

Using Service Cloud, you can expedite the entire service process. From the moment a customer inquiry is routed to an agent until the customer needs a renewal on her entitlement for support, Service Cloud aligns to and streamlines the process every step of the way.

Service Cloud offers various opportunities for automation:

- Using Salesforce assignment rules, you can automate how calls are routed to agents or queues based on a range of criteria.
- Case creation is also automated via email or web forms.
- Email templates streamline outbound communication.

✔ Escalation rules let you set up a structure that automates when and to whom a case is escalated.

✔ Approval processes allow you to determine the criteria for knowledge base article editing cycles.

Service Cloud leverages automation in different ways to orchestrate a system with moving parts, expediting your call center and making your agents better at what they do.

Chapter 2

Navigating Service Cloud

· ·

In This Chapter

▶ Selecting the right Service Cloud edition

▶ Accessing Salesforce.com

▶ Navigating the Home page

▶ Creating and editing records

▶ Finding the Help and Setup menu

· ·

*F*irst things first: Salesforce Service Cloud comes in several editions, and we start this chapter by helping you choose the right one for your business. Then we show you how to log in to Service Cloud, as well as offer a few administrator-level tips for password management. We cover the Home page and its components, and give you a brief introduction to creating and modifying records in Service Cloud. Finally, we cover where you can go for help.

Choosing the Right Edition of Service Cloud for Your Business

If you already use Sales Cloud (Salesforce's platform and product for sales organizations), Salesforce offers bundle pricing that integrates both the Sales Cloud and Service Cloud platforms. Otherwise, there are three Service Cloud editions that you can choose from. Regardless of the edition you choose, the *interface* — the way it looks and feels — is the same, but each edition has slightly different functionality and pricing:

> ✔ **Professional:** The Professional Edition is great for smaller contact centers. You get the core features of Service Cloud, such as case management and tracking, the Service Cloud Console, asset tracking, Chatter, auto-assignment and escalation rules, web and email-case capture, mobile access, contract management, email template management, and reports and dashboards.

Chatter is a social collaboration tool that functions as a private social network for your business. It lets you stay in contact and collaborate with everyone you work with. For example, using Chatter you can post documents for an entire team to look at and even download.

✔ **Enterprise:** The Enterprise Edition is the most popular and is intended for larger companies. Features include everything that's available in the Professional Edition, as well as offline access, Force.com pages and Visualforce for custom development, integration via web services API, record types, and social media integration, as well as workflow and approval processes.

✔ **Unlimited:** The Unlimited Edition gives you access to 24/7 customer support; unlimited online help, training materials, and videos; increased storage; and much greater capacity for tailoring and customization. That means that if something goes awry at 4 a.m. on a Sunday, you can contact Salesforce.com agents with your questions. This edition is great for large companies with complex business processes. The Unlimited Edition requires a devoted administrator to take advantage of all the functionality it offers.

Salesforce also offers a Developer Edition, which is a free Salesforce instance with limited licenses that has full functionality for administrators and developers who need to test configurations and code customizations.

The best part about Service Cloud is how easy it is to use. Depending on the way your business works, you can choose an edition that suits your needs. And, because you're in the cloud, you can simply add more licenses as your company scales or upgrade to another edition if you change your mind.

Logging In to Service Cloud

Because Service Cloud is entirely cloud-based, all you really need in order to access it is an Internet connection. (Well, you'll also need a username and a password, but we'll get to that.) You can log in from your office and then pick up where you left off in your hotel while traveling in Tokyo. Salesforce has many security measures in place to protect your identity and ensure that your company's sensitive data is not at risk.

Open sesame: Setting up a password

The first thing you have to do in order to set up your password is to have your administrator click a button on your user record that generates a

Salesforce system email with the subject line "Salesforce.com password confirmation." This email provides you with your username and a temporary password. The email contains a link that you can click, and it will take you to a page where you can change your password.

Open the email and then follow these steps:

1. **Click the link that appears after Log In Automatically by Clicking.**

   The Change Password page appears, welcoming you to Salesforce and prompting you to set a password for your account.

2. **Fill in the required fields and click Save.**

   The Home page (shown in Figure 2-1) appears. The Home page is the initial entry page you see after logging in to Salesforce. It has multiple components that are customizable based on your preferences and role in the organization.

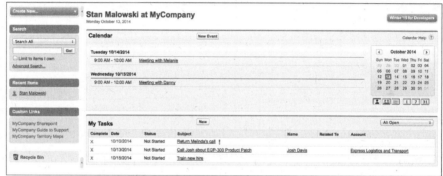

Figure 2-1: The Salesforce Home page.

I call do-over!: Resetting your password

You're bound to need to reset your password someday. If you lost or forgot your password, you can click the Forgot Your Password? link after failing an attempted log in. You'll need to enter your username and then you'll get an email with a password reset link; click that link, answer your security question, and reset your password.

If you want to change your password and you remember what the current one is, log in and follow these steps:

1. **Click the down arrow next to your name and then click Setup.**

   You may not have access to this area if you aren't an administrator. If this is the case, contact your administrator and have him reset your password for you.

2. **From the sidebar, under My Settings, click the + (plus sign) to the right of the first drop-down, Personal.**

A drop-down list of personal information settings expands.

The *sidebar* is the vertical panel running down the left side of the screen. It contains quick links to recent items and other at-a-glance, useful information.

3. **From the expanded selection, click Change My Password.**

The Change My Password page (shown in Figure 2-2) appears.

4. **Enter the requested information in the appropriate fields and click Save.**

The main Personal Information page appears and your password is changed.

Periodically change your password to protect your data. If your company's administrator chooses to have passwords expire automatically after specified periods, you'll be required to change your password periodically.

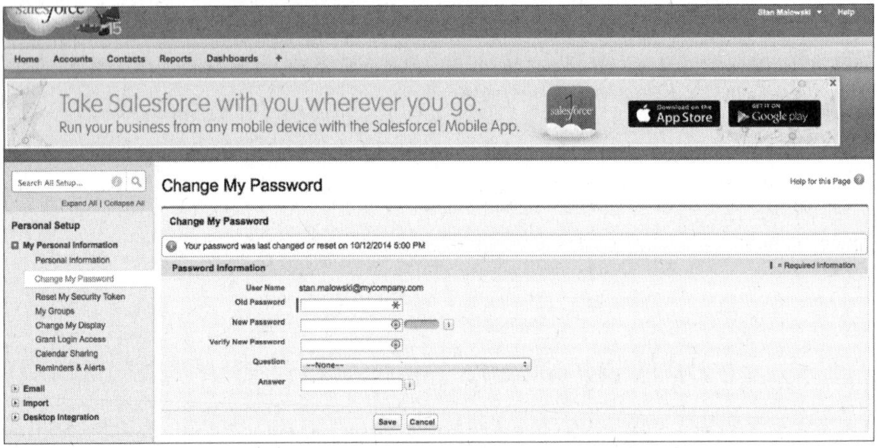

Figure 2-2: The Change My Password page.

Logging in and authenticating

Logging in to Salesforce is very similar to logging in to any other software as a service (SaaS) application, such as your email service. To log in to Salesforce, open your web browser and follow these steps:

1. **Type** `http://login.salesforce.com` **in the address bar and press Enter.**

The login page (shown in Figure 2-3) appears.

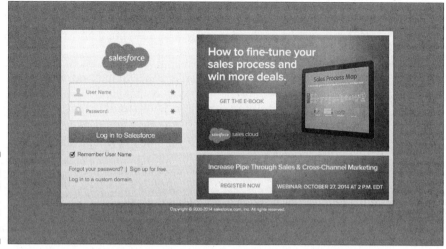

Figure 2-3:
The Sales
force.
com login
page.

2. Enter your username and password.

3. Click Log In to Salesforce.

The Home page appears.

If you're logging in from a computer that Salesforce doesn't recognize, you may be prompted to enter a verification code and authenticate your computer. If so, Salesforce will send an automated email or text message to the email address or phone number associated with your username. The message contains a verification code that you can type where prompted in Salesforce. This way you authenticate your computer and Salesforce verifies your identity.

Navigating the Home Page

When you log in, the Home page is the first page you see. It's designed to have the most pertinent and readily available information to reduce the number of clicks it takes you to get to where you need to go. You can navigate to any tab or app at the top of the page. You can also click shortcuts in the sidebar, check your calendar, and manage your open tasks before starting your day.

A *tab* is a table of data that holds relevant records and represents a collection of information. Tabs appear at the top of any page in Salesforce. *Apps* (short for *applications*) are a collection of tabs that are logically grouped under an umbrella in which a particular team or role can work from and default to.

The look and feel of the Home page is very similar (if not identical) for all users, but the information contained within the Home page is specific to you. For example, your calendar will be different from your peers' calendars. Similarly, your open tasks probably differ from those of your colleagues.

Like most elements within Salesforce, your administrator can customize the Home page to show only the information that is relevant to you or your role within the organization. For example, your support reps probably don't need to see items for approval if that's not part of their job. Depending on how your Home page is customized, you may also see dashboards.

Using the sidebar and custom links

Let's start off on the left side of the page. The sidebar column, shown in Figure 2-4, appears on almost all Salesforce pages. In this section, we look at the various features of the sidebar.

Figure 2-4:
The sidebar
column.

If your sidebar looks different or contains certain components that we don't cover here, your organization probably uses or develops third-party applications to enhance basic Salesforce functionality. For example, if your support agents use a softphone within Service Cloud, you may find that your organization supports computer telephony integration (CTI) and integrates a softphone third-party add-on.

Creating new records

Using the Create New drop-down on the Home page, you can quickly create new records and save yourself a bunch of clicks. Just click the drop-down and choose the type of record you want to create on the fly. On the individual tab Home page (the initial landing page you're taken to after clicking a tab), you see a Quick Create section in the sidebar. This section lets you create a new record pertaining to that tab, such as a new Account, with only having to enter a few fields, as shown in Figure 2-5. Yes, it's that easy and it can save you loads of time in the long run.

Although Quick Create is great for creating lots of records quickly, beware of data integrity issues. You can find yourself with many records with missing information. For example, if you have required fields upon the creation of certain records, users can bypass this requirement using the Quick Create feature if the field doesn't appear. If this is a problem for your organization, an administrator can disable the Quick Create feature.

Searching from the Home page

You can use the Search function on the Home page sidebar to perform quick search queries with one click. Just follow these steps:

Collapsing the sidebar

If your administrator turns on the Collapsible Sidebar feature, you and every user can choose for yourselves whether you want to expand or hide the column. If you're an administrator and you want to enable this feature, follow these steps:

1. **Click the arrow next to your name at the top of the page and then click Setup.**

    You're now in the administrative setup menu.

2. **On the left sidebar, under Build, click Customize and then click User Interface.**

    User Interface should be the last option in the list that is not bolded.

3. **Under the Sidebar section, click the Enable Collapsible Sidebar check box and click Save.**

    You and the other users now have the option to expand and hide your sidebar from any page where it's available.

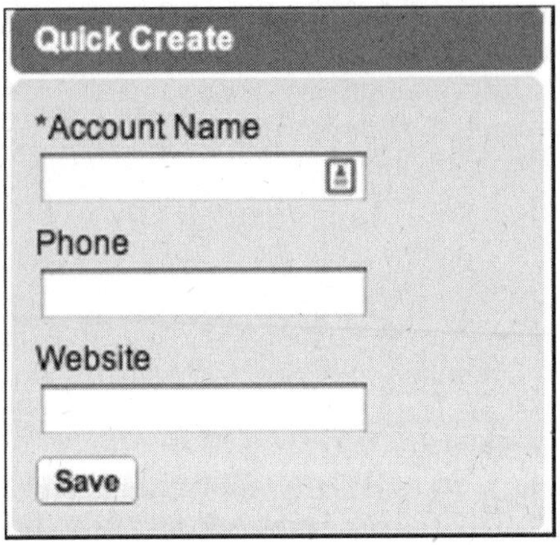

Figure 2-5:
The Quick
Create sec-
tion on a tab
Home page.

1. **Enter the keywords you want to search for in the Search field.**

2. **If you want to search only records you own, click the Limit to Items I Own check box.**

3. **Click Go.**

    Salesforce's Search Results page (shown in Figure 2-6) appears, display-
    ing different lists organized by object type, such as accounts, contacts,
    opportunities, and so on.

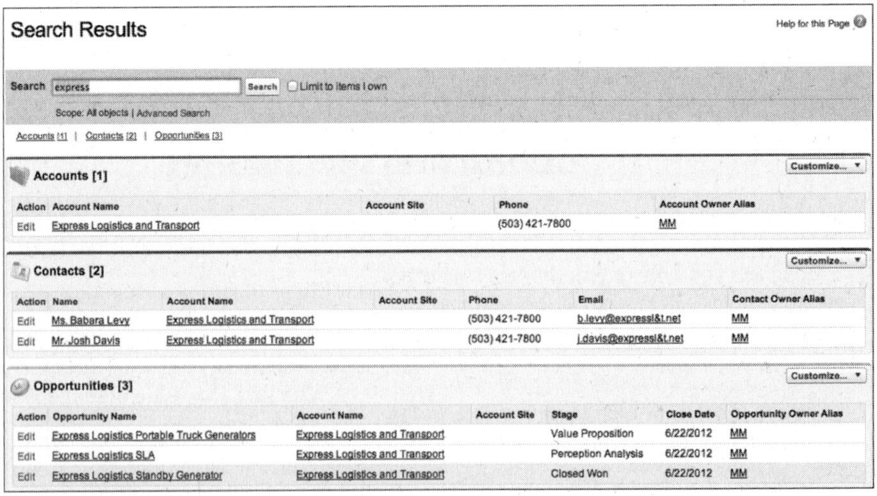

Figure 2-6:
The Search
Results
page.

4. **To select a record from one of the lists, click the record from the Name column.**

   The record's detail page appears. The *detail page* is the actual layout of a record and displays the information of that particular record.

5. **If the type of record you're looking for is not available, click the Advanced Search link.**

   From here, you can expand the scope of your search by selecting additional objects to search, as shown in Figure 2-7.

 If you don't find a particular record you're looking for, before sounding the alarms, remember that your administrator may have limited your privileges. Check with your company's Salesforce administrator if you can't find what you're looking for.

Reviewing your Recent Items list

The Recent Items list shows you a list of the last ten records you've viewed. You can click any of these records to quickly revisit them. This is especially useful if you log out and then log in again and want to quickly get to where you were. Sometimes the Recent Items list is a good reminder of what you've been doing.

Advanced Search

Search

| express | | Search |

Advanced Options

✓ Use enhanced search capabilities [i]
☐ Limit to items I own
☐ Exact phrase

Scope

Select All | Deselect All

☐ Accounts	☐ Contacts	☐ Leads
☐ Opportunities	☑ Cases	☐ Case Comments
☐ Service Contracts	☐ Contract Line Items	☐ Entitlements
☐ Campaigns	☐ Contracts	☐ Orders
☐ Assets	☐ Tasks	☐ Events
☐ Notes	☐ Attachments	☐ Ideas
☐ Reports	☐ Users	☐ D&B Companies

Figure 2-7: The Advanced Search screen allows you to broaden the scope of your search.

Saving time with custom links and components

You can add custom HTML elements or displays for other users, such as images and logos or special messages. If you use other websites for certain aspects of the job, shortcut links that appear on the sidebar can save you time. An administrator can also choose to expose these links to specific user profiles in your organization or show it to everyone in the company. For example, if your company uses a content or inventory management tool outside of Salesforce, an administrator can easily add a link to it in the sidebar.

Using the Recycle Bin

The sidebar also contains a Recycle Bin, which gives you the ability to search for (and recover) recently deleted records for up to 15 days before they're permanently purged.

Using the Chatter feed

If you don't see the Chatter feed on your Home page, it's not turned on for your organization. Contact your administrator to turn it on for you. If you are the administrator, you can enable Chatter by following these simple steps:

1. **At the top right next to your name, click Setup to go to the Setup menu.**

2. **Under Build, click Customize and then click Chatter.**

   Assuming Chatter is not enabled, only Settings will appear between Chatter and Files Connect.

3. **Click Settings.**

   The Chatter Settings page (shown in Figure 2-8) appears. Review the instructions on the page.

4. **Click the Edit button, click the Enable check box, and then click Save.**

   Once you click the Enable check box, many more settings appear on the page. Don't worry about these additional settings for now.

When Chatter is enabled for your organization, your Chatter feed appears in the center of the Home page (see Figure 2-9).

Now you and your team have access to Chatter, a way to communicate and collaborate with other members of your team or organization. Here you can add a status, post an important link, or upload files and documents to get your team involved in projects and tasks.

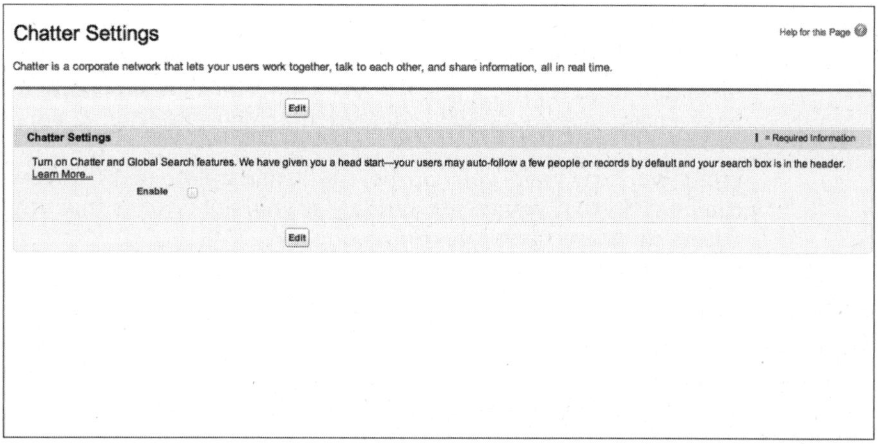

Chatter Settings

Help for this Page

Chatter is a corporate network that lets your users work together, talk to each other, and share information, all in real time.

Edit

Chatter Settings

| = Required Information

Turn on Chatter and Global Search features. We have given you a head start—your users may auto-follow a few people or records by default and your search box is in the header.
Learn More...

Enable

Edit

Figure 2-8:
The Chatter
Settings
page.

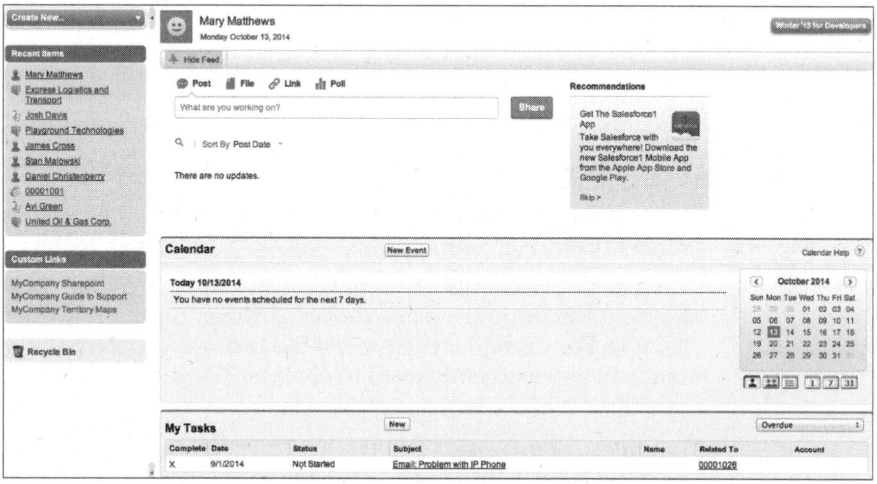

Figure 2-9:
The Home
page with
Chatter
enabled.

Even if you love Chatter and want it everywhere possible, sometimes it takes up too much screen real estate (especially in instances of those long back-and-forth posts between coworkers). If you want to hide the feed from your view to reduce excessive scrolling, simply click the Hide Feed link above the Post link.

Managing My Tasks and Calendar

A *task* is an activity that doesn't typically have a specific time and duration; an *event* does have a specific time and duration. Events and tasks are both considered *activities* in Salesforce. The My Tasks section shows your tasks, while the Calendar section displays your events.

Using My Tasks

The My Tasks section (shown in Figure 2-10) is your personal list of open tasks that need to be completed. An example of an open task may be calling back a customer on a specific date or attaching a relevant document to a case.

From the Home page, you can view, edit, and create tasks and events. These can be tasks that you create and set for yourself or ones that others assign to you or Salesforce generates automatically.

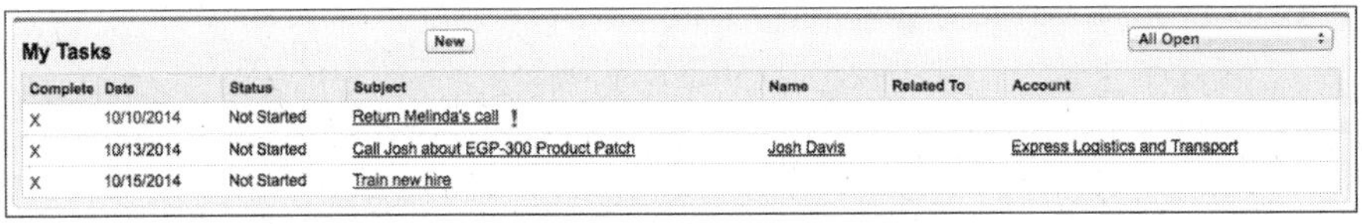

Figure 2-10:
The My
Tasks sec-
tion displays
all open
tasks.

More specifically, in the My Tasks sections, you can

- ✔ **Create new tasks quickly.** Click the New button and create your task.

- ✔ **View a list of open tasks assigned to you.** You can view up to 15 tasks on the Home page. By clicking View More, you can see the maximum.

- ✔ **Change your task time frame.** You can choose to see your tasks for different periods of time using the list at the upper right of the My Tasks section. For example, you can set the task view to look at overdue tasks that you more urgently need to complete, or view all your tasks that are due this month.

- ✔ **Complete your tasks.** Click the X to the left of a task to mark it completed. This will bring you to the Edit page (where you can modify a record), but it will automatically set the Status to Completed.

- ✔ **Review and edit tasks.** Choose any task in the list by clicking the link in the Subject column to view the task detail page. Click the Edit button to edit your task information. To edit a task directly from the Home page, you can click the X to complete it. Just make sure you change the status back to whatever it should be if it's not, in fact, completed.

Managing your events with the Calendar

The Calendar section stores your personal, team, or company events in Salesforce. It defaults to displaying the current month on the Calendar and shows you events in the upcoming week, as shown in Figure 2-11.

Figure 2-11:
The
Calendar
section
shows you
your sched-
uled events.

Like tasks, events in your Calendar are either created by you or assigned to you. You can choose which events you want to share with your Home page, as well as the view. You can choose from a daily, weekly, or monthly view of the Calendar. You're also able to customize who you want to share your calendar with and the level of detail they see by clicking on the Share My Calendar link, clicking the Add button, and selecting the user(s), role(s), or public group(s) you want to grant access to.

In the Calendar section, you can do the following:

✔ **Create new events quickly.** Click the New Event button and fill out the details to create your event.

✔ **View an actual calendar.** For the sake of familiarity, Salesforce has a visual representation of a calendar. You can toggle the month displayed by clicking the side arrows or click on individual dates to check out the events you have scheduled on them.

✔ **Use different views of your Calendar.** Click the icons underneath the small calendar to view a daily, weekly, or monthly calendar.

✔ **Change views of your events.** You can view your events as a list view, a multi-user view that shows the events assigned to multiple users, or a single-user view that shows you your assigned events.

✔ **Review and edit events.** Click an actual event in your Calendar list to display the event detail page. Click the Edit button to modify the event information.

Visualizing analytics with Dashboard snapshots

If your organization has customized your Home page, you may see a Dashboard section there. The Dashboard section displays the top three components of a selected dashboard.

A *dashboard* is a chart or graph that helps you visualize complex information about your business. These are representations of existing reports in Salesforce that display some key data you should have access to. For example, you may have a report of the average age of a case before it's resolved, broken down by support rep or geography. A dashboard can take the report and show you a bar chart, making the data more digestible. (See Chapter 18 for more information about dashboards.)

If the Dashboard section appears on your Home page, you can also do the following:

- ✓ **Change the Dashboard displayed on your home page.** Click the Customize Page link and select any dashboard you have access to. The Home page displays only the three components at the top of the dashboard you choose.

- ✓ **Refresh the Dashboard.** You should also remember to refresh the data that the Dashboard displays to see the most current information by clicking the Refresh button.

- ✓ **Drill down into your data.** Click a chart or table in the Dashboard to drill into the source report the Dashboard is visualizing for you.

Getting Started with Records

One of the basic building blocks of Salesforce is the record. *Records* are individual pieces of data that fall under tabs, or collections of pertinent records. They hold fields that display certain information. For example, a case record may have fields pertinent to the person the case is servicing, his address, his phone number, and the urgency of the issue. In this section, we explain how to create, view, edit, and delete records.

Creating new records

Salesforce offers a number of ways to create a new record. As mentioned earlier, you can always use the Create New drop-down list in the sidebar of most pages by doing the following:

1. **Click the Create New drop-down in the sidebar.**

   A list of available objects appear where you can choose which type of record you want to create, as shown in Figure 2-12. *Objects* are representations of database tables that contain your organization's information. For example, accounts, contacts, and cases are all standard Salesforce objects.

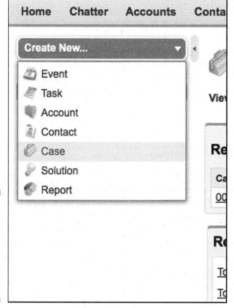

Figure 2-12:
The Create
New drop-
down menu
in the
sidebar.

2. Click the object, or type of record, you want to create.

The edit page of a new record appears with mostly empty fields (some fields may be pre-populated).

3. Enter information into the fields in Edit mode and click Save.

The detail page of the record appears, detailing the record you've just created.

Assuming you have the proper permissions, you can also create a record through the Object tab by following these steps:

1. Click the Object tab related to the record you want to create.

The tab Home page appears. For example, to create a new case record, click the Cases tab to get to the Cases Home page.

2. Click the New button in the Recent list for that object.

This list shows you the most recent records you've viewed pertaining to the tab you're in. For example, in the Recent Cases list, click the New button, as shown in Figure 2-13. The Case Edit page appears.

3. Complete the fields and click Save.

The detail page of the case record you've just created appears.

Congratulations! Now you can create records in Salesforce. You also see how painless and intuitive it is. Let's look at making the most out of the record you just created to understand the detail page.

Editing or deleting records

Editing and deleting records is even easier than creating them.

To edit a record, navigate to the detail page of the record you want to modify, and follow these steps:

1. **Click the Edit button at the top of the Detail page.**

   The Edit page appears with editable fields.

2. **Edit the fields you want to edit.**

3. **Click Save.**

   The record's Detail page appears, displaying the updated information.

If your administrator enables the inline editing feature in Salesforce, there is an even easier (yes, it's true) way to edit fields that can save you time and clicks. The inline editing feature allows you to edit fields directly from the Detail page without even clicking the Edit button. To edit a field inline, follow these steps:

1. **On a record's Detail page, hover your cursor over the field you want to edit.**

   An icon appears to the right of the field, indicating your level of access to it:

   - *Pencil:* You can edit this field inline, and the field is highlighted.
   - *Padlock:* You can't edit this field, and it isn't highlighted.

- *None:* You can edit the field, but not using inline editing. You'll have to use the traditional method of editing, detailed earlier.

2. **If the pencil icon appears, double-click the field and update the information.**

   Figure 2-14 shows how to update the Subject field on a case using inline editing.

3. **Click Enter to complete editing that field if you want to continue editing others; otherwise, click Save.**

   The record is saved with all your modifications.

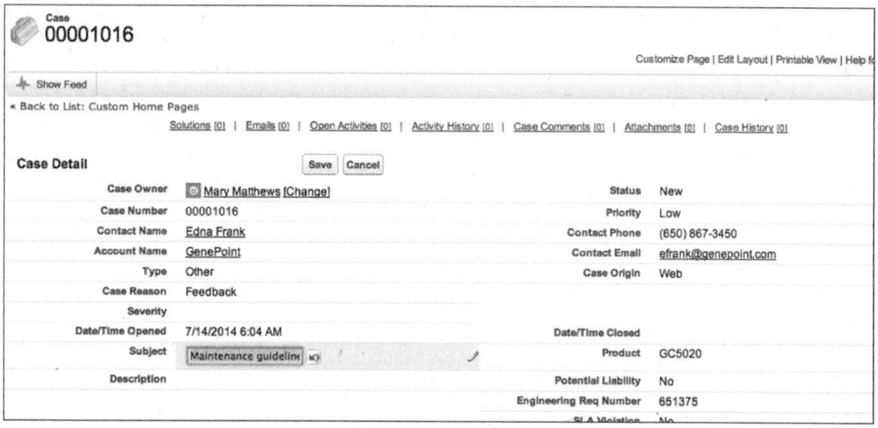

Figure 2-14:
Editing a
field inline.

Removing records from the Recycle Bin

If you accidentally delete a record or just want to restore one, thank the almighty Salesforce creators for the Recycle Bin. As long as 15 days haven't elapsed, you can bring the record back to business, so to speak.

To restore a deleted record, follow these steps:

1. **Navigate to your sidebar and click the green Recycle Bin.**

   The Recycle Bin page appears with the record in view.

2. **In the Action column, click the check box next to the record you want to bring back.**

   You can also select all the records by selecting the top check box near the word Action.

3. **Click the Undelete button.**

   You aren't redirected to any page, but the record you restored appears in the Recent Items list in the sidebar.

To delete a record, on the Detail page, simply click the Delete button. Don't worry — Salesforce will ask you if you're sure, in case you change your mind. If you do, just click Cancel to return to the Detail page. If you click OK and delete the record, it will move to the Recycle Bin for 15 days before Salesforce permanently deletes it.

Getting the most out of the Detail page

Let's look at a few features on the Detail page (shown in Figure 2-15) that can help you get the most out of Salesforce:

- ✔ **Hover links:** *Hover links* are quick links to jump to corresponding related lists that appear farther down on the page. The links appear above the buttons at the top of the Detail page, like Edit or Delete. You can hover over a link to open a sneak peak of the records in that list. If you hover over the link, it will bring you to the corresponding list on the page.

  If you don't see the links, contact your administrator to turn on this feature.

- ✔ **Related lists:** A *Related list* is a customizable list display on the lower part of the Detail page. The Related list itemizes the associated records of that object on another record. So, for example, a case Detail page can have an Open Activities Related list, itemizing all the open activities (emails, calls, and so on) associated with that case. Related lists are one of the many ways Salesforce provides a 360-degree view of the customer with minimal clicks.

- ✔ **Printable view:** You can't export a Detail page, but you can view a printable version of it in a new window. To do this click the Printable View link at the top right of the page.

- ✔ **Back to List:** If you've been working from a List view, click the Back to List link to return to that page. This is useful if hitting the Back button of your web browser won't take you to the list but to the Edit page, for example. The Back to List link appears at the top left of the page, below the Chatter feed and above the hover links.

- ✔ **Sharing a record:** To share the record with other users, click the Sharing button. This button doesn't appear on all records.

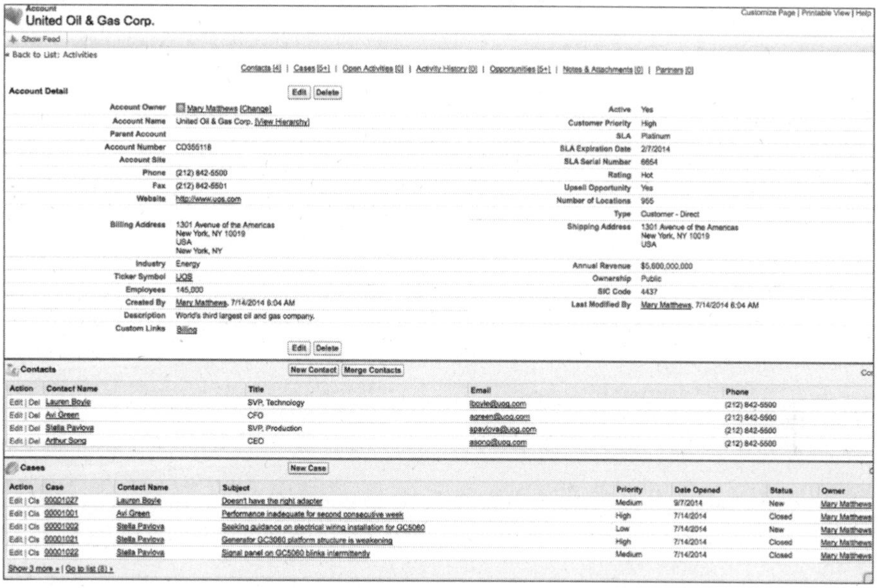

Figure 2-15:
The Detail
page.

Finding the Help and Setup Menu

We've already alluded to this, but the top right of any Salesforce page, to the left of the App menu, is where all the administrative magic happens. If you click the Setup link, you'll find a drop-down list with the following options:

- ✔ **Force.com home:** Force.com home is the "backend" of Salesforce, where administrators configure and customize native features of Salesforce for their companies.

- ✔ **Logout:** Click Logout to log out of Salesforce.

Apart from the Setup menu, there is the Help link. You can click this link to take you to a page containing Salesforce's official Help & Training.

Chapter 3

Personalizing Service Cloud

In This Chapter

▶ Understanding My Settings

▶ Customizing the Personal section

▶ Working remotely and offline

▶ Updating Chatter settings

*O*ne of the best parts of getting a new gadget is making it your own. When you've changed things around to best fit your preferences and personal patterns, the gadget really feels like you own it!

Salesforce was built to be customizable, so you can play around with features so they make more sense for you. You can modify what you want to see so that your system is yours and aligns with the way you do business and manage your day.

In this chapter, we make sure you understand the My Settings menu and options for customization so that you make the most of Service Cloud. Then, we discuss how you can customize your personal display to show exactly what you want to see. Finally, we show you how you can work with Salesforce at any time and from anywhere.

Understanding the My Settings Page

The My Settings page is the first section in a long list of customization tools Salesforce provides its users. The general Setup menu is not always available to every user — this is wholly dependent on the access the user has. However, the My Settings menu is available to each user, regardless of his or her profile. Salesforce gives each user the power to personalize his or her own experience to drive adoption and increase efficiency.

The list of tools and options available in the My Settings menu is fairly extensive, so let's get started and look at them at a high level. Luckily, they're all located in one centralized area.

To get to the My Settings, follow these steps:

1. **Click your name at the top right of any page in Salesforce.**

   Depending on your organization's settings, the Setup link will either be displayed to the right of your name in the header or as a drop-down option beneath it, as shown in Figures 3-1 and 3-2.

Figure 3-1:
Seeing the separate Setup link in the header.

Figure 3-2:
The Setup link appears under the username in the header.

2. **Choose My Settings.**

   A sidebar appears on the left side of the page with a My Settings menu, as shown in Figure 3-3. The main page has Quick Links and Desktop Add-Ons that provide users easy access to common settings.

3. **In the sidebar, click all the plus signs (+) to the right of the headings to expand them, as shown in Figure 3-4.**

   All the options appear in the sidebar under their respective headings.

4. **Under Personal, click the first menu item, Personal Information.**

   Your user detail record appears, showing you your user information in Salesforce. The next section of this chapter details how to edit it.

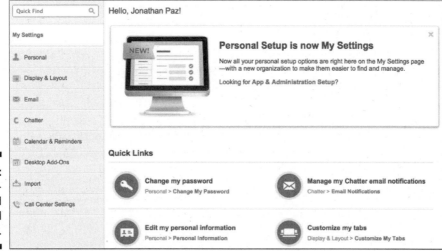

Figure 3-3:
The side-
bar and
Personal
Setup menu.

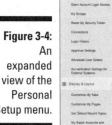

Figure 3-4:
An
expanded
view of the
Personal
Setup menu.

To quickly find a specific heading or subheading in the My Settings menu, go to the Quick Find bar at the top of the sidebar and start typing what you're looking for. Salesforce will filter down your options as you type, saving you substantial time.

Now that you know how to navigate the My Settings menu, we walk you through the options you have within them.

Updating Your Personal Information

The Personal section in the My Settings page allows you to change your user record, password, display, language, time zone, and personal information, among other things. In this section, we take a deeper look at these options.

Modifying your user record

Each user in Salesforce has a user record, detailing that user's personal contact information, preferred language, and time zone, as well as a few different fields that work together to determine the user's level of access in the system. To edit your user record, follow these steps:

1. **Click Personal Information.**

   Your user detail record appears in the body of the page, defaulting to Edit mode. In Edit mode, you can change certain fields that are available to you for editing.

2. **Click Save.**

   Your user detail record appears again and reflects the updated information.

Remember to update your information in this section if you move offices for work, change your phone number, or get promoted.

At the bottom of the user record, while in Edit mode, you can update your time zone if you're traveling often or moving around a lot. Don't forget to save.

Changing your password

If you want to change your password, follow these steps:

1. **In the Personal section, click Change My Password.**

   The Change My Password page appears with empty fields and an informational header indicating the last time your password was changed or reset.

2. **Type in your old password and type your new password twice.**

3. **Choose a security question in case you forget your password and the answer to it.**

4. **Click Save.**

   The My Settings main page appears and your password is updated.

An option under the Personal section is Reset My Security Token. In Salesforce, a *security token* is an automatically generated alphanumeric key that you have to add to the end of your password to log in to Salesforce via an API or desktop client. From the Reset My Security Token page subsection, click the Reset Security Token button to reset it and have the new token sent to your user's email address.

Creating personal groups

In Salesforce, a *group* is simply a set of users. A group can contain individual users, other groups, or roles (which we discuss in greater depth in Chapter 19). There are two types of groups in Salesforce:

- ✔ **Public groups:** As the name suggests, these groups are public and can be used by anyone in the organization. Only administrators can create public groups.
- ✔ **Personal groups:** Anyone can create a personal group for his or her personal use (for example, to share records with a certain set of users or groups that you specify).

In this section, we discuss personal groups.

To create a new personal group, follow these steps:

1. **Click My Groups in the Personal section of the sidebar.**

   The My Groups page appears, showing you a list of your personal groups.

2. **Click the New Group button.**

   A New Personal Group Edit page appears with empty fields.

3. **Name the group in the required Label field.**

   Use an intuitive name so that you and the other users in your group easily understand it.

4. **From the Search drop-down, select the type of user collection you want to search for to add to your group.**

   You can choose from another public group, a role, a role and all the roles beneath it, or a user. Also, depending on your licenses, you can select portal users. As you click on your choice, the Available Members column will populate with a list corresponding to it.

5. **Click the user or group of users you want to add, and click the Add arrow so it moves from the Available Members column to the Selected Members column.**

   Keep doing this until you have everyone you want in your personal group, as shown in Figure 3-5.

6. **Click Save when you're finished.**

   The My Groups Home page appears again and your new group now appears in the list.

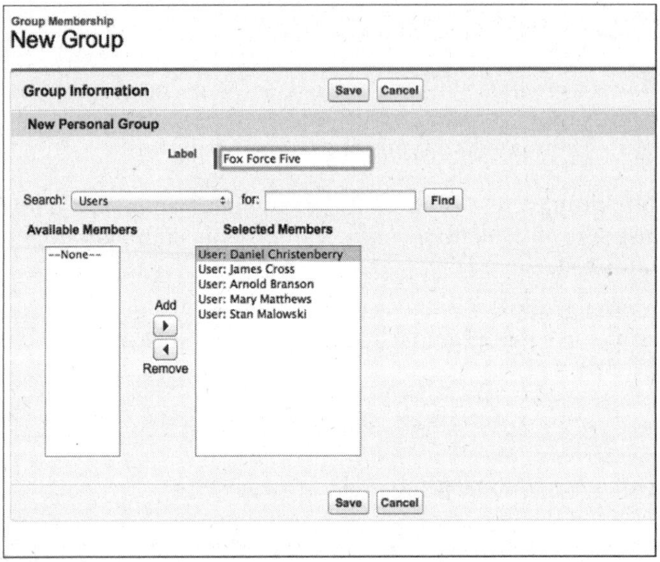

Figure 3-5:
Creating a
new per-
sonal group.

Changing your display

Your *display* is what you see on certain pages in Salesforce and should be modified based on how you do your business. If you don't use most of what's on your screen every day, change your display to work with only what's most relevant to you.

The display allows you to modify two things in Salesforce:

✔ Your tabs

✔ The related lists that appear on your records and their locations

REMEMBER

Your administrator holds more Salesforce power than you do (unless, of course, you are another administrator) and can override your personal page customizations.

Customizing your tabs

Salesforce Service Cloud already comes with standard tabs and groups them into apps that you can choose from at the top right of any page. Your company or administrator may also create new tabs and apps. Either way, it's likely that you don't need to see all the tabs at the same time, and there are some that you'll never use.

To customize the tabs you see, follow these steps:

1. **Click the Display & Layout section of the My Settings page's sidebar.**

   The section expands.

2. **Click the Customize My Tabs link.**

   The Customize My Tabs page appears.

3. **Use the Custom App drop-down to choose an app (you have access to) whose tabs you want to modify.**

   The lists in the Available Tabs and Selected Tabs columns will change, depending on the custom app you choose. You may want to add more tabs to the app you normally work from and/or remove a few.

4. **Select a tab you want to add or remove and use the Add or Remove arrow buttons to do so, as shown in Figure 3-6.**

   If you're a support rep working out of the Service Cloud Console every day, you probably don't need to see the Leads tab. You also may decide that you'd like to add the Contracts and Chatter tabs to access these more easily.

5. **To change the order in which your tabs appear, highlight the tab in the Selected Tabs column and use the Up, Down, Top, and Bottom arrows to move them.**

6. **When you have your tabs looking the way you want, click Save.**

   The Change My Display page appears again

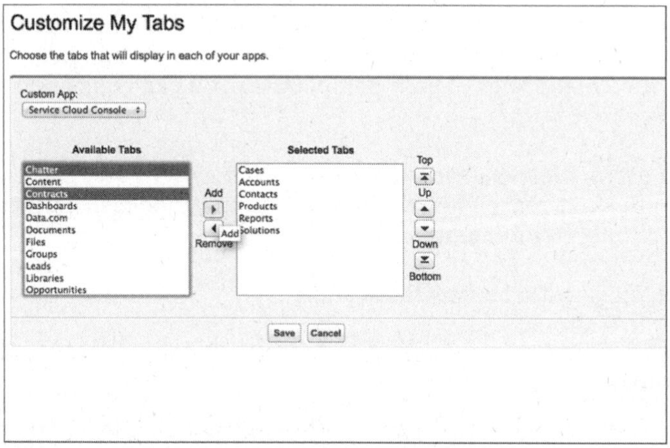

Figure 3-6:
Customizing
your tabs.

Customizing your pages

From the Display & Layout section, you can customize the order of your related lists on a record page. You may do this to minimize scrolling if your particular job rarely looks at certain related lists but you want to keep others top of mind and as high up on the record as possible.

To customize your page display, follow these steps:

1. **From the Display & Layout section, click the Customize My Pages subsection. Select a page in the drop-down and click the Customize Pages button beside it.**

   The Customize Pages page that is specific to the tab you've chosen appears.

2. **Select the lists you want to add or remove and use the Add or Remove arrows to do so.**

   For instance, if you have a knowledge base and don't use Salesforce Solutions, you can remove the related list from the Case detail page.

3. **Click the up and down arrows to change the order the lists appear on your page layout.**

4. **Click Save.**

   The Customize My Pages page appears again.

Granting others login access

In Salesforce, you can grant login access to system administrators and Salesforce support personnel so they can log in as you and help troubleshoot things with a better idea of your perspective. You can choose the duration of this access.

This is a useful tool when you have issues that either party can't remediate, or at the very least when they could use an inside peek at your view of Salesforce to better understand your problem.

To grant login access, follow these steps:

1. **Click Grant Account Login Access in the Personal section of the My Settings page's sidebar.**

   The Grant Login Access page (shown in Figure 3-7) appears.

2. **Choose an expiration date from the Access Duration drop-down that pertains to the party you want to grant access.**

That party will only be able to log in as you for the duration of the time you specify.

3. Click Save when you're done.

The Grant Account Login Access visually confirms that the changes were successfully saved.

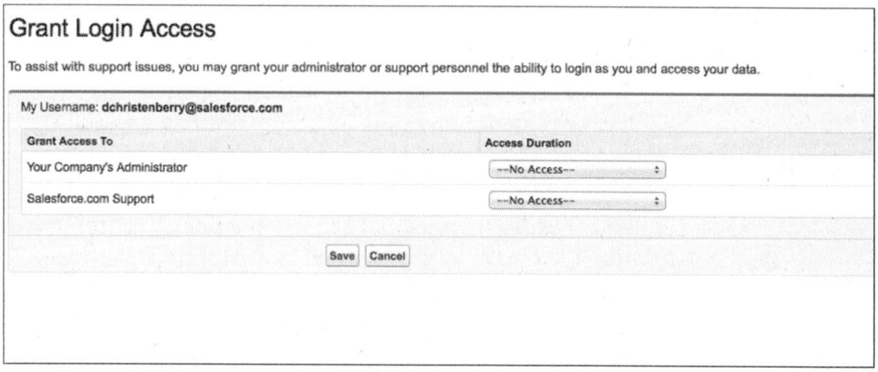

Grant Login Access

To assist with support issues, you may grant your administrator or support personnel the ability to login as you and access your data.

My Username: dchristenberry@salesforce.com

Grant Access To	Access Duration
Your Company's Administrator	--No Access-- ⇕
Salesforce.com Support	--No Access-- ⇕

Save   Cancel

Figure 3-7: The Grant Login Access page.

As an administrator, to log in as a user who has given you this access, choose Setup⇨Administer⇨Manage Users⇨Users, and choose Active Users from the list view drop-down. Then click the Login link to the left of the user's name. You now see Salesforce from that user's perspective. As soon as you log out, it will return you to the Users page as the administrator again.

Using Calendar sharing

You can grant access to your Calendar by sharing it with users, groups, all users in a role, or all users in a role and all the roles subordinate to it. You can choose who you want to share your calendar with as well as how.

To share your calendar, follow these steps:

1. Click Calendar Sharing from the Calendar & Reminders section of the My Settings page's sidebar.

The Calendar Sharing page appears with your username (meaning you have access to your Calendar). If you want to first take a quick look at what's on your Calendar, click the My Calendar link at the top left of the page.

2. **Click Add to share your Calendar with others.**

   The New Sharing page appears.

3. **Choose the user or group of users you want to add, and click the Add arrow so it moves from the Available column to the Share With column.**

   Keep doing this until everyone you want to share your Calendar with is in the column, as shown in Figure 3-8.

4. **Use the Calendar Access drop-down to select how you want to share your Calendar.**

   You may or may not have the following options for sharing, depending on how your administrator has set organization-wide sharing rules for calendars:

   • *Hide Details:* Others can see when you are or aren't available, but don't see why or any details.

   • *Hide Details and Add Events:* The same as Hide Details, but other users can add events to your Calendar.

   • *Show Details:* Others can see details about events in your Calendar.

   • *Show Details and Add Events:* The same as Show Details, but other users can add events to your Calendar.

   • *Full Access:* Others can see details about events in your Calendar, can add events to it, and can edit existing events in it.

5. **When you're done, click Save.**

   The Sharing Detail page appears, showing the newly added members you now share your Calendar with.

Reminding and alerting yourself

In the Calendar & Reminders section of the My Settings page you can access Reminders & Alerts, intended for customizing settings for event and task reminders.

These reminders and alerts serve as alarms to alert you if an event or task was triggered since the last time you've logged in. By default, a window pop-up reminds you (assuming your browser settings allow this) and a sound chimes. You can change these settings here.

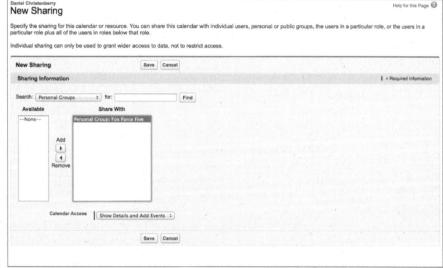

Figure 3-8:
Sharing
your
Calendar
with your
personal
group.

Customizing your email settings

The Email section of the My Settings page is all about emailing with Salesforce. To get here, choose *Your Name*⇨My Settings⇨Email⇨My Email Settings. Here, you can modify outgoing email settings, such as the following:

- ✔ **Email name:** Modify the name that appears on outgoing email from Salesforce.

- ✔ **Email address:** Change the email address that returned emails are automatically sent to.

- ✔ **Automatic Bcc:** You can have Salesforce automatically bcc emails to your return address.

- ✔ **Email signature:** Add a signature to the bottom of your outgoing emails.

Beyond the basic email settings, the Email section of the My Settings page also lets you manage:

- ✔ **Email templates:** Email templates expedite outbound communication to your customers.

- ✔ **Active mass emails:** See your mass email queue.

- ✔ **Stay-in-Touch settings:** Stay-in-Touch is a specific email template to request contact information updates from your customers.

Working with Salesforce Remotely and Offline

Maybe you're on the plane with a weak Internet connection. Maybe you're on a remote island on vacation. Either way, you don't always have an Internet connection. Salesforce.com planned for this and offers a way for you to update a subset of your records while you're offline.

Force.com Connect Offline is a downloadable client application that looks like the online version and allows users to create, read, edit, and delete from your *briefcase,* or a subset of available records. You can work anywhere, at any time, with literally no strings attached.

The first step is to install the application on your local hard drive. To do this, choose *Your Name*⇨My Settings⇨Desktop Add-Ons⇨Force.com Connect Offline and click the Install Now button. Make sure your administrator creates one or more offline briefcase configurations to hold the data available offline. When this is done, update the briefcase before running Connect Offline for the first time.

If you don't see an offline option in your Setup menu, you may be using Professional Edition. Force.com Connect Offline is only available for free on Enterprise, Performance, Unlimited, and Developer Editions, but you may still purchase it for an additional cost on the Professional Edition.

Changing Chatter Preferences

Under the My Settings menu is the Chatter section. Here you can manage your Chatter feed settings and choose how frequently Salesforce sends you Chatter email notifications.

When you follow records on Chatter, Salesforce sends updates to your Chatter feed when someone modifies the record. You can follow any record that your administrator enables for Chatter, such as accounts, cases, or contacts. To automatically follow records you create, follow these steps:

1. **On the My Settings page, click Chatter.**

   The section expands.

2. **Click My Feeds.**

   The My Feeds page appears where you can configure your Chatter feed settings.

3. **Click the Automatically Follow Records That I Create check box, and click Save.**

   You now have this setting enabled for your users.

You also have flexibility when it comes to the frequency of emails you receive following any kind of Chatter activity. You can receive emails when someone follows you, posts to a group you're a part of, mentions you in a post, and more.

The default is set to be more inclusive than exclusive, so if you don't want lots of Chatter email in your inbox, follow these steps:

1. **Under My Settings in the sidebar, choose Chatter⇨Email Notifications.**

   The Email Notifications page appears with all your options for receiving emails.

2. **Check or uncheck any of the check boxes to opt out of or into receiving emails.**

3. **When you're finished, click Save.**

   The My Settings page reappears.

Part II
Handling Customer Issues

Letterhead
MyCompany Logo

Preview your Letterhead details below.

Letterhead Detail   [Edit Properties] [Edit Letterhead] [Delete]

Letterhead Label	MyCompany Logo
Letterhead Unique Name	MyCompany_Logo
Available For Use	✓
Description	
Created By	Mary Matthews, 11/10/2014 6:01 AM

Modified By   Mary Matthews, 11/10/2014 6:18 AM

MY COMPANY

Find out how to build call scripts with Visual Workflow in a free article at
www.dummies.com/extras/salesforceservicecloud.

In this part . . .

- ✔ Find out about the case record and customize it to fit your needs.
- ✔ Handle customer issues with the case management lifecycle in Service Cloud.
- ✔ Manage your caseloads and collaborate internally to optimize efficiency in your call center.
- ✔ Understand communication and automation within Service Cloud to promote faster resolution.

Chapter 4

Creating and Managing Cases

• •

In This Chapter

▶ Creating cases for your customers

▶ Managing the case lifecycle

▶ Resolving and closing a case

• •

*I*magine you're on a call with a customer about a specific issue he's having with your product or service. After you've identified the customer on the phone, you want logging the issue to be incredibly simple — for good reason, too. In contact centers, every second counts. You need the ability to spin up cases on the fly.

Case management is the centerpiece of Service Cloud. It encompasses the entire lifecycle of your case — from the moment you create it until you close it, and all the touch points in between. The way you manage your cases in Service Cloud should map to your customized business process, and not the other way around.

We've all been in the customer's shoes before, trying to get an issue resolved without having to wait on hold multiple times and repeat our issues to every person we're transferred to. The bottom line is that no customer likes being shuffled around from agent to agent, and no service rep wants to be left unaware of customer activity and information. Learning to manage cases in Salesforce is the easiest way to avoid these common pitfalls.

In this chapter, we cover the basics of case management in Service Cloud. First, we show you how to create cases for your customers. We talk about the case record with its standard fields, while showing you how to customize case fields and layouts for your users. Next, we discuss how to manage those cases you've created, from detailing the case's information, to researching the issue, resolving it, and notifying your customer. Finally, we explain the customizable process for closing a case in Service Cloud.

Opening Cases for Customers

Cases are the foundation of Service Cloud. They're the focal point of your contact center and what your agents live and breathe on a daily basis. A *case* is a record of a service inquiry or support for a customer that details the issue and all the information surrounding it, as shown in Figure 4-1. From the case record, your agents manage the lifecycle of customer support and use these records as a hub for customer history and information.

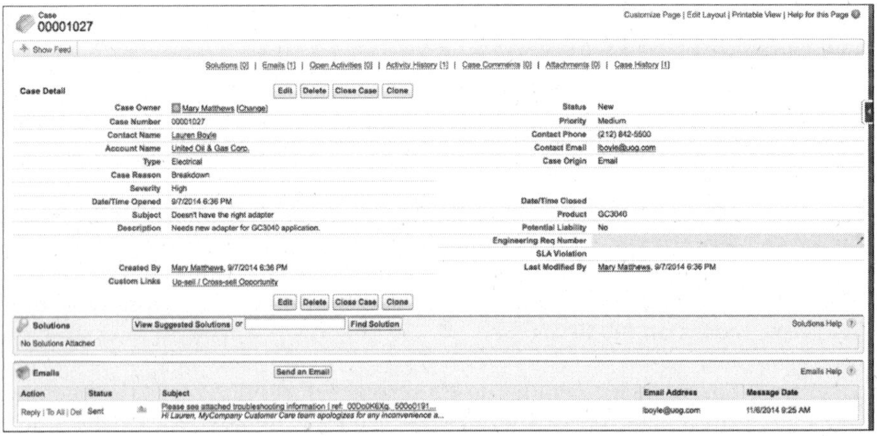

Figure 4-1: The case record.

In Service Cloud, creating a case is as simple as clicking a button. You can quickly create a case and enter all case details immediately, so that you can focus on helping your customer and not on figuring out cumbersome technology.

To create a new case in Salesforce for a support email or phone call, follow these steps:

1. **Navigate to the customer's account record.**

   You can use the global search to find it.

2. **Scroll down to the Contacts related list and click the appropriate contact record.**

   The contact record appears. Alternatively, if the contact from whom you're creating a case doesn't appear in the related list, click the New Contact button and create one first.

   In order to create a contact or a case, you need the proper security access. If you don't see these standard buttons, chances are, you need to talk to your administrator.

3. **On the contact record, scroll down to the Cases related list and click the New Case button.**

   The Case Edit page appears, with the Account Name and Contact Name fields prepopulated, as shown in Figure 4-2.

4. **After filling in the fields, click Save.**

   The case record appears and is created with the information entered.

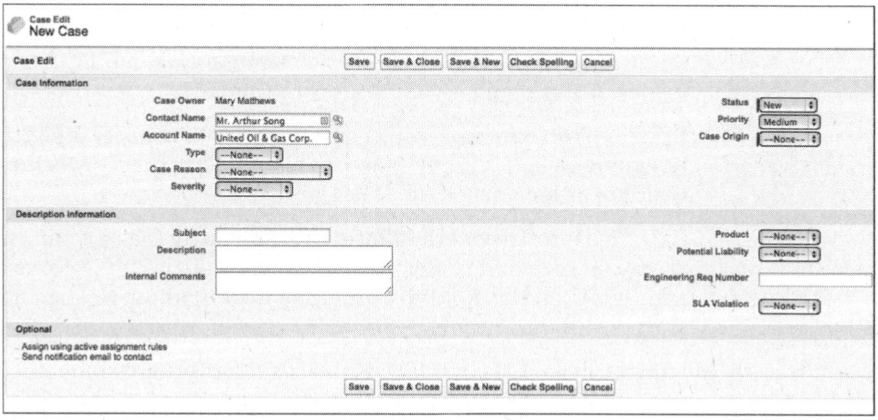

Figure 4-2: Creating a case in the Case Edit page.

Case Edit

Now that you know how to create a case and you see how easy it is to do, let's take a moment to discuss the case record.

For those one-and-done cases, where a case must be logged and tracked but solutions are immediately provided, instead of clicking Save, save time by clicking Save & Close. This saves the case info you just inputted and takes you to the Close Case detail page, discussed later in this chapter.

Understanding the case record

Because the case record is the central place for your support agents' work, it's important to make sure you understand the case record.

Getting to know standard case fields

Like other objects, the case object comes with standard fields out of the box. Let's take a look at some of these to understand what they're used for and how you can further customize them for your business.

Some standard case fields include

- **Account Name:** Look up the Account for whom the case is created.

- **Contact Name:** Look up the specific Contact (within the Account) for whom the case is created.

- **Case Number:** An auto-generated sequential number system, serving as a unique identifier for each created case.

- **Type:** You can have different case types and modify the picklist values, depending on your products or services.

- **Status:** You can have different case statuses and modify the picklist values, depending on your support process.

- **Priority:** You can rank your cases in order of priority and manage or assign them accordingly. You can also modify these priorities based on your business.

- **Case Reason:** There are different reasons why the specific case was created. You can modify the picklist values, depending on your business, and report on this field to determine how to improve specific areas of your customer service.

- **Subject:** This is the subject of the case that briefly states the issue. If you use Email-to-Case, the subject of the email maps to this field. If you use the Knowledge sidebar when creating a case in the console, it will use this field to automatically search for and suggest relevant articles.

- **Description:** This is the description that explains the subject of the case and details the issue.

- **Case Origin:** You can use this field to identify where the case comes from, usually by phone, email, or web. This is important for companies that want to see metrics on where cases are coming from and which channels to invest more in.

Customizing case fields and page layouts

Now that you have a good grasp on the case fields that come out of the box in Service Cloud, let's look at the basic customizations of these fields and page layouts to better align with your business.

Modifying case fields

You can modify standard case fields or create custom case fields to map to your personal process.

To change the label, or the name of the field as is displayed to the user, go to the Setup menu and follow these steps:

1. **Under Build, click the toggle to the left of Customize.**

   An expanded list appears.

2. **Click the first option, Tab Names and Labels.**

   Another expanded list appears.

3. **Click Rename Tabs and Labels.**

   Here you see a list of tabs and their standard tab names in Salesforce. You can configure standard Salesforce nomenclature and terminology here. For example, if your company wants to use the term *Ticket* or *Service Request* instead of the standard Salesforce term *Case,* click Edit next to Cases and rename the label here, both in the singular and the plural. If your new label starts with a vowel *sound,* such as *SR,* click the Starts with Vowel Sound check box.

   Embrace the change. Too often, companies cling to old terms from legacy systems. Although it's not detrimental in the big picture, consider accepting Salesforce's terminology with your new system. It will reduce administrative difficulties in the long term when those responsible for your organization can easily connect with the Salesforce ecosystem and speak the same language.

4. **Click Next.**

   Step 2: Enter the New Field Labels page appears.

5. **Type what you want the standard field to be called in the empty field(s) near the standard name and click Save.**

   If applicable, don't forget to add an *s* in the Plural column field and click the Starts with Vowel Sound check box, as shown in Figure 4-3.

Customizing your pages

In Service Cloud, if you're on Enterprise or Unlimited Edition, you can use record types and page layouts to control the organization and layout of your records. This is a good way to segment the fields and data you want to capture. For example, if you want to have some fields related to RMAs or product returns on your cases, but you only want these fields to be shown to a certain team, you can segment them using record types and page layouts.

Additionally, you can customize fields related to your business process, such as Status on the case, to display different picklist values depending on the case type. For example, you can have one case type for administrative issues, such as login difficulties or credit card issues, one for enhancement requests, and another for more technical inquiries. Each of these case types can have

Rename Tabs and Labels   Help for this Page

Enter the new tab names and field labels to display in the selected language.

Step 2. Enter the new field labels   Step 2 of 2

                                                                    Previous Save Cancel

Please review all the auto-populated values below for grammatical accuracy. Edit any standard field labels and other labels for the selected tab and language.

Tab   Cases
Language English

Standard Field Labels   Other Labels

	Singular	Plural	Starts with vowel sound
Case Currency	Case Currency		
Case Division	Case Division		
Case Name	Case Name		
Case Number	Case Number		
Case Origin	Case Origin		
Case Owner	Case Owner		
Case Reason	Case Reason		
Comment	Explanation	Explanations	
Description	Description		
Escalation Date	Escalation Date		
Internal Comments	Internal Comments		
Parent Case	Parent Case	Parent Cases	
Priority	Priority		

Figure 4-3:
Renaming
a standard
case field in
Salesforce.

unique record types and page layouts that display different fields and even distinct values in picklist fields if they follow separate process flows. To learn more about how to create and modify record types and page layouts, see Chapter 20.

Identifying and qualifying your customers

If your company has service-level agreements (SLAs) and requires that your customers first be entitled to support before actually receiving any, you may want to qualify the person on the phone before opening a case for her.

The following steps outline the basic process of identifying a caller in Service Cloud:

1. **In the global search at the top of any page, type the name of the customer on the phone — either the individual's name (the Contact) or the business the person is with (the Account) — and click Search.**

   The Search Results page appears with either a contact name or account name. If no results appear on the page, you can either create an account record for the customer, or follow some other business process that is decided by your organization.

   Whatever the process may be, remember to keep usability, adoption, and speed of service in mind. You want your customers and agents to love you, right?

2. **Click the Account or Contact Name.**

   If your company has a defined process around authorizing service, these records are where that information should be captured and updated.

Authorizing customers to receive support in Service Cloud

Beyond capturing this information in fields, for customers using Enterprise or Unlimited editions that have more complex processes around SLAs and service authorization, Service Cloud offers a suite of functionality around Entitlements.

Entitlement management in Service Cloud is a way for you and your users to verify, before opening a case for a customer, that the customer is entitled to receive support. Using entitlements, you can do the following:

- ✔ **Verify a customer's support eligibility.**

- ✔ **Define service levels for different types of customers and build processes around them to ensure they're enforced.**

- ✔ **Create and update unique service contracts for customers.**

- ✔ **Allow customers to view their own service contracts and entitlements, as well as create cases with the appropriate ones through Communities.**

Managing Your Cases

When you've created your case for a validated customer, the bulk of the work begins. As a support agent, you have many cases that you have to manage simultaneously. To stay ahead of the curve, Service Cloud offers some tools to increase productivity and help you focus on the issues you need to solve quickly. The way you manage your cases is very dependent on your specific business process, but Salesforce makes it easy to do.

The steps in managing your cases may differ slightly depending on whether you're using the Service Cloud Console (see Chapters 8 and 9 for more details).

Capturing case details

Managing your cases is maintaining them. You need to ensure that each case contains the most current information so that you, your customer, and everyone else in the organization understand where you are in the process. To modify case information, follow these steps:

1. Find the case you want to update.

In the global search at the top of any page, you can search for a case number, keywords from the case subject line, or even the name of a customer, and find the associated case. Or you can choose a case you're working on from a personal list view (see Chapter 5) or even from the Recent Items list in the sidebar on the left side of your screen.

2. Click the Case Number link to open the case.

The Case Detail page appears.

3. Click the Edit button to start editing the case.

The Case Edit page appears with fields you can change. Alternatively, if your organization has inline editing turned on, you can edit your fields directly on the Case Detail page by double-clicking them. For more information on inline editing, see Chapter 2.

As shown in Figure 4-4, at the bottom left of the Case Edit page, you can click the Send Notification Email to Contact check box to automatically let your customer know that you've updated the case.

4. When you're done, click Save.

The Case Detail page reappears with the changes and updates you've made.

In the interest of time, from the Case Edit page, you can also click Save & Close, to close out the case, or click Save & New, if you want to save the case and immediately start working on a new one.

Figure 4-4:
Sending case updates to customers on the Case Edit page.

Case Edit				

Case Edit · 00001027 · Help for this Page

Case Edit — Save · Save & Close · Save & New · Check Spelling · Cancel

Case Information · | = Required Information

Case Owner: Mary Matthews
Case Number: 00001027
Contact Name: Lauren Boyle
Account Name: United Oil & Gas Corp.
Type: Electrical
Case Reason: Breakdown
Severity: High

Status: New
Priority: Medium
Case Origin: Email

Description Information

Subject: Doesn't have the right adapter
Description: Needs new adapter for GC3040 application.
Internal Comments:

Product: GC3040
Potential Liability: No
Engineering Req Number:
SLA Violation: --None--

Optional

Assign using active assignment rules
Send notification email to contact

Save · Save & Close · Save & New · Check Spelling · Cancel

Sometimes updating cases doesn't involve modifying actual case fields, but rather the related information captured in related lists. If you want to add information to a related list or case information that is not stored in a field, you can simply scroll to the desired related list on the Case Detail page and click a corresponding button, such as the New Task button on the Open Activities related list.

Researching and resolving the issue

As an agent, you need to know what tools are available to you in Service Cloud to make your job easier. More specifically, Salesforce offers two major issue resolution tools for customers and support agents alike, Solutions and Knowledge.

What's the difference, you ask? Before we explain the differences, here's what they have in common:

- ✔ Both Solutions and Knowledge Articles can be attached to a case.
- ✔ You can follow both in your Chatter feed for continuous collaboration and improvement.

Here are some differences between Knowledge and Solutions:

- ✔ Knowledge requires feature licenses, meaning that it costs more money per user, whereas Solutions come free out of the box.
- ✔ Knowledge gives you the capability to segment through articles and data categories. This allows you to show different sets of knowledge to customers, partners, or support agents, something that Solutions can't do.
- ✔ Knowledge comes with a much more advanced suite of enhanced reporting and analytics. You can get insights into article popularity by channel, frequency of article use, keyword search reports, and many more.
- ✔ Knowledge currently integrates nicely with the Service Cloud console and Live Agent Chat, and will assuredly become more integrated as other features are released moving forward.
- ✔ Knowledge articles allow for a comprehensive publishing approval process for quality control.
- ✔ Solutions is not being actively improved upon anymore, whereas Knowledge is.
- ✔ Knowledge comes with rich text-editing functionality, but Solutions does not.

For an in-depth look at Knowledge and its capabilities, see Chapters 10, 11, and 12. To learn about Solutions, check out Chapter 5.

If you have the Solutions related list on the case record, you can click the View Suggested Solutions button, which brings up relevant solution possibilities based on your case's subject field. Alternatively, you can type directly into the blank field on the related list and click Find Solution to search that way, as shown in Figure 4-5.

Beyond finding articles that contain solutions to attach to a case, agents can also leverage Chatter and specific groups within it to tap into internal knowledge and solve cases more quickly.

Figure 4-5:
Saving time by searching for solutions directly from the case record.

Solutions	View Suggested Solutions or	Model CXV-8764	Find Solution	Solutions Help
No Solutions Attached				

Communicating the solution

After you've found a viable solution for the issue, the next step in the process is letting the customer know you've solved it.

One method of updating the customer is updating the case status and comments and checking the Send Notification Email to Contact check box before clicking Save (refer to Figure 4-4).

The Send Notification Email to Contact check box is not standard on all page layouts.

Another way to notify the customer is to add Case Comments as the case progresses so that you and anyone who opens your case can see exactly what is occurring on your case, from beginning to end. If you have the Self-Service Portal or Communities enabled in your organization, you can click the Public check box when creating a Case Comment, which exposes the comment to the customer in the Portal or Community. This helps customers view the progress of their cases online and know when you've solved it.

Finally, you can use the good old-fashioned method of email directly from the case, using email templates or manually drafting an email to let your contact know the case is solved. To learn how, see the "Sending emails from the case" section, later in this chapter.

Ensuring consistency with email templates

How often do you find yourself copying old emails so that you can send them to others? Do you often put off writing emails? Writing emails takes time, especially when you have lots of customers to correspond with. Luckily, it's easy to create and send email templates in Service Cloud. Email templates are a great way to make sure that your emails are sent to customers in a timely and consistent manner.

Learning about email templates

In case management, you can use email templates in case assignment rules, in auto-response rules, or even just to send customers in response to their inquiries. You can also make these email templates match your company's marketing and branding with logos.

Email templates are stored in folders, and those folders can be shared with different users or groups of users. Organize your templates into intuitive email folders instead of letting them accumulate in the default Unfiled Public Email Templates folder. This approach takes more time upfront, but it'll save you headache and hassle down the road.

There are four types of email templates users can create:

- ✔ **Text:** These templates can be created by any user and are the easiest to use. They require no HTML and are basic, text-only templates.

- ✔ **HTML:** HTML templates use previously created letterhead to showcase your company logo and brand, and support HTML formatting, although knowledge of HTML is not required.

- ✔ **Custom HTML:** These templates require either knowledge of HTML or the previously created HTML code to paste into your template.

- ✔ **Visualforce:** These templates use a saved Visualforce page so their merge fields can come from multiple different objects. This requires knowledge of Visualforce.

We discuss the two types of templates here that are most often used: text and HTML with letterhead. We don't want to bore you with custom code.

Merge fields allow you to customize email templates dynamically so that your emails don't look canned. For example, instead of sending all your customers an email that begins with "To whom it may concern" or "Dear valued customer," you can start your template with "Dear (Merge field: Contact_First_Name)" so that the first name of the customer is dynamically inserted when the email is sent.

Creating personal email templates

Instead of copying and pasting certain sentences and phrases, create your own personal templates to improve your productivity. To create a personal email template, follow these steps:

1. **Click your username at the top right and choose My Settings⇨ Email⇨Email Templates.**

   The Email Templates page appears with a Folder drop-down.

2. **Choose My Personal Email Templates from the drop-down and click the New Template button.**

   Step 1 of the template wizard appears, presenting you with four options for template types.

3. **Choose the type of email template that suits your needs and click Next.**

   The next step of the template wizard appears, showing a different page depending on your template selection.

4. **If you selected a text template in Step 3, you'll have to fill out some information, as shown in Figure 4-6, and then click Save.**

   Make sure you click the Available for Use check box. You don't have to click it right away if you're creating lots of templates, but you won't be able to actually use the template until you do.

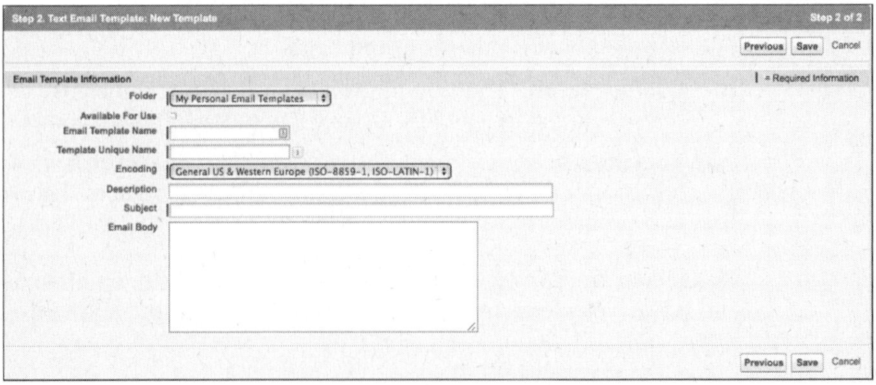

| Step 2. Text Email Template: New Template | Step 2 of 2 |

Previous | Save | Cancel

Email Template Information   I = Required Information

Folder | My Personal Email Templates |
Available For Use
Email Template Name
Template Unique Name
Encoding | General US & Western Europe (ISO-8859-1, ISO-LATIN-1) |
Description
Subject
Email Body

Previous | Save | Cancel

Figure 4-6:
Creating
a text
template.

The Text Email Template page appears, where you can preview and test the email template. Optionally, you can attach a file to your template in the Attachments related list.

5. **If you selected an HTML template in Step 3, you'll first have to create a letterhead or select a previously created one.**

   On the Letterhead Properties page, you can customize your letterhead's look and feel, as shown in Figure 4-7.

Letterhead
MyCompany Logo

Preview your Letterhead details below.

Letterhead Detail   Edit Properties   Edit Letterhead   Delete

Letterhead Label   MyCompany Logo
Letterhead Unique Name   MyCompany_Logo
Available For Use   ✓
Description
Created By   Mary Matthews, 11/10/2014 6:01 AM   Modified By   Mary Matthews, 11/10/2014 6:18 AM

MY COMPANY

Figure 4-7:
Creating a
letterhead.

If you're creating a letterhead from scratch, go to the Documents tab and create a new Document there, uploading an image file of your company's logo. You can use this on all your letterheads to make them look official. Fancy!

6. **Create the HTML template by using your letterhead, and adding the email content, including subject header, and copying and pasting merge fields in the content.**

You can only use merge fields from one object per email template. So if that's the case, you can only bring in fields from the case; otherwise, the merge fields won't populate in your email.

7. **When you're done, you can preview the template to make sure the merge fields are working and click Next.**

   Step 4 of the wizard appears.

8. **Create a text version of the same email template for those customers who can't or don't want to receive HTML in their emails.**

   Use the Copy Text from HTML version to speed this up if the text is similar or identical.

9. **Click Save.**

   The HTML Template detail page appears, with a preview.

Sending emails from the case

Now that you've created an email template or two, let's look at sending emails with and without them by following these steps:

1. **Navigate to the case record from which you want to send an email and click the Send an Email button on the Activity History related list.**

   If you don't see the Activity History related list, it's probably because it doesn't appear on your page layout.

   The Edit Email page appears with the From, To, and Related To fields pre-populated.

   If your organization has Email-to-Case, you can also use the Emails related list.

2. **If you're using an email template, before filling in the Subject or Body fields, click the Select Template button.**

   A pop-up appears, with a list of templates that are available to use, as shown in Figure 4-8. If you're not using an email template, go to Step 4.

3. **Select the template you want to use.**

   The Edit Email page refreshes with the Subject and Body populated.

4. **Modify and personalize the email, and then click Send when you're ready.**

   The case record reappears with the email logged in your Activity History and Emails related list, if applicable.

Before sending the email, click the Check Spelling button. Professionalism, folks.

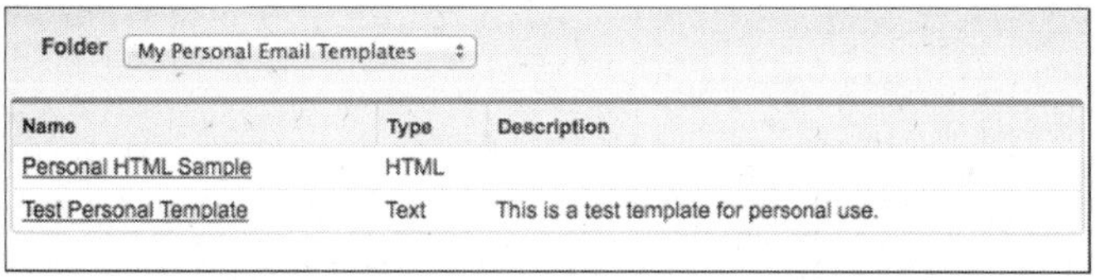

Figure 4-8:
Available
email tem-
plates.

Folder	My Personal Email Templates		
Name		**Type**	**Description**
Personal HTML Sample		HTML	
Test Personal Template		Text	This is a test template for personal use.

Closing a Case

This is definitely your favorite part of case management. The victory of case closure is sweet, especially in Service Cloud. To close a case, follow these steps:

1. **On the case record, click the Close Case button.**

   The Close Case Edit page appears, as shown in Figure 4-9. Alternatively, if article submissions are enabled in your organization and you want to capture the solution that helped you close the case, click the Save & Create Article button.

2. **Fill in the appropriate information, including the Status and other custom fields and information your organization wants to capture.**

   For example, you can add a custom field called Resolution to report on the most common ways cases are resolved.

3. **If you're using Solutions, fill out the Solution Information section to create a solution from this case.**

   Especially if the case is a great example for a particular issue, create a solution for it that you can reuse for similar cases. The solution will also be linked to this case.

4. **Click Save.**

   The case detail page reappears with a closed status. The case is now closed.

Easy enough, right?

More than likely, you'll want to customize the information and data you capture when an agent closes a case. You can add custom fields to the case object and move them onto the Close Case page layout so that you can report on these data points and get a better understanding of the problem, cause, and resolution of a customer inquiry.

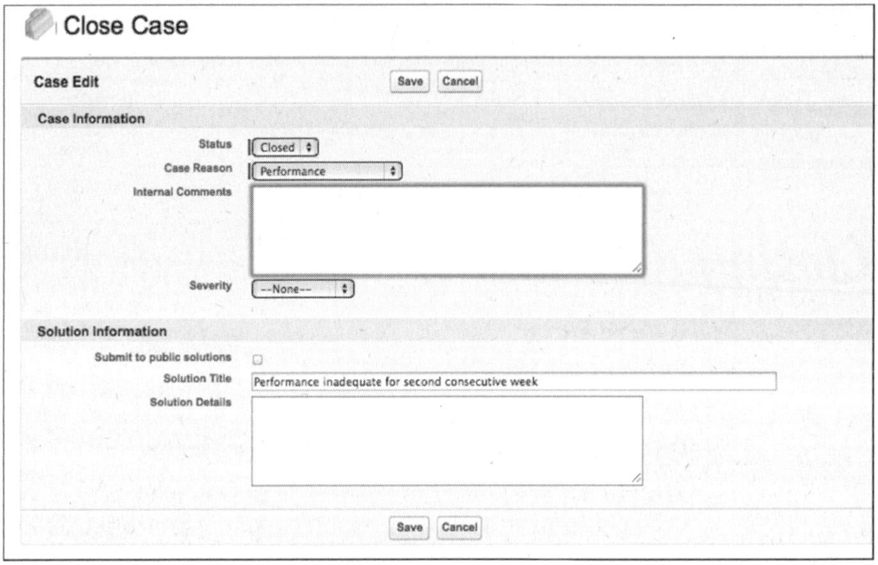

Figure 4-9:
The Close
Case Edit
screen
allows you
to capture
more case
details
before
closing.

To customize the close case page layout, choose Setup⇨Build⇨ Customize⇨Cases⇨Page Layouts, and follow these steps:

1. **Under the Close Case Page Layout list, click the Edit link to the left of the Page Layout Name.**

   The enhanced page layout editor appears, with the current page layout of the Close Case page.

2. **Use the enhanced page layout editor to drag and drop fields onto the layout, exactly where you want them.**

   The desired fields appear on the page.

3. **Optionally, to add a check box to the layout to choose to have your customers know when you close the case, click the Layout Properties button at the top of the toolbar and then click the Show on Edit Page check box, as shown in Figure 4-10.**

4. **Click Save when you're done.**

   The Case Page Layout screen reappears with your layouts.

To learn even more about how to create custom fields and modify page layouts, see Chapter 20.

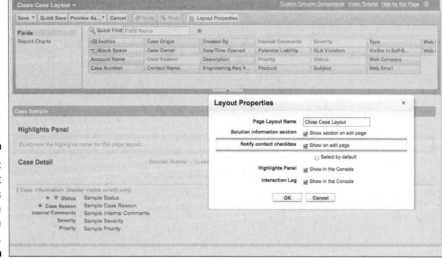

Figure 4-10:
Layout
Properties
on the close
case page
layout.

Chapter 5

Solving Cases Efficiently

. . . .

In This Chapter

▶ Creating custom list views

▶ Leveraging queues to manage cases

▶ Automating assignments and responses

▶ Taking advantage of organizational knowledge

. . . .

*W*ith Salesforce Service Cloud, not only can support agents quickly create and manage cases, but additional features and automation rest at your fingertips, just waiting to increase productivity, save you time, ensure customer satisfaction, and cut support costs across the organization. With additional, simple, point-and-click configuration options, your organization can quickly take advantage of the most powerful solutions in the industry to ensure consistent, quality communications with customers, decrease average case-handling times, and increase transparency throughout the case management process.

In this chapter, we review the fundamentals of views and queues. No matter your role in the organization, a basic understanding of views and queues can mean a great deal of time saved for you and your colleagues as you manage your case workload. Next, we reveal the powerful automation tools that Salesforce administrators can set up to cut busy work and generic communications out of the day for support agents, leaving them free to solve more cases. Then we explain how your organization's support teams can leverage three native Salesforce knowledge base options to quickly solve cases, efficiently reuse common solutions, and share resolutions directly with customers.

Managing Cases with Views and Queues

Sometimes the most efficient gains lie in the simplest solutions. If you can save seconds or even milliseconds on small tasks that you complete constantly, the savings will add up quickly over the course of a day, week, and year.

With Salesforce, learning the ins and outs of views and queues will help you help yourself whether you're a support agent, manager, or system administrator.

Creating a view

When you click into a tab in Salesforce to access a specific object (for example, Accounts, Contacts, or Cases), you find yourself on the object home page (for example, the Cases Home page if you select cases, as shown in Figure 5-1).

You see some larger, delineated rectangles on the Recent Cases, Reports, and Tools page. However, the first place your eye should land is the View drop-down at the top of the page.

When you navigate to the Cases tab, this View drop-down defaults to the My Open Cases option, as shown in Figure 5-1.

This exists on all object tabs in Salesforce and allows you to choose various views in list form, appropriately called *list views*. Each tab has a default list view that the page brings up when you first arrive. To change to a different view, you just need to make a new selection in the drop-down list.

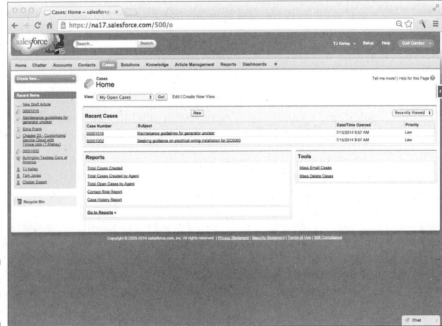

Figure 5-1:
The Cases
home page.

After you've made a choice, the page refreshes and displays the list view you've chosen. If you choose My Open Cases, you see a list of all cases that you're assigned to that are currently open issues, as shown in Figure 5-2.

Here are some of the default options available on the Cases home page:

- ✔ All Closed Cases
- ✔ All Open Cases
- ✔ My Cases
- ✔ My Open Cases
- ✔ Recently Viewed Cases

List views provide a quick, easy means of locating important records in the system. As mentioned, Salesforce provides a few useful options for you out of the box, but to realize the full potential of list views, you should create custom list views to display the records that are most important to your day-to-day activities.

Figure 5-2:
The My Open Cases list view.

For example, if you have a 72-hour service-level agreement (SLA), you should create a custom list view to display your open cases with the oldest created open case displaying at the top. Additionally, if you handle cases with multiple different priority levels, it may be worth creating a separate view altogether for high-priority cases.

Although very simple, custom case list views can be a huge timesaver as you manage your daily or weekly caseload.

To begin creating your own custom list view, click the Create New View link next to the View drop-down. You see the Create New View page, as shown in Figure 5-3. In Step 1 of the Create New View page, choose a name for your new view and proceed to the following sections to learn more.

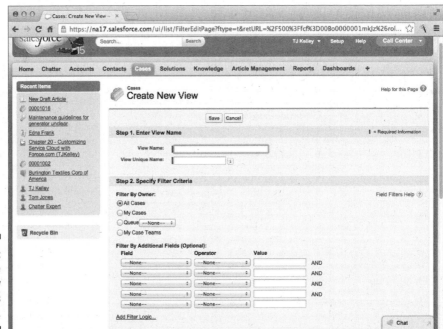

Figure 5-3:
The Create
New View
page, Steps
1 and 2.

Defining list view criteria

The first step on the road to list view independence is to create your own criteria. Take control of the data you see, and focus on the cases that matter most to you.

In Step 2 of the Create New View page (refer to Figure 5-3), follow these steps to define your list view criteria:

1. **Choose a filter by owner option.**

   For cases, you have the following choices:

   - *All Cases:* Displays all cases regardless of owner.
   - *My Cases:* Filters cases to look at only the ones you're assigned to.
   - *Queue:* Choose a specific case queue to look at for your view.
   - *My Case Teams:* Filters cases to look at only cases where you're on the case team.

2. **Optionally, filter by additional fields.**

   This step allows you to get very specific with your list view. You can choose from a wide range of case fields to filter for a subset of cases that matter most to you.

   Use the field drop-downs to create up to ten field filters for your list view. If you choose to go beyond five field filters in this section, you must click Add Filter Logic and use the Add Row link to add additional field filters.

3. **Optionally, click Add Filter Logic to further hone your results.**

   If you want to set criteria that are not united via "AND" logic, you'll need to add filter logic. For example, you may want to view cases where the priority is high and the status is new. You may also want to view high-priority cases that have been escalated in the same list view.

   In this example, you would set up the following field filters:

   - Priority equals High
   - Status equals New
   - Escalated equals True

   After you've created your field filters, you input the following filter logic: 1 AND (2 OR 3). This allows you to see high-priority cases that are either in the new status or have been escalated.

Exposing relevant data

When you're happy with the criteria for your list view, you need to choose what data to display on the view. When deciding what data to display on your list view, take a look back at Figure 5-2 and notice the columns of data that display in the list view. The fields you choose to expose will display on your list view, as shown by the columns in Figure 5-2.

If you're creating this list view for yourself, include only the fields that you find to be most relevant and helpful when quickly scanning cases. On the other hand, if you're creating this view for multiple users or a large group of users, be sure to fully understand the data that the users find most important and relevant so you can make the best choices to drive productivity.

In Step 3 of the Create New View page, shown in Figure 5-4, follow these steps to expose the most relevant data on your view:

1. **Use the Available Fields box to select the fields most relevant for your case list view.**

2. **Click the Add arrow to move fields from the Available Fields box to the Selected Fields box.**

3. **If you want to remove any fields from the Selected Fields box, click the field in the box and click the Remove arrow to add it back to the Available Fields box and leave it off of your view.**

4. **To the right of the Selected Fields box, use the Up/Down and Top/ Bottom arrows to choose the order in which the data will appear on your list view.**

    When you select a list view in the system, the fields appear from left to right as they're ordered from top to bottom in the Selected Fields box.

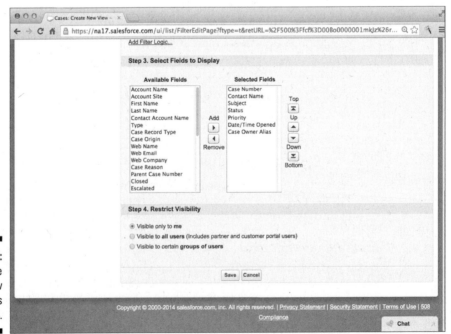

Figure 5-4:
The Create New View page, Steps 3 and 4.

Designating visibility

When you define your list view criteria and select the data you want to expose in the view, you need to decide who will have access to leverage the list view when they login and navigate to the Cases home page.

Only users with the Manage Public List Views permission enabled on their profiles will be able to designate visibility for list views. Also, this option is not available in Personal Edition.

Access to a list view doesn't necessarily give users access to all data rendered in the view. Users must have access to view case records through your security model in order to see the cases appear in a list view.

In Step 4 of the Create New View page, you can choose from the following options to designate visibility for your list view:

- ✔ **Only to me:** Visible only to the creator of the list view.

- ✔ **All:** Visible for all users in the system.

- ✔ **Visible only to certain groups:** Visible only to specified groups of users.

    Continue reading to learn more about how to restrict list view visibility to certain groups of users.

Managing your organization's views

If you have the Manage Public List Views permission enabled on your profile, you have the power to create, edit, or restrict custom list views for your organization. With great power, comes great responsibility.

If many users in the system have this permission, the available custom list views can quickly get out of hand if the users are frequently creating one-off views based on user requests and setting them as visible to all users.

If you have the "Manage Public List Views" permission, use your power to control and manage your organization's list views. If support agents log in and navigate to the Cases home page only to find a cumbersome list of a hundred custom list views, they won't have an easy time finding the list views most important to their jobs.

As a general rule, review your organization's custom list views once every six months and delete or restrict visibility as needed. Each support agent should have no more than ten list views available to him or her at any given time. This will save agents and, ultimately, customers time by allowing quick, easy access to the most important information.

Selecting users, roles, and public groups

When creating a list view, in Step 4: Restrict Visibility, you have the option to select for your list view to be visible to certain groups of users. When you make this selection, the page expands and presents you with a search filter, a search box, an Available for Sharing window, and a Shared To window, as shown in Figure 5-5.

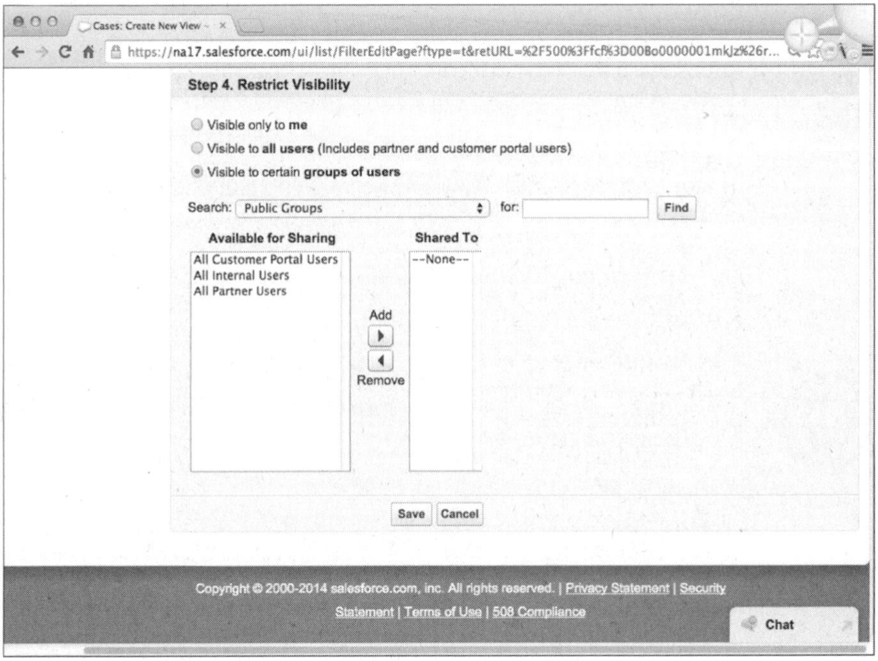

Figure 5-5:
Visible only to certain groups of users.

Follow these steps to select the groups of users that will be able to use your list view:

1. **Make a selection in the Search drop-down list from the following available options:**

   • *Public Groups:* A set of users that can contain individual users, roles, other public groups, or roles and subordinates

   • *Roles:* All users assigned to a specific role

   • *Roles and Internal Subordinates:* A role and all subordinate internal roles in your organization's role hierarchy

   • *Roles, Internal and Portal Subordinates:* A role and all subordinate portal and internal roles in your organization's role hierarchy

- *Portal Roles:* All users assigned to a specific portal role

- *Portal Roles and Subordinates:* A portal role and all subordinate roles in your organization's role hierarchy

2. **Type in the Open text box and click Find to search for roles and public groups that match or start with the words you typed into the text box.**

3. **Search through the options that display in the Available for Sharing window to locate the roles or public groups that you would like to share your view with.**

4. **Highlight the roles or public groups you want to share with and click the Add arrow to move them into the Shared To column.**

5. **Click Save when you're finished making your list view sharing selections.**

Creating public groups

Public groups are sets of users that may include individual users, roles, other public groups, or roles and subordinates. Public groups can be used to grant access to shared resources in Salesforce. Create public groups when you have sets of related users who will need similar access rights in the system. Groups are particularly effective when you have sets of related users who have varying roles, because they allow you to aggregate these users in one place, even though their roles may span the entire hierarchy.

To create a public group, follow these steps:

1. **From Setup, choose Manage Users⇨Public Groups.**

   The Public Groups home page displays.

2. **Click New.**

   The Group Membership edit page appears.

3. **Choose a label and unique name for your group.**

4. **Make a selection in the Search drop-down list from the following available options:**

   - *Public Groups:* A set of users that can contain individual users, roles, other public groups, or roles and subordinates

   - *Roles:* All users assigned to a specific role

   - *Roles and Internal Subordinates:* A role and all subordinate internal roles in your organization's role hierarchy

   - *Roles, Internal and Portal Subordinates:* A role and all subordinate portal and internal roles in your organization's role hierarchy

   - *Portal Roles:* All users assigned to a specific portal role

- *Portal Roles and Subordinates:* A portal role and all subordinate roles in your organization's role hierarchy

- *Users:* Individual users

- *Partner Users:* Individual partner users

5. **Select options from the Available Members window and click the Add arrow to add them to the Selected Members window.**

6. **Click Save.**

Creating a case queue

Case queues in Salesforce provide your support organization with an easy, flexible solution to support and distribute the cases across different levels of the organization. You can create multiple queues for your different support tiers and assign cases to those queues manually or automatically with case assignment rules.

Continue reading this chapter to learn more about case assignment rules.

To create a case queue, follow these steps:

1. **From Setup, choose Manage Users⇨Queues.**

   The Queues home page appears.

2. **Click New at the top of the page.**

   The Queue edit page appears.

3. **Enter basic information for your queue.**

   Choose the following details for your queue:

   - *Label:* A label for your queue that users will see as the queue name.

   - *Queue Name:* A unique API name for your queue that will be leveraged by the system, but not seen by users. Salesforce will automatically fill in a default queue name based on the field label that you enter.

   - *Queue Email:* An email address associated to the queue. Use this to enter a group distribution list if you want to notify an inbox managed by a group of users when a new case gets added to the queue.

   - *Send Email to Members:* Check this box if you want to send an email notification to all queue members individually when a new case gets added to the queue.

4. **Select the Case object from the Available Objects window.**

   The Case object is highlighted.

5. **Click the Add arrow to move the Case object into the Selected Objects window.**

   The Case object appears in the Selected Objects window.

6. **Select queue members for your queue by searching in the Available Members window and adding members to the Selected Members window.**

   You can select members to add to your queue based on the following options:

   - *Public Groups:* A set of users that can contain individual users, roles, other public groups, or roles and subordinates

   - *Roles:* All users assigned to a specific role

   - *Roles and Internal Subordinates:* A role and all subordinate internal roles in your organization's role hierarchy

   - *Roles, Internal and Portal Subordinates:* A role and all subordinate portal and internal roles in your organization's role hierarchy

   - *Portal Roles:* All users assigned to a specific portal role

   - *Portal Roles and Subordinates:* A portal role and all subordinate roles in your organization's role hierarchy

   - *Users:* Individual users

   - *Partner Users:* Individual partner users

7. **Click Save.**

When you've defined a queue, Salesforce automatically creates a queue list view that will be available to queue members on the Cases home page. Additionally, you can now leverage your case queue with assignment rules. Read on to find out more about using your case queue to automate case assignments in your organization.

Using Automation to Your Advantage

Views and queues will help you solve cases more efficiently by saving you time when searching for the most relevant case records or ensuring that the appropriate groups receive cases that they're best suited to solve.

With Salesforce case assignment rules and auto-response rules, you can take your time saving to the next level by automating standard case assignment procedures and basic email responses to the customer.

Not only will this save time in your day, but also Salesforce automation will ensure quality across your support organization. Let's face it, sometimes the little things like letting a customer know his case has been received can get lost in the hustle and bustle of everyday activities. Take control of your team's quality and ensure customer satisfaction!

Assigning cases within your organization

Are you a customer support manager who spends hours each day managing the assignment of new support cases manually? Are you new to Salesforce and trying to figure out the best way to assign cases? In both situations, case assignment rules are your best bet to save time and money, while ensuring customer satisfaction when it comes to assigning cases in Salesforce.

With case assignment rules, you can ensure that cases are routed to the correct users or groups by predefining all possible case scenarios and the assignment route they should take based on specific case criteria.

For example, you can automatically assign cases based on location, agent skill set, products involved, customer support tier, or case priority level when new cases are created from any channel.

Creating assignment rules

A case assignment rule is really a grouping of rules that will help you automatically assign cases throughout your support organization based on criteria captured on the case records. Each assignment rule can have multiple rule entries. A rule entry represents a condition or set of criteria that, when matched, determines the assignment of a case.

To create an assignment rule, follow these steps:

1. **From Setup, under the Build section, choose Customize➪Cases➪Assignment Rules.**

   The Case Assignment Rules page displays.

2. **Click New.**

   The New Case Assignment Rule page appears.

3. Choose a rule name.

Leave the Active check box unchecked unless you want to activate your assignment rule immediately. We recommend leaving the rule inactive until you have the criteria clearly defined and set.

4. Click Save.

The Case Assignment Rules page reappears with your new rule saved.

5. Click the Rule Name link for your new rule.

The Case Assignment Rule detail page appears.

6. Click New at the top of the Rule Entries list to add a new rule entry for your assignment rule.

The Rule Entry edit page displays, as shown in Figure 5-6.

7. In Step 1 of the Rule Entry edit page, enter a Sort Order for your rule entry. If this is your first rule entry, enter 1.

You can reorder rule entries before activating your assignment rule.

8. In Step 2 of the Rule Entry edit page, select the criteria for your rule entry.

For example, you might choose to route cases based on priority. If so, you could enter a piece of criterion using the Priority field with the equals operator and set the value to High to create a rule entry for high-priority cases.

Refer to the "Creating a view" section for a more comprehensive overview of how to define the criteria in Step 2 here.

9. In Step 3 of the Rule Entry edit page, select the user or the queue that should be assigned to the case based on the criteria you entered earlier.

10. Optionally, in Step 4 of the Rule Entry edit page, set predefined case teams to be added to each case that matches the criteria for this entry.

To learn more about Case Teams, refer to Chapter 6.

11. Click Save.

The Case Assignment Rule detail page reappears with your saved rule entry. You can create more rule entries and use the Reorder button on the Case Assignment detail page to choose the order in which the entries should be evaluated when assigning new cases.

12. When you've finished defining and ordering your rule entries and you're ready to start saving time by automating case assignments, click Edit at the top of the case assignment rule detail page, click the Active check box, and click Save.

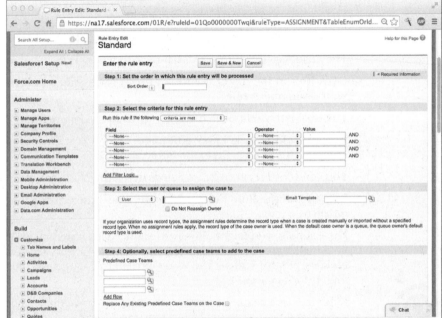

Figure 5-6:
The Rule
Entry edit
page.

You can create multiple case assignment rules, but only one rule can be activated in your organization at any given time. You may want to create multiple rules to use during different times of the year (if you have special holiday procedures, for example).

To ensure that your organization's cases are always being routed to an owner, create a final rule entry with blank criteria and assign it to a manager or manager-owned queue that can serve as a placeholder for any cases that sneak through your rule entries.

Setting up automatic responses for your organization

With Salesforce auto-response rules, you can predefine responses to your customers when cases come into your system from external channels.

You can set up automatic responses for cases captured through the following channels:

- ✔ Self-service portal
- ✔ Customer portal
- ✔ Web-to-Case form
- ✔ Email-to-Case message
- ✔ On-Demand Email-to-Case message

Defining auto-response rules

To create auto-response rules for cases, follow these steps:

1. **From Setup, under the Build section, choose Customize⟹Cases⟹Auto-Response Rules.**

   The Case Auto-Response Rules page displays.

2. **Click New.**

   The New Case Auto-Response Rules page appears.

3. **Choose a rule name.**

   Leave the Active check box unchecked unless you want to activate your assignment rule immediately. We recommend leaving the rule inactive until you have the criteria clearly defined and set.

4. **Click Save.**

   The Case Auto-Response Rules page reappears with your new rule saved.

5. **Click the Rule Name link for your new rule.**

   The Case Auto-Response Rule detail page appears.

6. **Click New at the top of the Rule Entries list to add a new rule entry for your assignment rule.**

   The Rule Entry edit page displays.

7. **In Step 1 of the Rule Entry edit page, enter a Sort Order for your rule entry. If this is your first rule entry, enter 1.**

   You can reorder rule entries before activating your assignment rule.

8. **In Step 2 of the Rule Entry edit page, select the criteria for your rule entry.**

For example, you might choose the Case Origin field as a piece of criteria and create different rule entries for cases originating from various channels.

Refer to the "Creating a view" section for a more comprehensive overview of how to define the criteria in Step 2 here.

9. **In Step 3 of the Rule Entry edit page, select the name and email address to use for the auto-response message that goes out to your customer. You can optionally select a Reply-to Address as well.**

10. **In Step 4 of the Rule Entry edit page, select an email template to use for the auto-response message.**

The email template selected will be the one used by auto-response rule entry to notify the customer of case information and updates.

To learn more about email templates, refer to Chapter 4.

11. **Click Save.**

The Case Auto-Response Rule detail page reappears with your saved rule entry. You can create more rule entries and use the Reorder button on the page to choose the order in which the entries should be evaluated when responding to new cases.

12. **When you've finished defining and ordering your rule entries and you're ready to start responding to customer inquiries automatically, click Edit at the top of the page, click the Active box, and click Save.**

Researching the Issue

In a dream world, for customer support organizations and customers alike, every single customer support agent would be able to answer any customer's question immediately. Well, while we're talking dream worlds, maybe there just wouldn't be any questions at all. Unfortunately, that's not the case. For the foreseeable future, people will continue to seek support when they're experiencing an issue with a product. They can only hope the agent on the other end has the power of Salesforce at their fingertips.

If you're an agent or a support manager, the good news for you is that even if everyone in your organization can't answer a customer's question off the top of his or her head, Salesforce provides a number of efficient and easy ways to store and access your organization's internal knowledge.

With Salesforce, you no longer need to rely on tribal knowledge to solve cases. There's no need to send an email blast around asking if anybody else has the answer. Instead, you can rely on yourself and the knowledge solution that your organization has chosen to leverage.

In this section, we review Salesforce CRM Content, Salesforce Solutions, and Salesforce Knowledge as options for solving cases. Your organization may leverage more than one of these simultaneously.

In order to most effectively leverage these tools for customer support cases, your organization must actually *use* the tool. Each tool serves as a conduit for organizational knowledge, but as conduits, they require a group on either end: one to aggregate, organize, and submit the information, and the other to consume the information and, ultimately, to share that information with the customer.

Investigating Content

Salesforce CRM Content provides an easy-to-use, flexible solution to house and access organizational knowledge. In order to leverage Content as a document management system, or knowledge base, make sure that your organization has access to Content.

Content libraries are available in the following editions of Salesforce:

- ✔ Contact Manager
- ✔ Group
- ✔ Professional
- ✔ Enterprise
- ✔ Performance
- ✔ Unlimited
- ✔ Developer

If you're an agent and you're new to using Content, or your organization is still evaluating possible tools, get familiar with the following Salesforce CRM Content user capabilities so you know what's possible:

- ✔ **Publishing and sharing official files throughout the organization:** Create and share knowledge in any file format.

- ✔ **Creating content packs:** Aggregate multiple files into what's known as a *content pack* to share with customers or internal agents. For example, you could create an FAQs content pack with individual files containing frequently asked questions about specific products.

- ✔ **Organizing Salesforce CRM Content with fully searchable content libraries:** These Content libraries can be enabled with custom security settings and permissions, features labeled for faster searching, and the ability to create personal or private libraries. For example, you can create individual libraries for a support group that focuses on hardware your company sells, and another group that focuses on software. This differentiation will ultimately help your agents locate relevant information more quickly.

✔ **Subscribing to files or content packs to ensure you're notified if the owner uploads a new version:** The subscribe feature can be very effective to communicate organizational changes to agents or for dedicated support agents to receive updated product information to share with customers.

✔ **Enabling users to contribute new content or update existing content to make improvements or adjustments:** Empower support agents in your organization with the ability to take ownership of organizational knowledge and make additions or updates where necessary.

✔ **Share these files directly with your customers:** Use content deliveries to share information directly with customers.

Keep reading to find out more about content deliveries.

✔ **Uploading any file type:** Create, publish, and share knowledge in any format.

When you're working a case, to locate and share valuable information from the Content library with your customer, follow these steps:

1. **Navigate to the case record you're working on, scroll to the bottom of the Case detail page, and locate the Related Content related list, shown in Figure 5-7.**

   Your organization must add the Related Content related list to Case page layouts in order to leverage Salesforce CRM Content directly from Case records. See Chapter 20 for more information on modifying page layouts.

2. **If this is a new case, and there is no existing related content, click Find Content or Search All.**

   Salesforce searches all the content libraries that you have access to regardless of which button you choose, however, the search results will differ based on your choice.

   When you click Search All, the results display all content in your libraries. If you click Find Content, Salesforce performs a directed search for content that relates to the following attributes on the case record:

   - Case Reason
   - Subject
   - Account Name
   - Industry

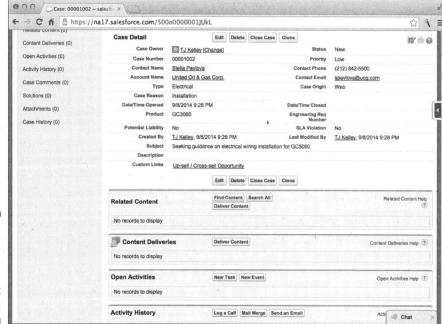

Figure 5-7:
Working
with the
Related
Content
related list.

3. **Review your search results and filter the results by entering additional search terms or selecting filter criteria in the sidebar.**

4. **When you locate a piece of content that is relevant to your case, click Attach.**

   Salesforce attaches the file to your case record.

5. **Click Back to return to the case record.**

   The case record displays.

6. **Check the Related Content related list to ensure that your file attached correctly.**

   The file displays in the related list.

7. **Click Deliver next to the file or content pack that you want to send to your customer.**

   The Content Delivery Wizard displays on the Define Settings step, as shown in Figure 5-8.

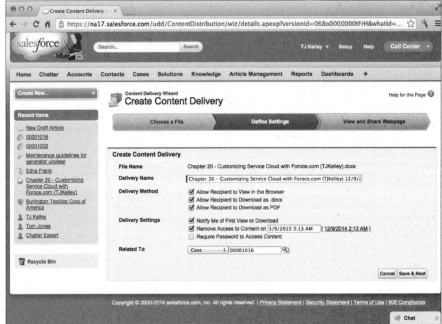

Figure 5-8:
The Content
Delivery
Wizard.

8. **Define the settings for your content.**

   Salesforce CRM Content provides you with a number of flexible delivery methods and security options. You'll also notice that Salesforce associates the content delivery to the support case. This delivery will be tracked on the Content Delivery related list (viewable if added to the page layout) on the case record.

9. **Click Save & Next.**

   The content delivery generates a custom web page for the content that will be shared with the customer.

10. **Optionally, preview the web page and click the Previous button to go back and change the settings.**

11. **When you're satisfied and ready to send the content to the customer, copy and paste the URL in the yellow Deliver window and email it to the customer.**

12. **Click Done when you're finished.**

    The case record displays.

Solving cases with suggested solutions

Salesforce Solutions present a knowledge base solution that is targeted more specifically to service organizations than Salesforce CRM Content is. Support organizations that use Solutions rather than Content will find a tool that aims to answer specific customer inquiries instead of only providing the relevant content to search through and find the answer.

With Salesforce Solutions, you can empower your support organization with a powerful issue resolution tool while saving money. A key feature of Solutions called Suggested Solutions can help to cut costs by reducing case resolution times and enabling self-service for your customers via your Self-Service Portal, Customer Portal, or Customer Community.

In order to leverage Suggested Solutions, you must ensure that your organization can do so. Suggested Solutions are available in the following editions of Salesforce:

- ✔ Professional
- ✔ Enterprise
- ✔ Performance
- ✔ Unlimited
- ✔ Developer

If your organization uses Suggested Solutions, when researching a customer's issue or problem, follow these steps:

1. **Navigate to the case record you're working on, scroll to the bottom of the page, and locate the Solutions related list, shown in Figure 5-9.**

   Your organization must have the Solutions related list available on Case page layouts in order to leverage Suggested Solutions directly from case records. Refer to Chapter 20 for more information on modifying page layouts.

2. **If this is a new case, and you haven't already attached a solution, no solutions will appear in the related list. Click View Suggested Solutions or type some key search terms in the text box and click Find Solution.**

   Salesforce searches for all relevant solutions that your organization has created.

   When you click Find Solution, Salesforce searches for relevant solutions based on the information found on the case record.

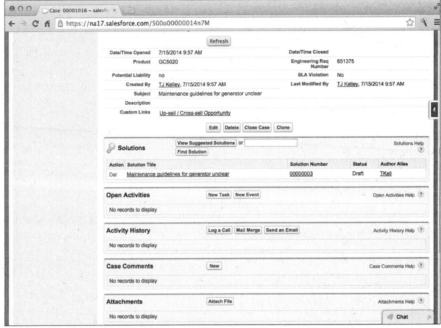

Figure 5-9:
The
Solutions
related list.

When you click View Suggested Solutions, the results will return relevant results based on a powerful search that incorporates the following into a scoring system for solutions:

- Word frequency

- Word proximity

- Case similarity (for solutions with cases attached already)

- Related solutions

3. **Review the relevant solutions on the Suggested Solutions page for the case, as shown in Figure 5-10.**

4. **Click Select in the Action column next to the solution you want to leverage for this case.**

Salesforce attaches the solution to the case record.

5. **Communicate the solution back to the customer to resolve the case.**

Communicate the solution back to the customer according to your company's procedures. Here are some of the possibilities for communicating and resolving the case:

- Email the solution to the customer.

- Call the customer and communicate the solution.

- If your organization has set up the appropriate workflow rules, you may be able to update the case status or close the case to generate an automatic email alert to the customer with Suggested Solutions included.

- If your customer has access to the case record and solutions via a Customer Portal or Customer Community, she can access the case record directly to view the attached solution.

6. **If you can't locate a corresponding solution in Salesforce, but you discover a resolution, you can close the case and create a new solution for future occurrences of similar cases, as shown in Figure 5-11.**

If you choose to create a new solution, be sure to complete Step 5 and communicate the solution to the customer.

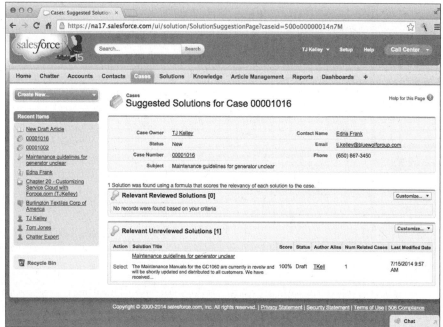

Figure 5-10:
The Suggested Solutions page.

Using Knowledge

Salesforce Knowledge provides the most expansive and flexible suite of options for creating, storing, maintaining, and sharing your organizational knowledge. Salesforce Knowledge provides the following capabilities:

✔ Create and manage content with Knowledge articles.

✔ Share unique knowledge datasets with internal users, customers, partners, and even the general public.

✔ Define a publication process for your organization's knowledge articles and exercise fine-tuned, transparent controls over each step of the process from creation to publication.

✔ Supports all file types.

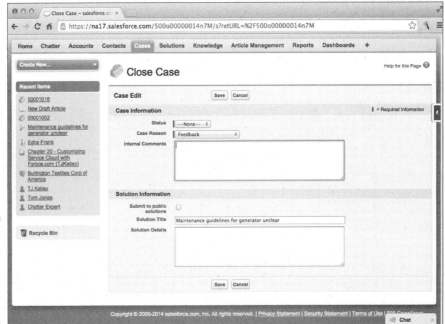

Figure 5-11:
Create a new solution when closing a case.

For more information on licensing, costs, and features, turn to Chapter 10. For detailed information on implementing Knowledge, jump to Chapter 11. And to see how to manage your organizational knowledge with Salesforce, refer to Chapter 12.

If your organization has implemented Salesforce Knowledge, you can research and solve customer support cases using Knowledge articles by following these steps:

1. **Navigate to the case record you're working on, scroll to the bottom of the page, and locate the Articles related list, as shown in Figure 5-12.**

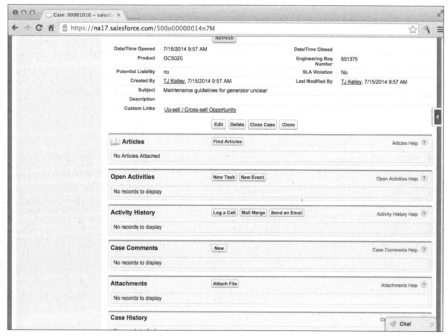

Figure 5-12:
The Articles
related list.

Your organization must have the Articles related list available on Case page layouts in order to leverage Articles directly from case records. Refer to Chapter 20 for more information on modifying page layouts.

2. Click the Find Articles button on the Articles related list.

The Knowledge tab displays with search results.

The subject of the case will be used automatically in order to provide some initial search results.

3. Review your search results and refine them if needed.

For more information on searching for articles, turn to Chapter 12.

4. When you find an article that fits to solve your case, click the drop-down arrow next to the article's title and select Attach to Case.

Salesforce attaches the article to your case.

5. Click the Back to Case link above the search bar to return to your case.

The case record displays.

6. Scroll down to the bottom of the page, locate the Articles related list, and ensure that the article you selected has been attached to the case.

In addition to searching for articles from the Articles related list, Salesforce Knowledge enables support agents to complete the following actions with articles:

- ✔ Automatically view suggested articles.
- ✔ Send article PDFs directly from the Articles related list.
- ✔ Create new articles when closing a case.

Salesforce Knowledge is the newest feature (newer than Content and Solutions), and, as such, it's likely to get a greater investment of time and energy from Salesforce over the coming years. Keep this in mind if your organization is still evaluating your options — Knowledge will almost certainly continue to evolve and improve at a rapid pace, but the same can't be said for Content and Solutions.

Chapter 6

Collaborating on Cases

In This Chapter

▶ Getting assistance with case teams

▶ Escalating a case

▶ Leveraging Chatter on cases

*E*ven the best agents can't do everything alone. A large part of successful case management depends on collaboration. Remember being the newbie at your latest job? How did you get all your questions answered? Likely, you had to ask someone, and this happened informally by the water cooler or via email. Organizations typically have a lot of tribal knowledge that isn't recorded in one central repository. This makes ramping up more difficult than it needs to be. On the other hand, over-communication and constant email blasts can be overwhelming. Salesforce recognizes this and moves toward greater collaboration in each feature release.

The importance of working together in call centers can't be overstated. People are usually too swept up in daily tasks and caseloads to work any way but independently. Getting assistance at critical points in the case management process can be vital to keeping that customer. Finding answers to questions already posed in one central repository benefits everyone.

In this chapter, we discuss how Service Cloud bridges the gap between efficiency and collaboration in a way that makes working together second nature and spreading (or requesting) information effortless. We talk about predefining case teams to facilitate coordination and collaboration in working cases. Then we take a look at escalation processes in Service Cloud and how to set them up according to your business rules. We walk you through Chatter on cases and the best way to use the collaboration tools Salesforce provides out of the box.

Getting Assistance with Case Teams

Sometimes you need team members to help out with specific issues that you just don't have the expertise or authority to solve. One of the ways agents can work together in Service Cloud is by using the Case Teams functionality.

A *case team* is a team of users who work together on a case, with each user playing a different role that determines his or her level of access for the case. For example, if you need a manager and a seasoned technical rep to work with you on a specific case, you can include them on your case team.

Case teams aren't necessary for every business, but if you foresee a situation where a case owner needs hands-on assistance and you don't want to transfer case ownership (effectively reassigning case resolution responsibility to someone else), case teams are a powerful tool.

Defining case team roles and access

The first step in using case teams is to define your case team roles. Clearly defining each user's role in the management of a case gives you an easy way to establish accountability.

Another great thing about case teams is that they're standard filters in list views and reports, so they can be easily referenced, as shown in Figure 6-1.

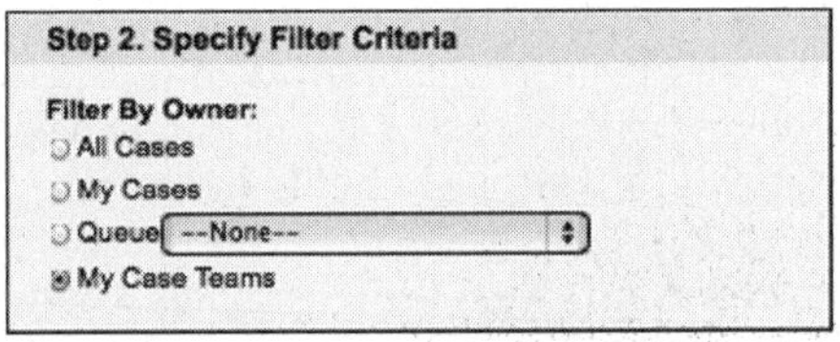

Figure 6-1:
List view filter criteria referencing case teams.

Step 2. Specify Filter Criteria

Filter By Owner:
- ⊙ All Cases
- ⊙ My Cases
- ⊙ Queue [--None-- ⬦]
- ⦿ My Case Teams

Because the roles that users play in your case team dictate the level of access they have, start by planning who needs the ability to do what. There are three levels of access for each case team role:

- ✔ **Read/Write access:** Users with Read/Write access can see and edit the case, including adding notes, attachments, and records in related lists.

- ✔ **Read Only access:** Users with this access can see the case but can't edit it or add notes or attachments. They can still add records in related lists.

- ✔ **Private:** Users cannot access the case.

Setting up case teams

Now that you know all about case teams, let's set them up. Choose Setup⇨ Build ⇨Customize⇨Cases⇨Case Teams⇨Case Team Roles and follow these steps:

1. **Click the New button.**

   The New Case Team Member Role page appears, as shown in Figure 6-2.

2. **Fill in the Member Role Name and select the level of access for that role from the Case Access picklist.**

3. **Optionally, click the Visible in Customer Portal check box.**

   Check this box if you have the Customer Portal and want the member in the role to be visible to users there.

4. **Click Save when you're done.**

   Alternatively, click Save & New to save the role and immediately create another.

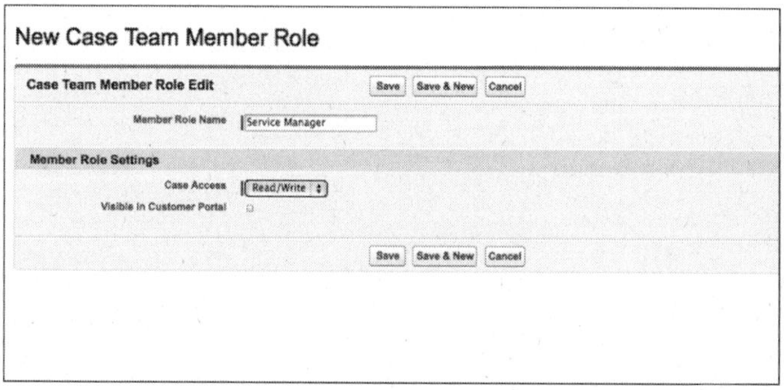

Figure 6-2: Creating a new case team member role for a manager.

After you have a few case team roles set up, make sure the Case Teams related list appears on your case page layout(s). To do this, choose Setup⇨ Build⇨Customize⇨Cases⇨Page Layouts, and follow these steps:

1. **Click the Edit link on the left side of the case page layout(s) you want to modify.**

   The enhanced page layout editor appears for the selected layout.

2. **On the top-left toolbar of the layout editor, select Related Lists.**

   The page automatically scrolls down to the related list section of the layout and the available related lists appear in the editor, while the lists in use appear grayed out, as shown in Figure 6-3.

3. Click Case Team from the available related lists, and drag it wherever you want it to appear on the page.

The Case Team related list appears on the page.

4. Click Save when you're finished.

The system asks if you want this change to overwrite the personal customizations of your users. Click Yes or No depending on your preference. The Case Page Layout page appears again.

Now that you've set up case teams for your organization, your case owners can add collaborators to their cases.

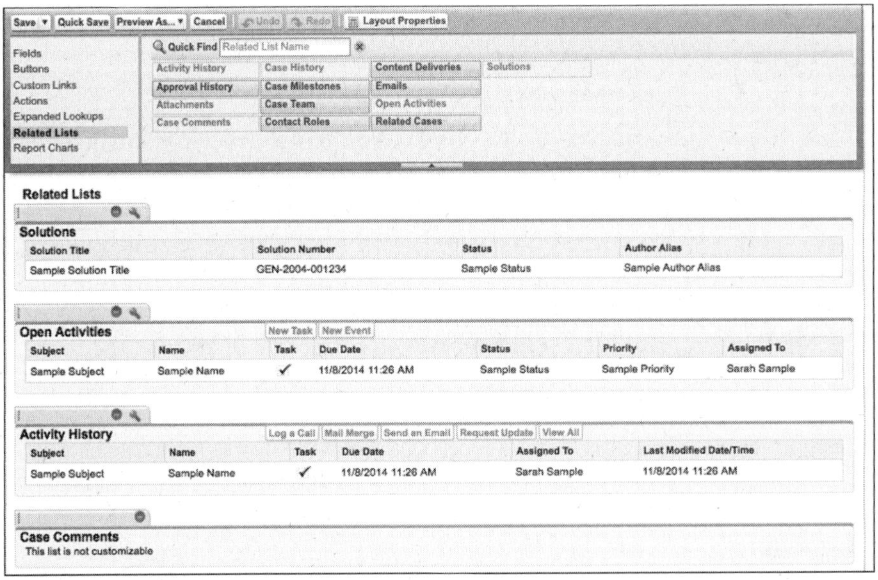

Figure 6-3:
Using the Related Lists section of the page layout editor.

Using predefined case teams

To make the process of adding team members to your case even easier, Service Cloud offers predefined case teams. Your users can create case teams to collaborate on cases consistently and efficiently.

To create a predefined case team, choose Setup⇨Build⇨Customize⇨Cases⇨ Case Teams⇨Predefined Case Teams, and follow these steps:

1. Click the New button.

The Add Predefined Case Team page appears.

2. **Fill in a name for your team in the Team Name field.**

3. **Click the lookup icon to the right of the first Team Member field in the list.**

   A lookup dialog pops up with a list of Recently Viewed Users.

4. **Select a user from the list or search for and select a specific user you want to add to the team.**

   The lookup dialog closes and the selected user appears in the field.

5. **In the Member Role field, select a member role for the user.**

   The Case Access field should auto-populate with the specified access for that role. The Case Team roles you created in the previous steps are what members can be assigned to. That is, a member role isn't new — it's just derived from the Case Team role but pertains to that specific team member.

6. **Click Save when you're done.**

   The Predefined Case Teams page appears with your new predefined team.

Adding team members to your case

Now that there are case teams with member roles and predefined case teams in the system, let's put them to use from an agent's perspective.

From a case you're working, follow these steps:

1. **Scroll down to the Case Team related list and click the Update Case Team Members button.**

   The Update Case Team Members page appears, with a section to add individual case team members and their respective roles, as well as a section to add predefined case teams.

2. **Click the lookup icon to the right of the Team Member field.**

   A lookup dialog screen pops up with a list of users.

3. **Select a user from the list or search for and select a specific user you want to add to the team.**

   The lookup dialog popup closes and the selected user appears in the field.

4. **In the Member Role field, select a member role for the user.**

   The Case Access field should auto-populate with the specified access for that role.

5. **To add a predefined case team as well, click the lookup icon next to the Predefined Case Team field in the bottom section of the page and select a case team you've already defined.**

   The Update Case Team Members page appears with your selection(s), as shown in Figure 6-4.

6. **Click Save when you're done.**

   The case record reappears with your case team member(s) in the Case Team related list.

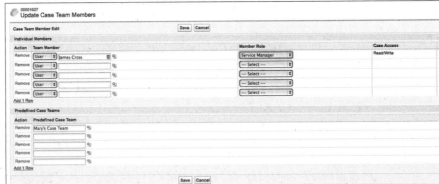

Figure 6-4:
Updating
team mem-
bers for
your case.

Escalating a Case

It's really important to make sure that cases don't fall through the cracks. Still, in a fast-paced high-volume environment, humans make mistakes. Escalation rules are Service Cloud's answer to this concern. By automating how and when cases are escalated, managers can rest assured that cases are handled efficiently and receive the attention they deserve.

Escalation rules are really just containers for rule entries and rule actions. Rule entries are a set of criteria the case must meet to trigger those rule actions. You can have multiple rule entries. Escalation rules are used to reassign cases and optionally notify users when a case has not met certain criteria. For example, you can create escalation rules for the following scenarios:

- ✔ If a case is not resolved 40 business hours after it's opened, automatically reassign the case to a second tier.

- ✔ If a case opened for any high-value customers is not updated at least once daily, automatically reassign it to a manager.

Reassigning a case

By their very definition, escalation rules reassign case ownership when they meet certain criteria. We discuss in detail how to automate that process here. There are a few other options for transferring case ownership as well.

The first option is the manual reassignment of a case. Nobody likes to do a lot of manual work, so this option makes the most sense when performed on a case-by-case basis (pun intended). What we mean is that while escalation rules are used as a catch-all for cases that have predefined attributes, manually transferring cases should be reserved for one-off situations where a case doesn't necessarily meet specific criteria but needs to be quickly reassigned or escalated in the interest of time.

In this section, we explain how to manually transfer case ownership to a user or a queue. Before outlining these steps, it's important to keep a few things in mind:

- ✔ **To transfer individual records, you need the Transfer Record permission enabled on your profile.** To see if you have this permission, go to a case record and check if you see a Change link next to the Case Owner field. If you don't, contact your administrator to give you this permission.

- ✔ **The new owner of the case record needs to have at least Read permission on the case object to be an owner.**

- ✔ **When you change case ownership, all notes, attachments, and activities associated with that case are also transferred to the new owner.**

To transfer a case owner, go to the case record whose owner you want to reassign and follow these steps:

1. **Click the Change link to the right of the Case Owner field.**

   The Change Case Owner page appears, as shown in Figure 6-5.

   If you don't see the Change link next to the owner field, you don't have the necessary permissions to change the case owner.

2. **From the picklist, choose whether the case owner should be an individual user or a queue.**

3. **Click the lookup icon, search and select the user or queue to whom the case should be transferred.**

   Optionally, click the Send Notification Email check box to notify the new user of the change.

4. **Click Save when you're done.**

   The case record reappears with the selected owner in the Case Owner field.

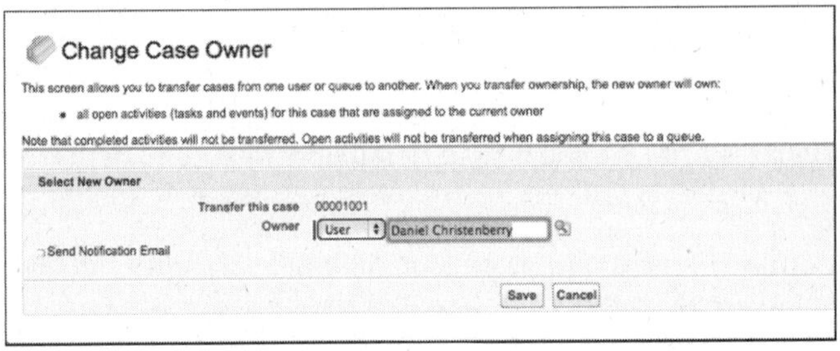

Change Case Owner

This screen allows you to transfer cases from one user or queue to another. When you transfer ownership, the new owner will own:

• all open activities (tasks and events) for this case that are assigned to the current owner

Note that completed activities will not be transferred. Open activities will not be transferred when assigning this case to a queue.

Select New Owner

Transfer this case 00001001

Owner [User ▼] [Daniel Christenberry] 🔍

☐ Send Notification Email

[Save] [Cancel]

Figure 6-5:
Reassigning
a case
owner.

Now you know how to manually transfer a case owner in those times when all else fails. Another way to reassign a case is through workflow rules. These work in a similar way to escalation rules, but are not specific to cases or to reassignment. See Chapter 20 for more information on when to use workflow rules and how to build them.

Creating escalation rules by criteria

To automate case escalation, create some escalation rules. Choose Setup➪ Build➪Customize➪Cases➪Escalation Rules, and follow these steps:

1. **On the Case Escalation Rules page, click the New button.**

   The New Escalation Rules page appears.

2. **Give the rule an intuitive name, click the Active check box if you want this to be the one active rule, and click Save.**

   The Case Escalation Rules page reappears with the rule.

   Although you can create many escalation rules, you can only have one active escalation rule at a time. The other inactive rules won't be in effect.

3. **Click the rule name for the escalation rule you created.**

   The Rule Detail page appears.

4. **Click the New button under Rule Entries.**

   The Rule Entry Edit page appears.

5. **In the Sort Order field, enter a number for the order in which this entry should be processed.**

   Service Cloud evaluates each rule entry in the sort order you specify and stops when it finds a match.

6. **In Step 2 of the Rule Entry Edit page, choose the attributes a case must have to trigger this rule entry.**

   For example, if you have a distinct escalation process for high priority customers, you can select "Account: Customer Priority equals High."

7. **In Step 3, specify how business hours apply to escalated cases:**

   - *Ignore business hours:* Select this radio button if you want the escalation rule to remain in effect at all times.

     If you choose to ignore business hours, the escalation rule will always remain in effect, even during holidays and weekends.

   - *Use business hours specified on the case:* The escalation rule will only run during the business hours on the specific case or the default business hours.

   - *Set business hours:* Use this to select specific predefined business hours during which the rule will run.

8. **In Step 4, specify how you want escalation times to be set. In other words, number of hours since:**

   - *The case is created.*

   - *The case is created, unless it's been modified.* Once it's been modified, the case will never get escalated.

   - *The last modification time of the case.*

9. **After you've selected at least one field for each step on the Rule Entry Edit page, as shown in Figure 6-6, click Save.**

   The Rule Entry page appears with your selections.

Setting up escalation actions

After creating your escalation rule entries to specify the criteria required to escalate a case, you need to choose what actions these criteria trigger. To do this, set up escalation actions. If you're no longer on the Rule Entry Edit page, go back to it by choosing Setup➪Build➪Customize➪Cases➪Escalation Rules, and follow these steps:

1. **Click the Rule Name you want to add actions to.**

   The Case Escalation Rule page appears with your Rule Entries related list.

2. **Click the Edit link to the left of the rule entry.**

   The Rule Entry Edit page appears with an Escalation Actions related list.

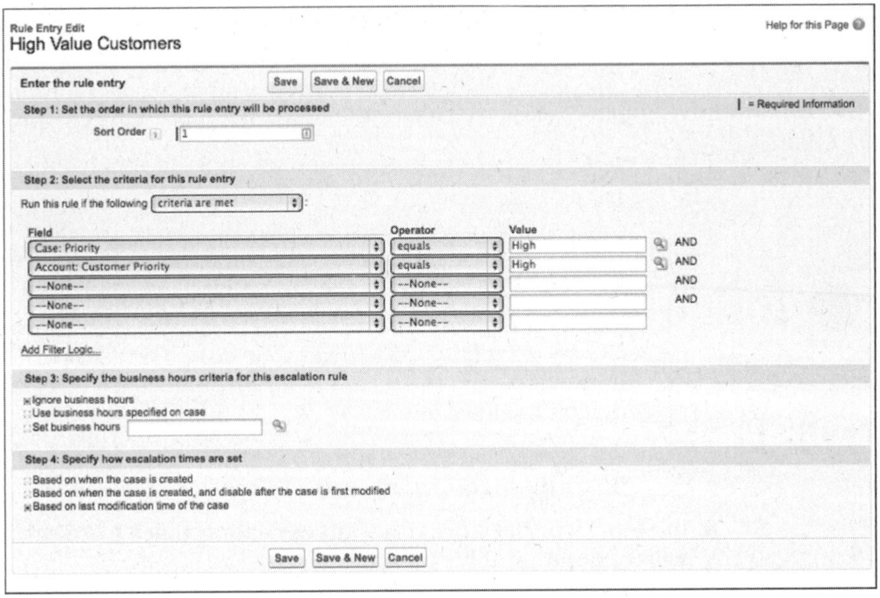

Figure 6-6:
Creating a
new case
escalation
rule.

3. **Click the New button in the Escalation Actions related list.**

   The Escalation Actions Edit page appears, as shown in Figure 6-7.

4. **Specify the number of business hours after which a case is escalated in the Age Over field.**

   You can also indicate 30-minute intervals in the associated picklist.

5. **Click the lookup icon to choose the user or queue to which the case is escalated after it matches the criteria.**

6. **Select an email template to use for notifying a user that the case is escalated.**

7. **Click the Notify Case Owner check box to notify the case owner that the case is being escalated.**

   Optionally add up to five more email addresses that should also be notified.

8. **Click Save when you're finished.**

   The Rule Entry Edit page reappears.

Congratulations! Now you can set up automatic escalation rules and actions that will help your users work together and ensure that all cases are handled in a timely and consistent manner.

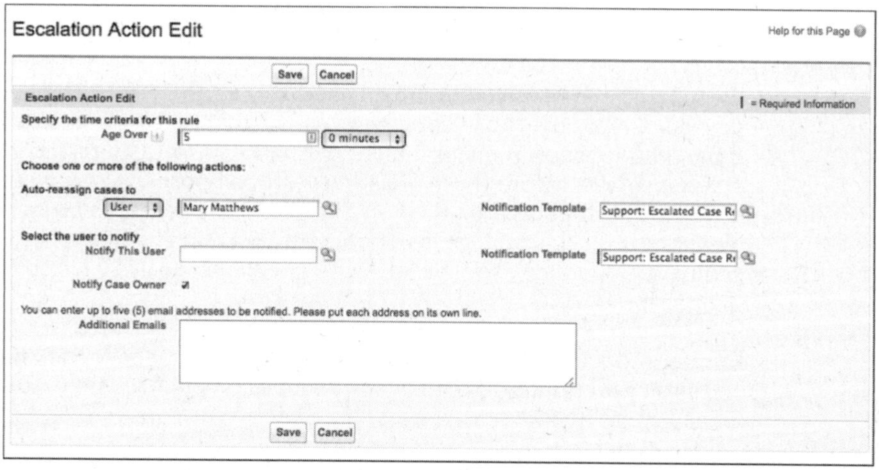

Figure 6-7:
Creating
escalation
actions for
your rule.

Leveraging Chatter on Cases

One of the most common problems employees face internally is finding information quickly. Whether it's trying to find out specifics on your company's 401(k) plan or identifying the best person to contact for a broken computer, chances are, you'll have to do some digging and emailing. Fragmented processes and the inability to work across organizational silos hurts your business. Not only is it a colossal waste of time, it hurts employee satisfaction, onboarding, and ultimately your bottom line.

Chatter's value proposition is a user's ability to quickly reach staff, tap into the social aspect of public knowledge sharing, and resolve cases even faster.

Collaborating on cases has never been easier. Chatter provides a central place where users can post and respond to questions, update others with statuses, and see recent activity on records to connect with people and share business information securely and in real time.

If you're an administrator, turn on Chatter by following these steps:

1. **Choose Setup➪Build➪Customize➪Chatter➪Settings.**

   The Chatter Settings page appears.

2. **Click the Enable check box and click Save.**

   A larger menu of configurable settings appears.

Tapping into internal knowledge

If you're a veteran at your company and you've come in contact with lots of new employees over the years, you've probably been asked the same question multiple times. A major benefit of Chatter is the aspect of knowledge sharing. Where before these questions were all posed in person or via email, now the question can be asked on Chatter. What does this mean for you? It means that this knowledge is no longer trapped in email inboxes, but instead can be seen publicly, so that the same questions won't be asked over and over again.

Chatter reduces email (or increases it if you don't manage the Chatter email settings appropriately), keeps your teams accountable, and makes project management easier.

Using Chatter groups

You can use Chatter to collaborate with everyone in your company, with specific individuals, or only within certain groups. You can create specific groups for various use cases. Here are some examples:

- ✔ **Groups for specific teams or departments:** If you're working a case and you need some technical knowledge about a specific product, you can post directly to the engineering team Chatter group or to a product management Chatter group. Those teams can then see your question and provide answers in real time. Also, you can ask benefits-related questions on an HR Chatter group.

- ✔ **Groups for events:** If your company is having a retreat, fundraising event, or holiday party, create a chatter group for the event. Using this group, you can communicate updates, answer questions, and boost company morale.

- ✔ **Groups for projects:** Create a group for a specific project and invite your project team. You can share project-related files and information, and collaborate on it together without cluttering your inbox.

- ✔ **Groups to maintain confidentiality:** You can set up private groups where team members can discuss sensitive information outside their normal Chatter feed.

- ✔ **Groups for skills:** Sometimes it's tough to know who you should ask. Create Chatter groups for specific skills to help your agents' questions get to the right people more quickly. The power of Chatter really becomes apparent when you leverage it with global support teams and experts in different places.

Chatter groups have different levels of access. Posts made to a private Chatter group can only be seen by members of that group.

To create a Chatter group, follow these steps:

1. **In the top-right App picker, choose the Salesforce Chatter app and click the Groups tab.**

   Alternatively, you can click the Chatter tab and then the Groups link in the sidebar. The My Groups page appears, listing your existing groups and membership within them.

2. **Click the New Group button.**

   The New Group Edit page appears, as shown in Figure 6-8.

3. **Type the name of the group.**

4. **Select a setting for automatic archiving.**

   You have the option to archive the group automatically if no posts or comments are added in a 90-day period.

5. **Set the group access level:**

   • *Public:* Anyone can join the group and see the group's Chatter feed.

   • *Private:* Only members can see group activity and contribute to the feed. A user needs to request membership and get approval from the owner or manager of the group.

   • *Allow Customers:* The owner and manager of the group can invite customers to join private groups.

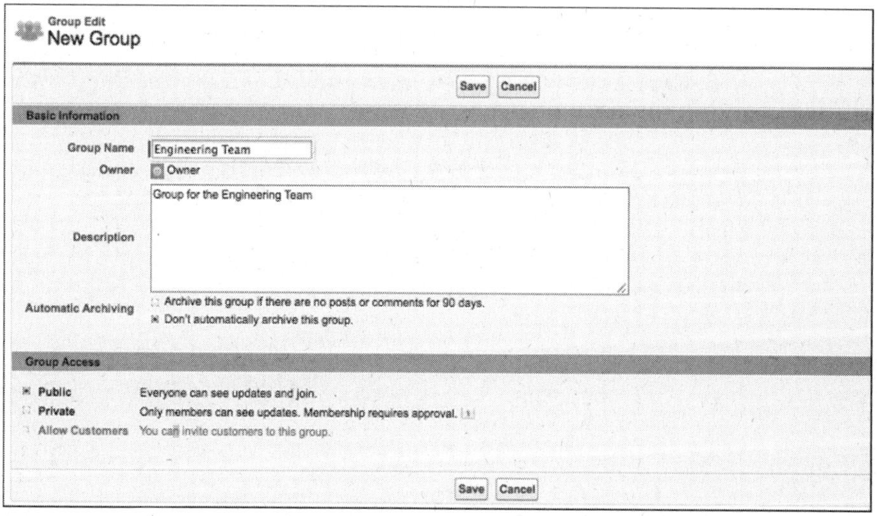

Figure 6-8:
Creating a new Chatter group.

   6. **Click Save when you're done.**

   The new group's home page appears. You can now add members to it by clicking the Add Members link on the right side of the screen.

Tracking in Chatter

With the follow feature, you can quickly follow records and people in Chatter to get updates about them on your home page feed. Before you can follow anything, your administrator has to enable Chatter for specific objects. *Objects* are types of records that are usually represented by those tabs at the top of your Salesforce page, like Cases or Contacts. Feed tracking allows users to follow records of that object.

Within each object, you can also choose specific fields to track so that users who follow a record will be updated when those fields change. For example, if you have feed tracking enabled on the Status field on cases, a manager following an important case is immediately updated on his or her case feed when the case's status changes.

You can select up to 20 fields per object to track in Chatter.

To enable Chatter for certain objects, follow these steps:

   1. **Choose Setup⇨Build⇨Customize⇨Chatter⇨Feed Tracking.**

   The Feed Tracking page appears, as shown in Figure 6-9.

   2. **Select the name of the object you want to follow on the left sidebar.**

   The fields for that object appear in the body of the page.

   3. **Click the Enable Feed Tracking check box.**

   4. **Select the fields you want to track with Chatter.**

   5. **Click Save when you're done enabling feed tracking for the records you want to be able to follow.**

Topics is another clever tracking tool in Chatter that allows you to associate your posts or updates with other posts of the same topic by using the hashtag symbol (#) followed by the topic, with no spaces in between. In this way, you can easily organize updates, ideas, or topics of conversation and increase their visibility.

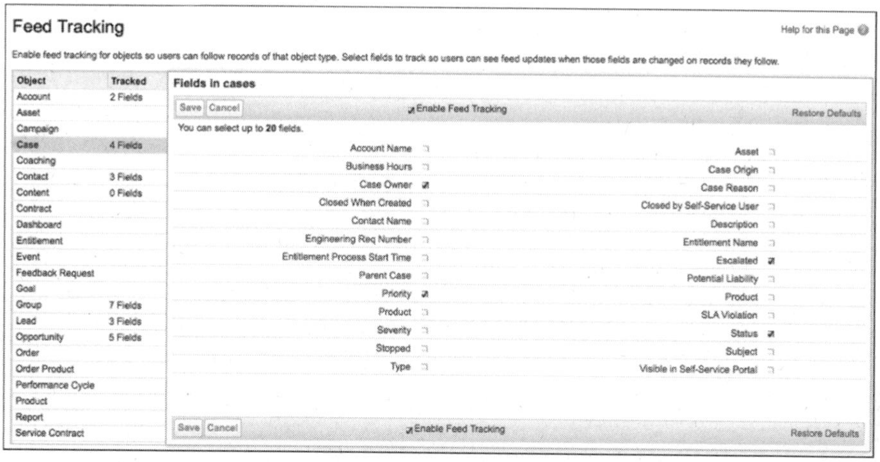

Figure 6-9:
Select the object to follow and the fields to track in Chatter.

Communicating with customers and partners

Internal Chatter activity should not be publicly visible to your customers. Sometimes you want to swarm with others on a particular case. Maybe the sales team follows a case that you've updated to reflect an expired contract and they want to jump in for a renewal opportunity. In either case, you don't want external customers to see this activity. Public Chatter groups aren't exposed to customers for this reason.

In other situations, Chatter makes sense for communicating quickly with your partners or customers. Chatter customers are users outside your company's email domains. They can only see the groups they're invited to and collaborate with those groups' members.

To set this up, first configure the Chatter group's settings to allow customers (see the earlier section, "Using Chatter groups," for a quick reminder). Then make sure your administrator sets up the customer or partner as a user in Salesforce. If this is the only reason you're creating a user record for the customer, he or she can use a Chatter Free license, which is free and only provides Chatter access with no access to records or data. (See Chapter 19 for more on how to create a user.)

Now that you've set it up, all you have to do is invite the customer or partner, and you can start collaborating with him on Chatter!

Part III

Improving Your Service Organization's Effectiveness

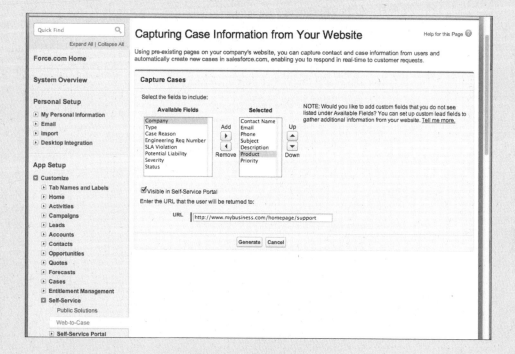

Find out how to create mini-page layouts for the Service Cloud Console in an article at www.dummies.com/extras/salesforceservicecloud.

In this part . . .

✔ See the many channels through which you can service your customers with Service Cloud.

✔ Get to know the Service Cloud Console, its terms and functionality, as well as some considerations to keep in mind before implementing it.

✔ Set up Email-to-Case and Live Agent for quicker support.

✔ Set up the Service Cloud Console for your organization to turn your high-volume call center into an efficiency machine.

Chapter 7

Capturing Cases in a Multi-Channel World

In This Chapter

▶ Understanding the multi-channel approach

▶ Implementing Web-to-Case

▶ Setting up Email-to-Case

▶ Considering computer telephony integration

▶ Using Live Agent chat

▶ Exploring social channels

Case management is the heart of any support strategy, and Salesforce Service Cloud highlights this by giving you the tools to provide excellent customer service through a wide range of channels. In an increasingly connected world, conventional (and more operationally expensive) service channels such as call centers can no longer be the only source of service.

Today's consumer wants immediate service around the clock through a variety of devices and channels, without having to listen to hold music or repeat the issue to multiple reps. The modern customer leaves public feedback, making the customer's experience critical to your company's image and success.

No matter which channel(s) your business employs, Salesforce Service Cloud gives you the tools to successfully support your multi-channel strategy to deliver consistently high-quality customer support anytime anywhere.

In this chapter, we lay out the common service channels that serve as touch points between you and your customer. We show you how to implement several of the more popular channels, such as Web-to-Case and Live Agent, as well as introducing computer telephony integration (CTI) and Salesforce Social Customer Service.

Offering Multiple Service Channels

Multi-channel support is an obvious boon to any organization with loyal customers. Offering your customers various means to reach the same end — issue resolution — has two main benefits:

- ✔ **Increased customer satisfaction:** Customers can interact with your business the way they want to.

- ✔ **Decreased operational cost:** Providing answers via multiple avenues keeps call volume down and your agents focused on more complex cases.

In the past, each channel lived in its own silo — marketing owned social data, with call center managers overseeing daily call volumes, and IT departments managing web traffic. Salesforce Service Cloud offers a holistic view of customer activity and real-time analytics in the utilization of each channel. Now executives and key decision-makers have visibility into channel popularity and can nimbly pivot toward more frequently used channels and divest from those left in the dust. Agents see customers' preferred method of contact and engage with them the way they like.

Today, customer service is more important than ever before when it comes to securing loyal consumers. As excellent customer service becomes an expectation and not a luxury, consumers are becoming more demanding than ever. Companies need to be proactive — they can no longer afford to be reactive.

One of the most effective ways to be proactive is by making your service about your customer. Let your clients choose the way they want to get in touch with you. Provide different options for your customers to receive consistent service, regardless of where they are or what time it is. This is the essence of true customer support, and it's the purpose of offering a multi-channel strategy.

Setting Up Web-to-Case

In addition to using the phone, your customers may want to reach you directly from your website. With the Web-to-Case feature in Salesforce, your customers fill out a brief form on your company website that automatically creates a case in Salesforce for agents to start working. You can quickly generate a standard HTML form to put on any web page; then, when the customer clicks Submit, the form is sent to Salesforce's servers, which converts the information to a case. Web-to-Case is one of the fastest ways a customer can submit an inquiry and one of the easiest ways to increase agent productivity and response time.

Web-to-Case is a must-have for customer service because customers immediately navigate to a company's website when they have problems or need help. That said, Web-to-Case does have a few limitations (which we cover next), and you do need to do some upfront prep work before diving in and implementing it. But Web-to-Case is one of the most common tools businesses use to automate case creation directly from their sites, and after setting it up, you'll see how easy it is to do in Service Cloud.

Recognizing the limitations of Web-to-Case

Before jumping in and discussing how Web-to-Case works and how to set it up, we want to cover a few of its limitations so you know what to expect:

- ✔ **Your company can only get 5,000 cases per 24-hour period.** If the number of cases entered via Web-to-Case exceeds 5,000, Salesforce sends an email to the address associated with the default case owner containing the additional case details. Salesforce queues these additional cases in a pending request queue and then submits them once the 24-hour period is over. If your organization requires the ability to capture more than 5,000 cases via your website daily, submit a request to Salesforce.com customer support to increase the limit.

- ✔ **Customers can't send attachments.** As of this writing, Web-to-Case does not support adding attachments. This can be an issue because, in certain situations, customers may need to attach a screenshot or log file indicating the issue with your product.

- ✔ **The Web-to-Case forms don't offer rich text.** Adding rich text fields on Web-to-Case forms is possible, but the information captured within them is saved as plain text when the case is created in Salesforce, which defeats the purpose.

- ✔ **Web-to-Case doesn't have any spam filters.** In other words, Salesforce accepts it all and doesn't natively filter out spam, although you can set up validation rules and workflows to filter out cases that appear to be spam.

Preparing to enable Web-to-Case

Before enabling Web-to-Case, take the follow steps to make the setup as smooth as possible:

- ✔ **Create an email template for the customer.** Make sure you have an available default email template that your customers receive when they submit a case. Include a case number or confirmation that the customer can reference. (See Chapter 4 for more information about email templates.)

- ✔ **Create active case assignment rules.** Build assignment rules to assign a case to a default user or queue. If you don't have active assignment rules or if the case doesn't meet the rules' criteria, the owner on a web-generated case will default to the owner indicated in your organization's support settings. (See Chapter 5 for more on setting up assignment rules.)

- ✔ **Customize your support settings.** Use support settings to select a default case owner that serves as a net for those cases that don't meet your assignment rule criteria. To do this, choose Setup ➪ Build ➪ Customize ➪ Cases ➪ Support Settings, and locate the Default Case Owner field. Then click Edit, and select the desired user or queue.

Now you're ready to set up Web-to-Case for your organization.

Enabling Web-to-Case

To set up Web-to-Case, choose Setup ➪ Customize ➪ Self-Service ➪ Web-to-Case, and follow these steps:

1. **On the Capturing Cases from Your Website page, review the listed steps and then click the Generate the HTML link.**

2. **Move the fields you want to display on the Web-to-Case form from the Available Fields column to the Selected column by clicking the Add arrow, as shown in Figure 7-1.**

3. **Enter the URL to which the user returns after submitting the form, and click Generate.**

   Most web forms direct users to a thank-you/submitted page or a support page.

4. **Copy and paste the provided HTML code on your website or into a page hosted on your web server, and click Finished.**

You can also paste the output into your computer's text editor, save it with a `.html` suffix, and then open the file from the web browser to see and test it. Also, it doesn't have any design to it on purpose so that your company's web developer can easily incorporate your branding in it.

If this step seems too technical for you, copy and paste the code into an email and send it to someone on your web services or IT team.

5. **After the web form is up and running, test the form by filling it out and clicking Submit.**

   Make sure it routes to the appropriate party in Salesforce and captures the information entered.

Your organization is now able to auto-generate cases via a simple HTML web form that integrates directly into Service Cloud.

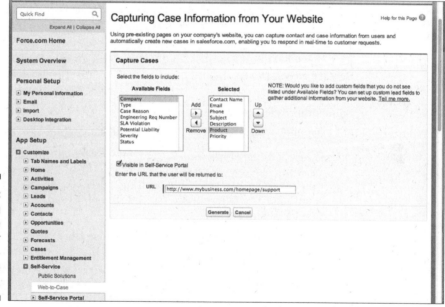

Figure 7-1:
Capturing the case fields for your Web-to-Case form.

Implementing Email-to-Case

Salesforce Service Cloud allows agents to quickly and efficiently manage cases through email as well. By sending an inquiry to an email address set up for your support team, Salesforce automatically creates a case in Salesforce and auto-populates relevant case fields, including any attachments the customer sends. If the sender's email address matches a Contact's email address in Salesforce, Email-to-Case will associate the new case with that Contact record, as well as the Contact's Account record. What's more, agents can reply to the email directly from the case, capturing the entire email thread and customer interaction in one place.

Salesforce helps you better manage the inbound and outbound flow of email communication through two slightly different methods: Email-to-Case and On-Demand Email-to-Case. We focus on the latter here.

Set up On-Demand Email-to-Case by choosing Setup ➪ Customize ➪ Cases ➪ Email-to-Case. Then follow these steps:

1. **On the first informational page, click Continue.**

2. **On the Email-to-Case Settings page, review the differences between Email-to-Case and On-Demand Email-to-Case.**

   If you need the ability to accept emails larger than 25MB from customers, Email-to-Case is for you.

3. **To continue enabling On-Demand Email-to-Case, click the Edit button and check both the Enable Email-to-Case and Enable On-Demand Service check boxes, customize other relevant settings, and then click Save.**

   Some other relevant settings include

   • *Enable HTML Email:* Helps your agents see emails in HTML format.

   • *When Sending Email from a Case, Insert Thread ID in the Following Sections:* You can choose to insert the Thread ID into the email subject or body. This helps both the agent and the customer see a unique ID to differentiate multiple email threads that may have similar subject lines.

   • *Failure Response Settings:* You can choose the system's behavior when your email count goes over the daily limit and the email can't become a case. Bouncing the message will have it reply to the sender with a reason for the rejection, whereas discarding the message will have the email go away without letting the sender know. Requeuing the message puts it in a holding bin to be processed in the next 24 hours. If you only want a certain subset of people to be able to send emails that become cases, set what happens when an unauthorized person sends an email in the Unauthorized Sender Action field.

When you enable Email-to-Case, you can't disable it. You can disable On-Demand Email-to-Case, however.

4. **At the bottom of the page, click the New button under Routing Addresses, ensuring the dropdown to the right of the New button is set to Email2Case.**

   The Email-to-Case Routing Information page displays the settings for your routing addresses, or the email addresses of your support team(s). An example of how to complete these settings is shown in Figure 7-2.

5. **Fill in the routing information, email, task, and case settings.**

   You can choose to accept email only from certain email addresses or domains, as well as auto-create tasks for case owners, and pre-populate case information on cases converted by a routing address.

6. **After completing the information for one or all of your routing address(es), click Save.**

   A popup window details the final steps for activating the routing address. Salesforce sends an email to the indicated routing address with directions on how to verify it for activation.

7. **After you verify the email, configure your mail server so that it forwards messages received at the email address you provided to the unique email service address that Salesforce provides and lists for you.**

   Now send a test email to your unique Salesforce email address and ensure that Service Cloud converts it into a case with the relevant fields pre-populated and assigned to the correct case owner. After your email is linked to forward to the long Salesforce-provided email, a customer can send an email to your email (for example, `support@mybusiness.com`) and it'll turn into a case in your org.

8. **Add your new configured email address to your company support site.**

   Make the news official to your customers — and advertise it well.

9. **On the Cases page layout, add the Emails related list.**

   Choose Setup ⇨ Customize ⇨ Cases ⇨ Page Layouts, click the Edit hyperlink near any or all page layouts you want to modify, choose Related Lists in the top enhanced page layout editor, and drag Emails to the Related Lists section. Then click Save.

   If you want Salesforce to send an immediate email acknowledgement to the email sender after she emails an issue, you can set up auto-response rules.

Congratulations! Your organization now accepts cases via email. Your customers will be thrilled that they can log issues with no long hold times or frustrating repetition, while your agents (and pocketbook) will be grateful that you've significantly reduced inbound calls to your contact center.

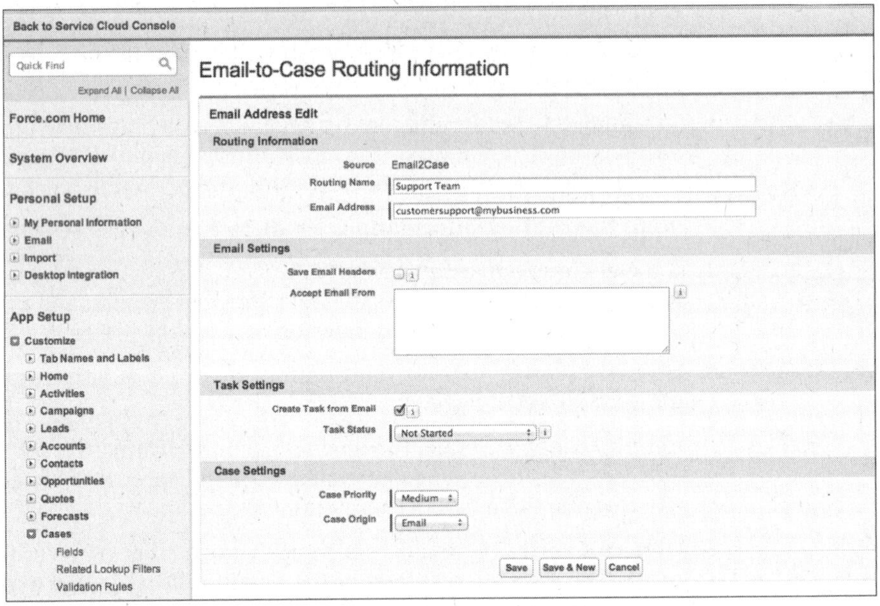

Figure 7-2:
Entering
a routing
address and
selecting its
settings.

Discovering Computer Telephony Integration

The more traditional support channel, the telephone, is not going away any-time soon. Salesforce Service Cloud also supports phone inquiry efficiency in call centers, which is just as important as more modern channels.

Computer telephony integration (CTI) is technology that facilitates the inter-action between or integration of telephone and computer. It's commonly used in call centers. CTI comes in many shapes and sizes but generally has the same objective: enabling agents to respond to customers as quickly and effectively as possible with very little needed from the customer.

One of the main considerations when implementing CTI is choosing whether a vendor integrates your current phone system or using a cloud-based phone system. Having a *softphone* (software that allows your users to make calls over the web), integrated with Service Cloud saves a significant amount of time for all parties involved. For example, when a customer calls, before even answering the phone, the agent has access to pertinent caller information, such as the name, location, purchase and support history, and so on. This is one of the most common and useful features of CTI and is normally set up in an informational popup window.

Salesforce offers Open CTI, enabling developers familiar with JavaScript to customize and build CTI systems that integrate with Salesforce. In other words, partners and customers can embed third-party web apps directly into Salesforce, opening up a world of possibilities. Open CTI eliminates the need for CTI adapters and desktop software requiring ongoing maintenance. It also allows you to standardize the call center in the Service Cloud console for a uniform and intuitive experience, from both the agent and customer perspectives.

Open CTI is an additional feature that costs money.

Implementing Live Agent Chat

Another way Salesforce allows your customers to reach you without picking up the phone is through chat. Live Agent Chat is a native chat application that is the quickest way to get in front of your customer and at the lowest cost to you. How customized you want your Live Agent Chat to be is up to you, and it can range in complexity depending on that decision. In this section, we cover the basics to get your baseline chat up and running for your business.

In order to implement the feature, you have to enable Live Agent, create Live Agent users by giving them access to it, and customize it according to your preferences and settings.

Enabling Live Agent

To enable Live Agent for your organization, choose Setup ➪ Customize ➪ Live Agent ➪ Settings. Then select Enable Live Agent, and click Save.

If the Live Agent menu doesn't appear under Setup, contact Salesforce.com Support to enable this feature in your organization.

After enabling Live Agent for your organization, you have to either create or modify pre-existing user records to provide the relevant Live Agent permissions necessary for them to do their jobs. Different aspects of Live Agent permissions are enabled in different places.

Adding Live Agent Users

In order to have individual users work as Live Agents and support your customers through chat, they need some minor adjustments to their user records. Choose Setup ➪ Manage Users ➪ Users, and then follow these steps:

1. **Click Edit to the left of the user who will be a Live Agent.**

   Alternatively, click the New User button and create a new user.

2. **On the user record, click the Live Agent User check box, as shown in Figure 7-3.**

3. **Click Save.**

If you can't find the Live Agent User check box, your organization needs to buy more Live Agent feature licenses.

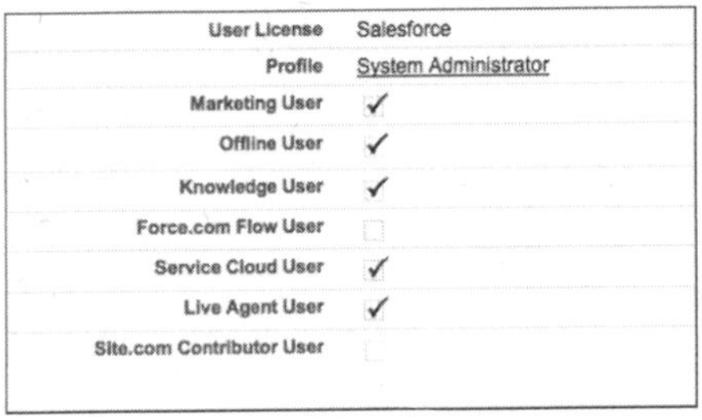

Figure 7-3:
The Live Agent User check box must be checked in order to create a Live Agent user.

User License	Salesforce
Profile	System Administrator
Marketing User	✓
Offline User	✓
Knowledge User	✓
Force.com Flow User	☐
Service Cloud User	✓
Live Agent User	✓
Site.com Contributor User	☐

Granting Live Agent users the right permissions

You've checked the Live Agent User check box on the agent's user record, but there's more. You also have to ensure that your agents have the permissions necessary to accomplish the tasks your company has set out for them. You can accomplish this in one of two ways:

✔ **Profiles:** Create or enhance a specific profile to contain these specific permissions bundled within it, and assign your Live Agent users to it.

✔ **Permission sets:** Create a Live Agent permission set that contains only Live Agent permissions and assign them to the relevant users.

How do you know which option is right for your organization? A good rule of thumb is to look at the number of users. Do you have 20 Live Agent users or 3? If you don't have many Live Agent users add a permission set. Otherwise, create a new profile for your Live Agent users. Just be wary of creating too many profiles — administrating an environment with a large number of pro-files can quickly become difficult.

If you go the permission-set route, here are the permissions your Live Agent users need:

- ✔ **Administrative permissions:** All Live Agent users need to have the API Enabled permission on their profile.

- ✔ **Standard object permissions:** The object-level permissions necessary for your live agents depend in part on the features you're implementing. For example, if agents need to see visitor and transcript records, they'll need (at the very least) Read permissions on the Live Chat Visitors and Live Chat Transcripts objects. In order for them to create Quick Text, users need full access (Create, Read, Edit, Delete) permissions on the Quick Text object, while seeing Live Agent Sessions requires at least Read permissions on that object, as shown in Figure 7-4.

Managers or supervisors may need a higher level of permissions, such as Edit, in order to modify records that agents are working on.

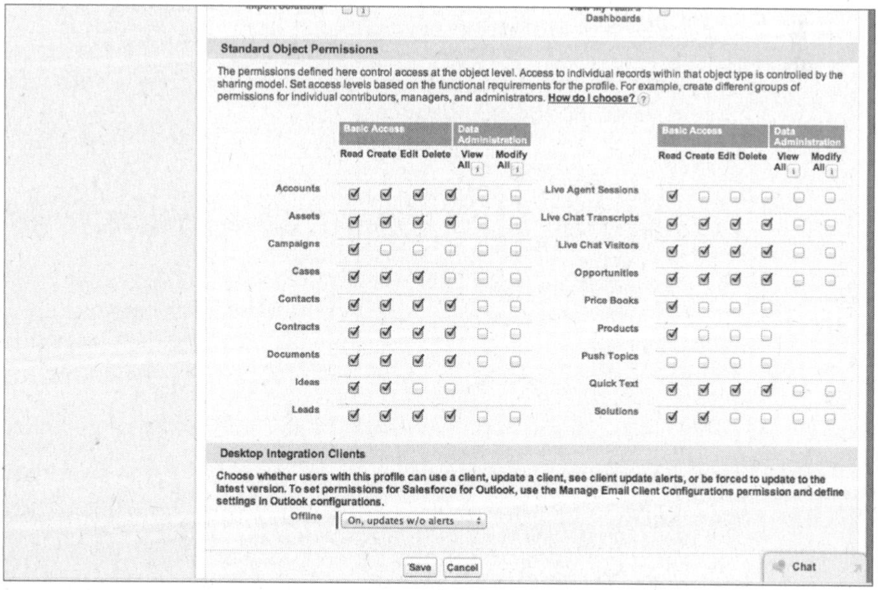

Figure 7-4:
Selecting various standard object permissions for Live Agent users.

Adding Live Agent skills

After setting up your Live Agent users, add Live Agent skills if your company segments agents into different skill groupings. For example, your customers are normally routed to a first-tier customer service representative for common issues (for example, resetting passwords, changing addresses, paying by phone, and so on), but more complex problems are directed to second-tier engineers (for technical assistance and troubleshooting). In this case, you would create two skills sets to segment those agents into the appropriate skill groups.

In Salesforce, you can identify and segment your agents' skills and then assign those users to the appropriate skill set so that Salesforce routes your customer requests accordingly.

To create a skill in Salesforce, choose Setup ➪ Customize ➪ Live Agent ➪ Skills, and then follow these steps:

1. **Click the New button.**

2. **Name the new skill.**

3. **Assign users and profiles to the skill.**

   You can assign both individual users that have the skill, as well as entire profiles, as shown in Figure 7-5.

4. **Click Save.**

   The skill you've just created appears on the screen, with its name and its assigned users and profiles.

Assigning Live Agent configurations

Live Agent configurations are packaged pieces of functionality that you must put together to manage Live Agent in the Salesforce console. Like Live Agent skills, Live Agent configurations are assigned at the user or profile level and are responsible for toggling certain settings in the console, such as:

- ✔ The number of simultaneous chat sessions an agent can have

- ✔ Notifications and sounds when the agent has a new chat request

- ✔ Whether an agent can transfer the chat to another agent or even receive files through the chat window

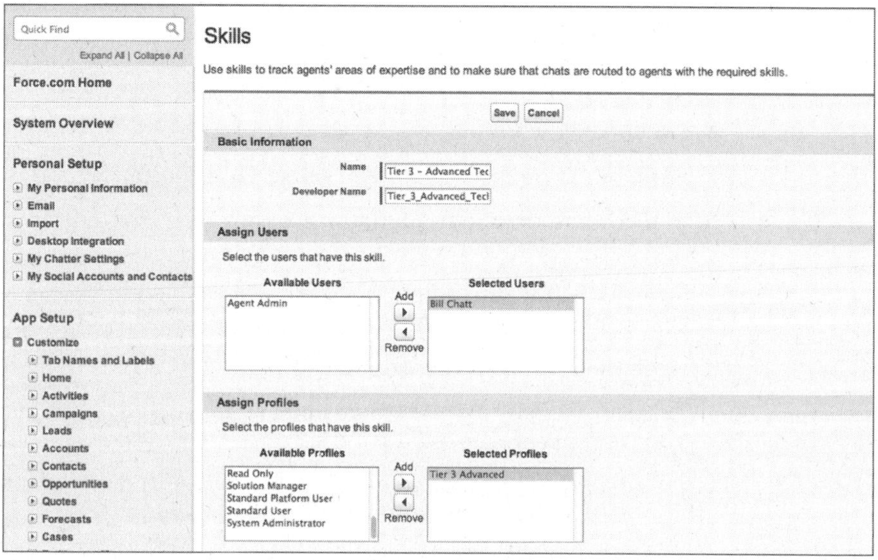

Figure 7-5:
Assigning
users and
profiles to a
skill.

You can assign different Live Agent configurations to different users and profiles, based on their level of experience or expertise. For example, a new agent who's still training should probably be grouped in a configuration that allows no more than three chats at any given time. Similarly, you can assign a seasoned agent on your team a configuration that allows for up to seven chats at once. You may want to disable chat transfer for some users while giving this configuration to others.

Creating Live Agent chat buttons and deployments

If you're intending to implement Live Agent Chat, your website visitors need a clearly visible button on your site that indicates live help is available if they need it. A chat button is what customers should click when they want to initiate a chat with one of your Live Agents.

Talk to your IT or web team before implementing chat buttons. To customize them, you need to either have a Force.com site set up or use some custom code.

You can put multiple chat buttons on your page or deployment, with each button mapped to a specific skill that you've already created. In this way, clicking an Internet Issues button won't route you to the same agent as clicking a Telephone Connectivity button.

Assuming you've already set up a skill or two, start building your button by choosing Setup ⇨ Customize ⇨ Live Agent ⇨ Chat Buttons & Invitations, and then follow these steps (see Figure 7-6):

1. **Click the New button.**

2. **From the Type drop-down list, select Chat Button.**

3. **In the Name field, enter a name for your new chat button.**

   The Developer Name field should auto-populate with the same name you provided in the Name field. The field will have underscores instead of spaces because it's an API name.

4. **From the Routing Type drop-down list, select a routing type.**

   This setting determines how customers are routed to various skills. Your options are as follows:

   - *Choice:* The inbound chat enters a queue and any agent who is assigned the appropriate skill can pick it up.

   - *Least Active:* The inbound chat is automatically routed to the least active agent (measured by number of open chats) who is assigned the appropriate skill.

   - *Most Available:* The inbound chat is routed to the most available agent (measured by chat capacity minus number of open chats).

5. **To associate specific skills with the button, select one or more skills in the Available Skills column and click the Add arrow to move them into Selected Skills.**

6. **From the Language drop-down list, select the language for the text in your chat window.**

7. **In the Push Timeout field, enter the time agents have to answer inbound chats before the chats are rerouted.**

   This only applies to you if you selected Least Active or Most Available from the Routing Type drop-down list.

8. **Fill in the remaining fields in the Basic Information section.**

   If you have a Force.com site to use for button customizations, enter the information in the Chat Button Customization section. ***Note:*** If you don't have a Force.com site, you can manually modify the button code.

9. **Click Save.**

   The button detail page is displayed with generated chat button code you can copy and paste into your site's HTML.

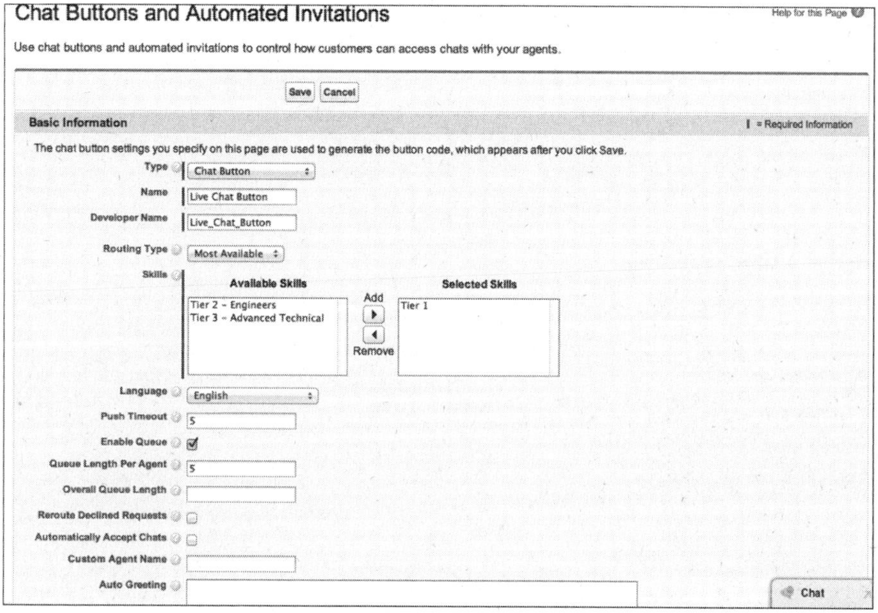

Figure 7-6:
Creating a
new chat
button for
Live Agent.

Deployments control what happens when someone clicks a Live Agent button. The button invokes Live Agent, but you can use code to control the look and feel of the chat window. You create deployments in much the same way as buttons. Like button creation, deployments also require copying and pasting provided code on each web page where you'll be deploying Live Agent. Figure 7-7 shows deployment creation.

Setting up live chat transcripts and visitors

Salesforce automatically creates a visitor and transcript record after each chat between a visitor and an agent. Live Agent Transcript records details of the chat between the agent and the customer. An example is shown in Figure 7-8.

Live Chat Visitor is an object whose record displays information about the visitor's computer and where the chat took place. An example of this record is shown in Figure 7-9.

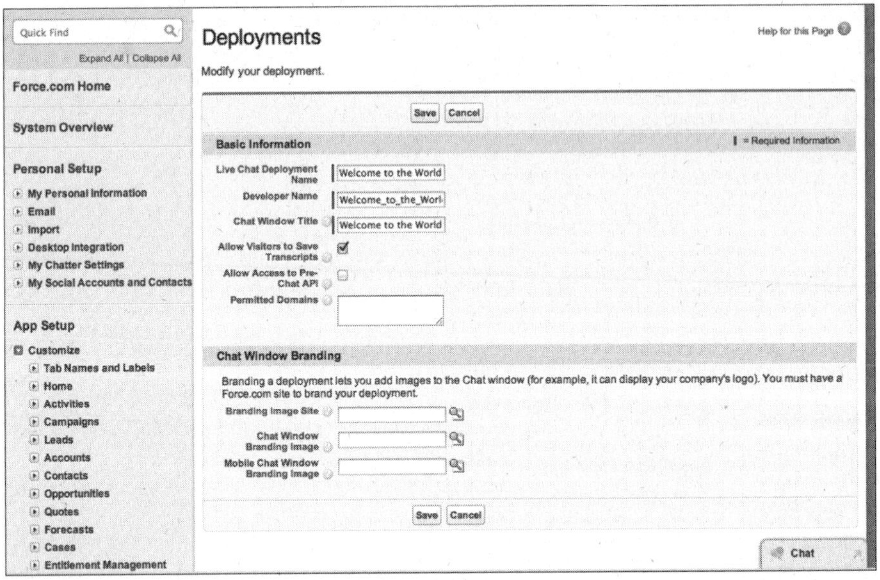

Figure 7-7:
Creating a
new deploy-
ment for
Live Agent.

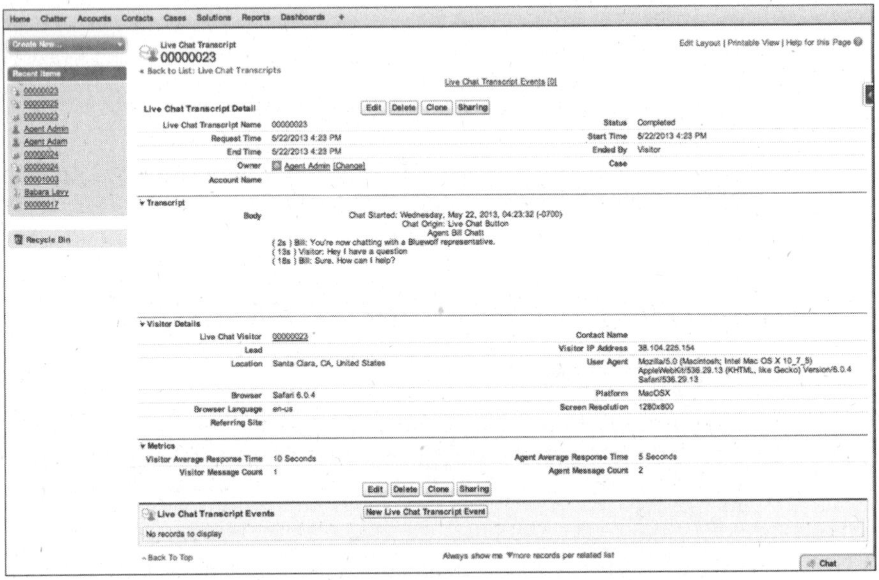

Figure 7-8:
The Live
Agent
Transcript
record.

Figure 7-9:
The Live
Chat Visitor
record.

Planning a pre-chat form

The pre-chat form is where your customers initiate a chat with an agent, entering pertinent information about the issue before the chat itself. This is done by creating a Visualforce page to host your form or simply developing the form on your own using code. You need to think about which information to capture that is most relevant, useful, and concise. The form is a delicate balance between arming the agent with enough information to provide a smooth experience for the customer, and getting your customer to an agent as quickly as possible without slowing the entire process down and deterring your customer from using it.

Reporting on Live Agent sessions

Live Agent reports don't come out of the box, but that doesn't mean that you can't create a custom report type to give you visibility into Live Agent sessions. Generally speaking, custom report types give you greater flexibility to report on custom objects and other permutations of standard objects because they relate to a primary object of your choosing.

Live Agent Session records are created each time an agent accepts a chat. These records contain pertinent information that is useful to report on. For example, managers or supervisors may want greater insight into their agents' average online chat time or the number of chats they field in a given week, month, or quarter. You can also see this information as it relates to a number of other related records, such as cases or contacts.

You can only create custom report types with records related to the primary object if that primary object has a relationship with those records. If not, create a lookup field to create that relationship.

Discovering Social Channels

Social media has become a choice marketing channel for a growing portion of business communication. Plus, customers are increasingly turning to social media to praise, bemoan, support, or question products and brands in the marketplace. A social customer service channel is an effective tool for gauging the pulse of your brand's reach and your customers' loyalty. Although it requires strategy, planning, and resources to execute properly, social customer service ultimately improves customer satisfaction, reduces call volume, and strengthens brand perception as your team publicly responds to and resolves issues in real-time.

Using Salesforce Social Hub, you can automate how Service Cloud scans through all the information about your company or product in online social posts for more efficient and meaningful customer interaction. Agents can interact with customers by responding to cases generated from Twitter and Facebook. Through the case feed, agents reply directly to tweets directed at your company or like and respond to Facebook posts, both privately or publicly. In this way, you can have a historical reference of your social interaction with customers, all from the contact record. Automating the routing of customer service issues from social media into Salesforce Service Cloud not only expedites customer interaction, it efficiently tracks and maintains a historical record of it in one centralized repository.

Salesforce's integration with Radian6 provides social insights that lead to actionable business objectives by measuring buzz around your brand or that of your competitors. Salesforce allows tracking of Social Personas (which represent a contact's profile on a social network) and Social Posts (which represent a post on a network) to give your agents the capability to monitor and moderate your managed Facebook page. They also provide the ability to determine which posts warrant case creation and which do not, in order to have a clean system that doesn't accept spam and waste precious agent time.

To use the Social Customer Service feature within Salesforce, you must purchase Social Hub licenses and ask Salesforce.com Customer Support to turn on Social for your organization.

Chapter 8

Managing a Contact Center with Service Cloud Console

In This Chapter

▶ Working in the Service Cloud Console application

▶ Understanding basic Service Cloud Console terminology

▶ Answering the right questions before implementing the Service Cloud Console

*T*hose who work in or manage high-volume contact centers frequently cite similar pain points and familiar daily struggles: high-stress environments compounded by painful processes to get the information necessary from and to large numbers of customers. On top of it all, many agents are expected to answer and resolve a certain number of issues every hour. Besides the more obvious measures a call center can take to solve these common problems (training programs, positive incentives, proper scheduling, and friendly competition), the Service Cloud Console also can greatly help manage an agent's workload out of the box.

The Service Cloud Console is a tab-based application interface that Salesforce Service Cloud uses to simplify case management by giving agents more access to key data using fewer clicks. In other words, less time finding important information and more time satisfying customers.

In this chapter, we first walk you through the typical tasks in an agent's day and tell you how these are made easier with the Service Cloud Console. Then we cover basic terminology for the console to give you a high-level understanding of it. We wrap up the chapter with a series of questions any call center should ask before implementing the console.

Using the Service Cloud Console

Specific tasks in any contact center vary from company to company, and your business is no exception. Although the details of your business process may stray from the tasks laid out here, you can probably find some similarities:

- ✔ **Answering inbound customer inquiries:** These inquiries can come in the form of emails, phone calls, web forms on your site, or even tweets. Additionally, you can "pick up" existing inquiries or cases that are queued for a specific team, location, or skill set.

- ✔ **Requesting customer information:** If you don't already know it, you'll have to locate the individual's information while simultaneously taking notes on the current problem.

- ✔ **Validating the customer's entitlement to service:** Most companies differentiate between authorized and unauthorized contacts. Warranties, service-level agreements (SLAs), and service contracts all fall under this category.

- ✔ **Creating or maintaining a case:** Agents and supervisors alike need a case record to serve as a one-stop shop, tracking all progress and interactions on any particular issue.

- ✔ **Researching the issue:** Collaborating with internal specialists, mining the knowledge base, and working the issues all lead to getting your customers answers.

- ✔ **Resolving the problem and notifying the customer:** After you resolve and communicate the resolution to the customer, you close the case and move onto the next one.

Essentially, customer service aims to field and resolve customer issues in a timely, personable, and consistent way that leaves the client feeling happy and satisfied with the decision to do business with you.

When you use the Service Cloud Console, answering inbound customer queries becomes second nature. Whether a CTI integrated popup alerts you of the name and information of the contact calling, or you receive a blind phone call and type the customer's name in the global search bar, the console provides the information necessary to identify the caller within seconds. Figure 8-1 shows the global search for a caller's name while in the console.

After you open the customer's contact record, you see the Cases related list that displays all the cases and inquiries the customer has had with your company in the past, as shown in Figure 8-2. All this and we're only at two clicks!

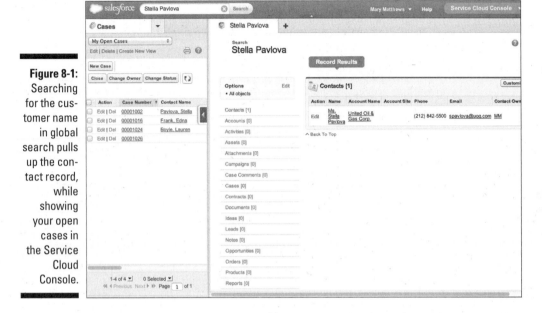

Figure 8-1:
Searching
for the cus-
tomer name
in global
search pulls
up the con-
tact record,
while
showing
your open
cases in
the Service
Cloud
Console.

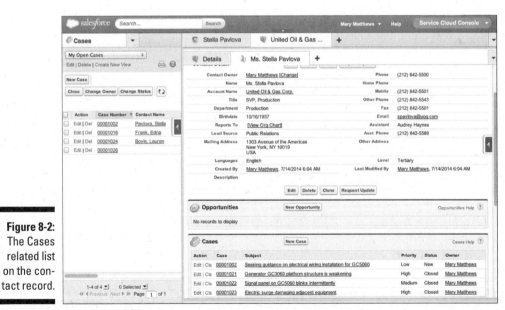

Figure 8-2:
The Cases
related list
on the con-
tact record.

Similar to the Cases related list, you can see the Entitlements related list on a contact record to determine whether a customer is entitled to receive support. If the customer's entitlement is active, go ahead and open a new case for him. If not, you can transfer him to your Renewals department to renew his contract. In either scenario, the Service Cloud Console makes it easy to see different pieces of pertinent information, without incessant clicking and wasted time. Figure 8-3 shows the Entitlements related list on a contact record.

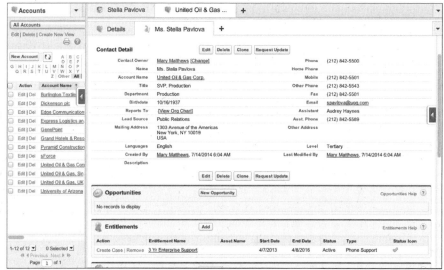

Figure 8-3:
The
Entitlements
related list
shows an
active enti-
tlement on
the contact
record.

Other great time-saving features of the console include the Interaction Log, which helps agents take quick notes on an interaction, while being able to simultaneously view other panes and customer information. Similarly, you can enable the Knowledge sidebar, which automatically scours your knowledge base for answers to common problems, using the standard subject field of your case as the keywords. Finally, communication with the customer is all tracked and recorded on the same case record as the rest of the activity pertaining to the issue in question for quick access and historical record.

Saving Time with Keyboard Shortcuts

Keyboard shortcuts exist for browsers, software, and many other applications. The Service Cloud Console is no exception. Because the console is designed for heightened efficiency, what better way to double the speed than with keyboard shortcuts?

One useful example of saving time with keyboard shortcuts is editing records. Just by pressing E on your keyboard, you can save yourself a click and get straight to editing the record you're on. You can also save time with other shortcuts like saving a record or switching between different tabs.

The first step is enabling keyboard shortcuts for the console. To do this, choose Setup➪Create➪Apps in Salesforce, and then follow these steps:

1. **Click Edit next to the Service Cloud Console for which you want to enable keyboard shortcuts.**

   If you haven't created a custom one, you'll see the Sample Console.

2. **Scroll down to Choose Keyboard Shortcuts and click the Customize Keyboard Shortcuts link.**

3. **Click the Edit button and then check the Enable Keyboard Shortcuts check box, as shown in Figure 8-4.**

4. **Select the prepackaged default shortcuts you want to enable.**

   Creating new custom shortcuts requires more significant customization and a developer to use the Salesforce Console Integration Toolkit.

5. **If you want to edit the key command for a default action, click the Edit link to the left of the check box and enter your desired key command.**

6. **Click Save.**

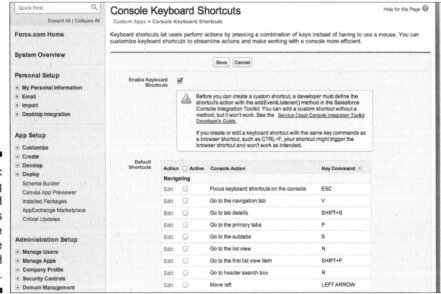

Figure 8-4: Enabling keyboard shortcuts for the Service Cloud Console.

Now go back to the console and test out your new time-saving keyboard shortcuts.

Existing keyboard shortcuts on the browser you're using may interfere with the console keyboard shortcuts.

Getting Familiar with Service Cloud Console Terms

Before we dive into the details of setting up the Service Cloud Console in the next chapter, we want to cover the basic console terminology. Figure 8-5 shows the basic Service Cloud Console interface. Familiarize yourself with these basic terms to understand the ins and outs of navigating in the console:

✔ **Service Cloud Console:** The console is the overall user interface that is a synthesis of various components usually seen separately within Salesforce.

✔ **Navigation tab:** This is a top-level customizable drop-down of objects available to view within the console.

✔ **Pinned lists:** A list of records belonging to the object chosen in the navigation tab. You can choose if you want the list to display at the top or on the left side of the Service Cloud Console (see Chapter 9 for more information).

✔ **Primary tab:** When you select a record from the list, it appears as a new primary tab.

✔ **Subtab:** Shows the main record you're currently working on and is related to the item in the primary tab. You can have multiple subtabs open and quickly switch between them.

✔ **Highlights panel:** Allows you to choose the most useful and relevant fields on a record to view them at a glance.

✔ **Interaction Log:** Where service agents or others can log quick notes on a record to account for a specific interaction relating to it.

✔ **Salesforce Console Integration Toolkit:** Steps up the level of customization possible for the Service Cloud Console through this API. The toolkit gives developers greater access to the console so that, together with the business, you can display other browser pages as tabs directly in the console.

Figure 8-5:
The
Salesforce
Service
Cloud
Console
interface.

Now that you're familiar with the basic uses, functions, and terms of the Salesforce Service Cloud Console, you can start planning your implementation of it.

Preparing Your Strategy for the Console

Before jumping ahead and implementing the Service Cloud Console, you need to ask yourself some important questions and do some planning. Here are a few basic questions to think about:

- ✔ **As an agent, how much time do you spend trying to identify a customer and a customer's entitlement to service?**

- ✔ **As a manager, what criteria do you expect to measure your agents against?** If time is a major factor, you want to ensure your customer service reps are not bogged down by the limitations of a system and are spending their time researching and resolving issues.

- ✔ **Do you have a high- or low-volume contact center?** Although the console may be useful in either situation, it's really built for a high volume of calls and customer inquiries.

✔ **Are you looking for a customized interface for your agents?** One of the best features of the Service Cloud Console is how extendable it is. You can add custom Visualforce component pages to it to jazz it up, but someone with Visualforce skills will need to help. Even without Visualforce, the console is quite extendable so that you can easily customize its look and feel.

✔ **Do you want to integrate the console with other systems?** CTI is one example, but the Developer Toolkit makes your options sizeable.

✔ **Which fields do you want to highlight on records within the Service Cloud Console?** If time is of the essence, you'll probably want to prioritize the minimum number of key fields needed to get the agent's job done.

✔ **Do your users need the ability to jot down quick notes while talking to customers?** The Interaction Log is perfect for exactly this.

Now that you've begun thinking about some important questions for your console implementation, we can show you how quickly and easily you can set up the Service Cloud Console for yourself. After implementing this powerful tool, you'll find that not only does it save time, but it also increases user adoption while decreasing onboarding time for new agents.

Chapter 9

Implementing the Service Cloud Console

....

In This Chapter

▶ Customizing the Highlights panel for the console

▶ Creating a Service Cloud Console app

▶ Setting up interaction logs

▶ Modifying the list display

▶ Turning on the Knowledge sidebar for the console

▶ Choosing the right users for the Service Cloud Console

....

*F*ast-paced environments are the nature of your business. Agents require attention to customer interaction; they shouldn't concern themselves with toggling between screens and unnecessary clicking. Enter the Salesforce Console. The console is a visual framework or application that simplifies an agent's job by aggregating related information onto one screen.

Salesforce's Service Cloud Console uses a tabbed environment to navigate different groupings of related records quickly and easily. By reducing time-consuming scrolling and clicking, an agent can find, update, and create records in seconds. With the Service Cloud Console, you can manage more customer cases at the same time with greater precision. And you don't have to waste valuable time changing screens or toggling back and forth between different browser windows. For example, if you're a customer service rep, you can use the console to log a case for a customer on the phone, while seeing her contact and account details and previously opened cases, and taking notes, all on the same page.

In this chapter, we show you how to implement and optimize the Salesforce Service Cloud Console to boost productivity in high-volume call centers. We show you how to build a custom application for the console in the

App Picker. You discover how to build highlights panels, interaction logs, and list displays. Then we discuss how to customize them in a manner that makes sense to you. Finally, we cover how to choose which users should work in the console.

Understanding the Service Cloud Console

The Service Cloud Console is a tab-based application interface in Salesforce that is optimized for speed and ease of navigation. Allowing agents to quickly toggle between subtabs and having multiple, easily accessible views into customer data greatly increases their effectiveness.

Figure 9-1 shows the components of the console, which is comprised of the Navigation tab, the Primary tab, and subtabs. Customizing the console also includes the ability to have a Highlights panel, interaction log, and Knowledge sidebar.

Figure 9-1:
Your customized Service Cloud Console user interface.

Navigation tap · Primary tap · Sub tap

Interaction Log

Enabling the Highlights Panel

Now that you're ready to set up your very own Service Cloud Console for your agents, your first step is setting up the Highlights panel on the Account page layout. The Highlights panel allows you to customize a table of up to four columns at the top of each Primary tab in the console, displaying key customer information at a glance.

To set up the Highlights panel on an account, choose Setup➪Customize➪ Accounts➪Page Layouts, and then follow these steps:

1. **Click Edit next to the Account page layout you want to modify.**

2. **Hover your cursor over Highlights panel (see Figure 9-2) at the top of the layout until a wrench icon appears and then click it.**

   Figure 9-2 shows the Highlights panel.

3. **Click a highlighted panel and choose a top and bottom field for each; then click OK.**

   Choose the fields that best suit your business needs. For example, if you or your agents look at the Status field first, this would be a good selection for the Highlights panel.

4. **Click Layout Properties at the top of the page layout editor and make sure to select Show in the Console next to Highlights panel.**

   Figure 9-3 shows the properties of the console to ensure its display.

5. **Click OK and then click Save.**

   You can follow these steps to customize Highlights panels for other object page layouts as well, such as cases.

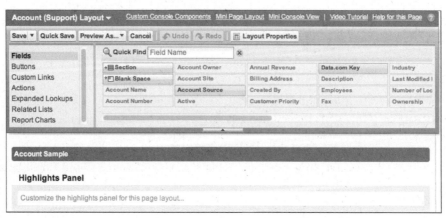

Figure 9-2:
The
Highlights
panel at the
top of the
Account
page layout

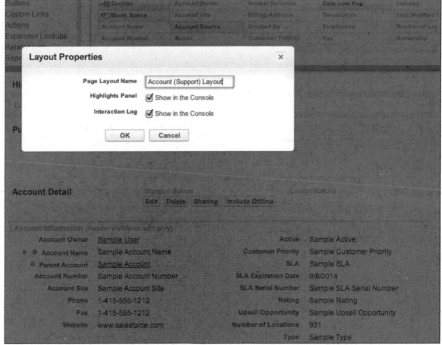

Adding an App for the Service Cloud Console

Now that you have turned on the Highlights panel for the console, let's look at building an actual application to make the Service Cloud Console easy to select. Agents in the console will be able to see these key fields quickly without having to waste time scouring for important information.

To build a new customized app for your console, choose Setup ➪ Create ➪ Apps, and then follow these steps:

1. **Click the New button.**

   Figure 9-4 shows how a user can start creating a custom app.

2. **Click the Console Type radio button and click Next.**

3. **Give your new app a name, such as Service Cloud Console, and click Next.**

4. **(Optional) You can choose to add a custom logo under 20KB for your new app.**

Figure 9-4:
From the
App menu,
click the
New button
to create a
custom app.

5. Select the objects to include in the console's Navigation tab by moving the Available Items into the Selected Items column, and then click Next.

Figure 9-5 shows how to customize Navigation tabs.

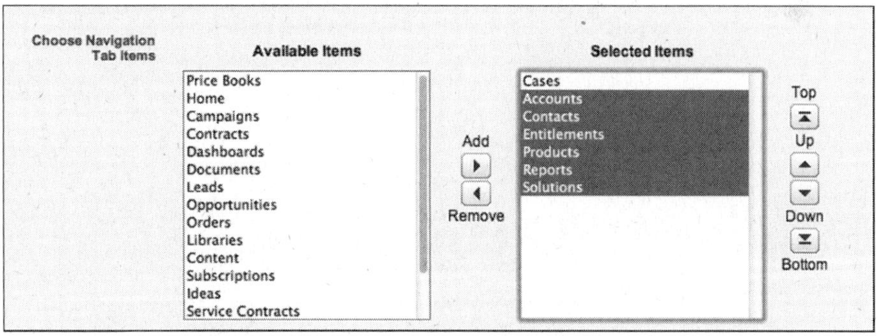

Figure 9-5:
Customizing
your
Navigation
tab items.

6. Customize how your chosen items will display when you don't select them from a primary tab or a subtab.

This means that you can choose how records will display when agents select them from a search result or any other list that is not one of the tabs in the console. For example, you can choose to always display cases as a subtab to an account, as shown in Figure 9-6.

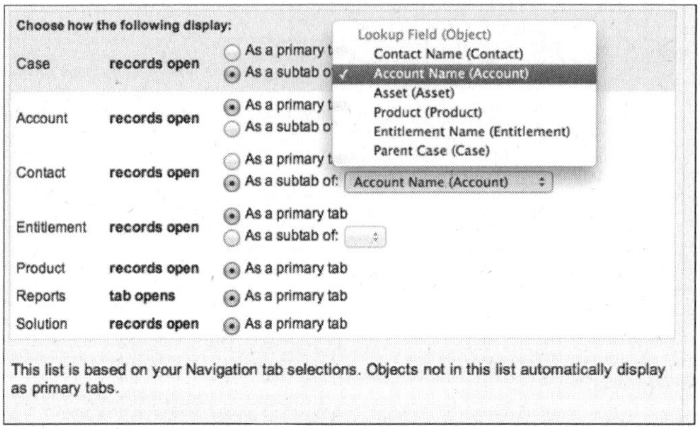

Figure 9-6:
Selecting
case
records will
display as
subtabs to
an account

7. **Choose how the other records will display and click Next.**

8. **(Optional) If Live Agent is enabled, you'll be prompted to choose Live Agent Settings. If Include Live Agent in This App is checked, agents using the Service Cloud Console while also administering chat sessions can work on the chat sessions within the SCC. If the box is checked, additional check boxes will appear to help determine what objects open as subtabs of each chat session. You can even include suggested Articles from Salesforce Knowledge in Live Agent, if you have that enabled.**

9. **Click the Visible check box next to each of your profiles that should have access to the console, and then click Save.**

When completed, the Apps page appears with your new Service Cloud Console app.

Building Interaction Logs

Interaction logs are another time-saving tool you can enable for your call center. These logs allow console users to take quick notes and update task fields on open records while on customer calls, without sacrificing visibility into important information.

Enabling interaction logs for the console

To enable interaction logs on a case, you must turn them on for page layouts, as you did earlier for the Highlights panel.

Choose Setup ⇨ Customize ⇨ Cases ⇨ Page Layouts, and then follow these steps:

1. **Click Edit next to the case page layout you want to modify.**

2. **Click Layout Properties at the top of the page layout editor and make sure to click Show in the Console next to Interaction Log, as shown in Figure 9-7.**

3. **Click OK and then Save.**

Customizing and assigning interaction logs

After enabling them, you can customize interaction logs to display the task fields that are most relevant to you or your agents. You can even create and customize multiple logs with distinct information and assign them to different users.

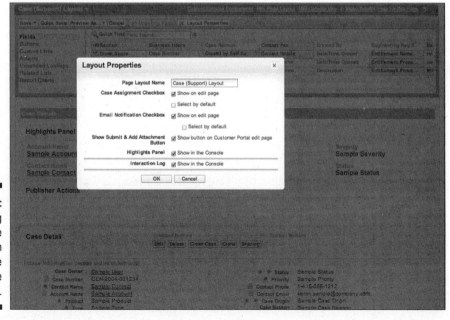

Figure 9-7: Enabling the console interaction log on the case page layout.

Choose Setup⇨Create⇨Interaction Log Layouts, and then follow these steps:

1. **Click Edit next to the Default Interaction Log, or click the New button to create a new one and give it a name.**

2. **Move the task fields you want to display on the interaction log from the Available column to the Selections column, as Figure 9-8 indicates.**

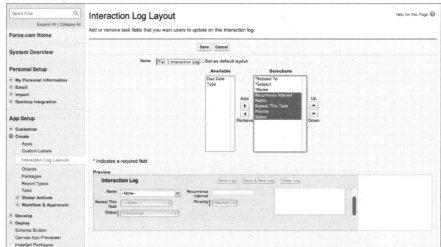

Figure 9-8: Customizing the interaction log layout.

3. **Click Save.**

   Now that you know how to create and customize the interaction log, assign the layout to specific user profiles.

4. **From the Interaction Log Layout screen, click the Log Layout Assignment button.**

5. **Select the interaction log you want to assign to each profile and then click Save.**

   Figure 9-9 shows how to assign interaction log layouts to users.

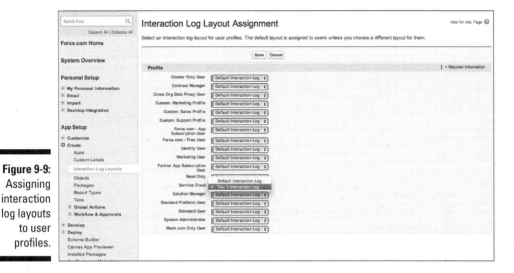

Figure 9-9:
Assigning
interaction
log layouts
to user
profiles.

Choosing a List Display for the Console

List displays are different interface styles available to agents to work on a specific list or subset of records. Depending on preference, you can choose between a few list placements on the console. Which list placement will help your agents view important customer information that much more quickly? Let's look at the options available and how to customize the way lists appear.

In the console, you can display lists in three different ways:

- ✔ **Full screen, unpinned:** Select this option if you never want to display the list pinned to a side of your screen. Lists only appear when you select the Navigation tab, and clicking a record will open a new tab.

- ✔ **Pinned to top:** This option pins a list to the top of the screen while a new tab opens for a specific record below this list.

- ✔ **Pinned to left:** Lists appear to the left of the screen while you work in a record to the right of it.

Figure 9-10 shows a pinned-to-the-left console display.

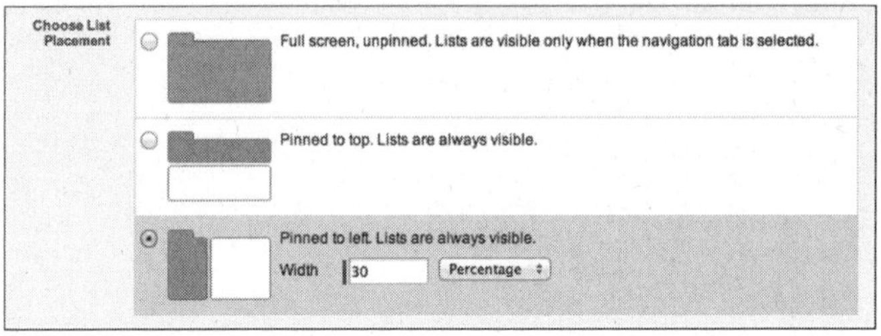

Figure 9-10:
Selecting a
pinned-to-
the-left list
display for
the console.

Choose Setup ⇨ Create ⇨ Apps to change how your lists display in Salesforce, and then follow these steps:

1. **Click Edit next to the console app whose list display you want to modify.**

2. **In the List section of the page, select the style that best suits you.**

3. **Set the width of the list display and click Save.**

   You probably shouldn't set the list display to a percentage greater than 40 percent of your browser. *Remember:* You want the ability to see these lists while you work, but focus on the specific record at hand.

4. **Click Save.**

Now that you have enabled and customized your console, let's briefly discuss how to enable the Knowledge sidebar before jumping into the considerations to make in determining who should be working in the console.

If Salesforce Knowledge is already enabled for your organization (see Chapter 13), you can enable the Knowledge sidebar for the console so that articles with keywords found in your case subject dynamically appear for an enhanced user experience.

Choose Setup ⇨ Customize ⇨ Cases ⇨ Page Layouts, and then follow these steps:

1. **Click Edit next to the case page layout for which you want the sidebar to appear.**

2. **Select Layout Properties.**

3. **Click Knowledge Sidebar.**

4. **Click OK and then click Save.**

In this way, you can turn on the Knowledge sidebar for only certain layouts that you can then assign to a certain subset of users who need it.

Selecting Users to Work in the Console

The Service Cloud Console is a powerful tool to expedite efficient customer service and delight your customers. Although all call center agents need access to a lot of information at once, there are certain considerations to keep in mind when choosing which users should be living and breathing the Service Cloud Console:

- ✔ **Case volume:** The first consideration to make is your case volume. What does an agent's daily caseload look like? Are you a relatively new business working on 2- to 30 cases a day? If so, the console will probably be less beneficial than working in a fast-paced support center answering hundreds of calls and logging thousands of cases weekly.

- ✔ **Agent hierarchy:** Another consideration is your agent structure or hierarchy. Normally, the first and/or second tiers or points of contact with your customers should be working in the console app. Escalating to more technical or managerial-level support probably requires less console use and more of Salesforce's standard apps.

Make sure you've assigned the Service Cloud feature license to the users you want in the console. This step and assigning the console to the proper profiles are necessary after you've made these considerations.

The beauty of Salesforce is that enabling the console is ultimately your choice. You can use the console whether you're a very small business or the manager at a Fortune 500 company.

Part IV

Leveraging Your Organizational Knowledge

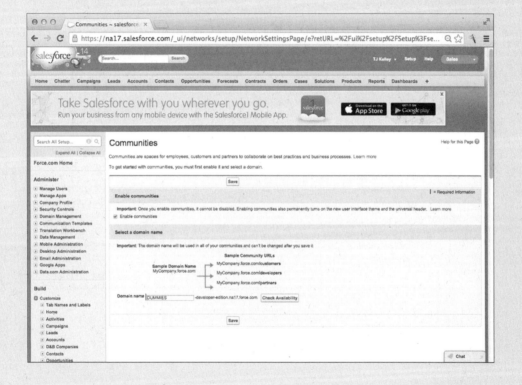

In this part . . .

✔ Learn the basic concepts and available features of Salesforce Knowledge.

✔ Find out exactly how to get a Salesforce knowledge base up and running in your organization.

✔ See the management and governance processes that are possible with Knowledge articles.

✔ Learn how to think about categorizing your organizational knowledge.

Chapter 10

Planning Your Knowledge Implementation

In This Chapter

▶ Understanding Salesforce Knowledge

▶ Getting familiar with Knowledge terms

▶ Planning the information your knowledge base will contain

▶ Considering how your users will interact with your knowledge base

▶ Determining controls around publication

▶ Thinking about the users in your system and the permissions they need

*Y*our organization surely has a great deal of institutional knowledge — well, at least *some* institutional knowledge, right? No matter the breadth or depth of your organization's knowledge, you need to ensure that your employees, customers, partners, and the public can interact with the information they need in the right moment, the right place, and the right format.

Salesforce Knowledge provides the framework for a knowledge base that can enable your organization to quickly create and easily manage information that you want to share with internal or external users.

 Before you embark on your Knowledge journey, make sure your organization can utilize Salesforce Knowledge. Knowledge is available for use in the Performance Edition and Developer Edition without any additional cost. Knowledge is also available for use in the Enterprise Edition and Unlimited Edition with an additional cost associated.

In this chapter, we help you recognize what exactly Salesforce Knowledge is and what new components it introduces to your organization. Then we walk you through the thought exercises you need to complete to prepare for a Knowledge implementation. Finally, we touch on the various users you can empower with Knowledge, as well as the permissions and licenses they need.

Understanding Basic Knowledge Terminology

Before you can begin planning and thinking deeply about your Salesforce Knowledge implementation, you need to understand the new terms that Knowledge introduces.

If you're working with a team, be sure to have a group meeting to review Knowledge terminology so that everyone can work with common definitions on the implementation.

Here are the most important terms you need to know when it comes to Knowledge:

- **Article:** An article contains information that you want to make available in your organization's knowledge base (for example, product information). Articles may contain information meant for your own customer support agents or information intended for direct consumption by customers, partners, or the public.

- **Article type:** All articles in Salesforce Knowledge must have an article type assigned to them. Examples of article types might include FAQ, How-To, or Troubleshooting articles. Article types enable your organization to differentiate between articles by the type of content they contain, the consistent structure and appearance of that content, and the groups of people that will be able to access that content.

- **Article-type layout:** Similar to a page layout, article-type layout allows system administrators to group fields on articles into specific sections and order them in the most efficient way for their users. Administrators also have the ability to make fields invisible or read-only for users. Only one layout is available for each article type.

- **Article-type template:** The article-type template determines how an article-type layout is presented to users. For example, an article-type template can specify if the article displays in separate tabs after being opened or if it displays on a single page. You can create custom article-type templates, but Salesforce provides two standard options:

    - **Tab template:** Renders sections of an article type's layout as tabs for the end-user.

    - **Table of contents template:** Renders all sections of an article type's layout on a single page. This template also includes hyperlinks to important related content.

✔ **Channel:** The avenue through which articles are made available. Salesforce offers four types of channels, as well as one custom option:

- **Internal app:** Articles are available to users via the Articles tab in your organization.

- **Customer:** Your customers can view articles via the Articles tab if it's available to them in either your Customer Portal or Customer Community.

- **Partner:** Your partners can view articles via the Articles tab if it's available to them in either your Partner Portal or Partner Community.

- **Public knowledge base:** You can provide articles to the public by using the Sample Public Knowledge Base for Salesforce Knowledge app, which is available on the AppExchange and will allow you to create a public knowledge base to share your articles.

   The AppExchange is a marketplace for business applications created for the Salesforce community. You can access the AppExchange at `https://appexchange.salesforce.com`.

   Creating a public knowledge base using this application will still require Sites and Visualforce development. Work with a developer at your organization if you want to create a public knowledge base to display your articles.

- **Your company website:** Articles can additionally be rendered through your own company website.

An article can have the following statuses:

✔ **Draft:** In-progress articles that are not visible via any channel. Article Managers are the only users who can view draft articles.

✔ **Published:** Available via the Articles tab and any other channel where you choose to expose articles. Published articles can be archived or changed back to draft status to ensure users and visitors no longer have access to them.

✔ **Archived:** Articles withdrawn from public visibility after being published. Articles can be archived manually or automatically using an expiration date.

Articles can also be organized into groups and categories:

✔ **Data category for articles:** Establishes criteria for differentiating, sorting, and categorizing articles (for example, product families or sales regions). Article authors can select categories for their articles and users can easily find relevant articles via the Articles tab by searching in specific data categories.

Administrators can also control the access users have to articles by restricting or opening data categories to specific subsets of users.

✔ **Category group for articles:** Arranges data categories into overarching, hierarchical groups. For example, you may want to create a products category group and organize your product hierarchies within the group using data categories. Your users will be able to filter by category when searching for relevant articles.

There are also additional types of users involved with Knowledge:

✔ **Article Manager:** Users assigned to the Manage Articles user permission. Article Managers gain access to the Article Management tab and can create, edit, assign, publish, archive, and delete any article in your system.

✔ **Knowledge Agent:** Users who interact with your organization's articles, but don't create, edit, or manage the articles in the database.

With Salesforce Knowledge articles, you can create content in multiple languages. The following terms are only relevant if your organization uses multiple languages in your knowledge base:

✔ **Draft translation:** Similar to draft articles, these are in-progress translations that have yet to be published.

✔ **Published translation:** Published and subsequently translated articles. Article Managers can view published translations from the Article Management tab.

Categorizing and Adding Article Types

Make sure that you thoroughly understand the purpose of your knowledge base. What purpose will your articles serve? Who will access these articles and how will they leverage the knowledge base? Answering these questions is imperative to building an effective knowledge base.

The answers to these questions will help you

✔ Identify the different types of articles your organization requires.

✔ Categorize these articles.

✔ Determine the roles and personas that will need access to the knowledge base, as well as the functions they need to complete.

For more detailed information on the various actions that your users will perform in the knowledge base, turn to Chapter 12.

One of the key first steps you need to take to plan your knowledge implementation is to determine the number of article types you need to create.

Article types serve as differentiators for your articles on multiple levels. They empower you to capture distinct information on each individual type. For example, you surely want to capture different information on a How-To article and a FAQ article. Additionally, article types allow you to display information differently for your users via article-type templates.

Article-type templates provide different options to render the sections from your article types to your users.

Finally, article types allow you and your users to search for articles more easily.

For more information on creating article types, refer to Chapter 11.

Although article types allow you to begin categorizing your articles at a high level, data categories and category groups take article organization to the next level.

If your organization only plans to use a few article types and there are little to no requirements for restricting access to these article types, we recommend that you consider skipping over data categories, because there may not be a valid need to use them. On the other hand, if your organization plans to create more than three article types or you need to restrict access to articles based on content, data categories are the right option for you.

When authors create articles, they can assign data categories to their articles, which allows your users, partners, or customers to search for articles by those categories. Additionally, administrators can leverage the data categories to restrict access to articles if needed.

Administrators can restrict article access by role, permission set, or profile. Before deciding to restrict article access by data category, you should perform a mapping exercise to understand which roles, profiles, or permission sets will have restricted access.

Figure 10-1 is an example of what a data category hierarchy may look like using products as the category group for articles.

To learn how to set up data categories, refer to Chapter 12.

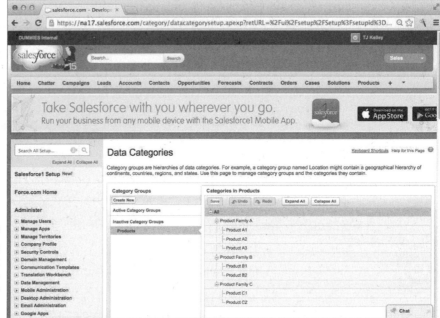

Displaying Articles and Layouts

When planning your Salesforce Knowledge implementation, you need to decide what information your articles will provide and how that information will be displayed to the consumers of the articles. Ask yourself the following questions:

- ✔ **What purpose will your articles serve?** Understanding the purpose of your articles allows you to create various article types to be most efficient for the authors. When you know exactly what information will be recorded in various article types, you can customize each by adding custom fields to capture the information you need. For example, on a Q&A article, you might simply create a custom field for the question and the answer.

  To see how to create custom fields for your articles, refer to Chapter 20.

- ✔ **Who will access these articles and how will they leverage the knowledge base?** Knowing the type of users who will be accessing various article types allows you to display that information in a manner that will allow them to interact with the information in a way that meets their needs. You can customize the order and positioning of fields using the article-type layout.

Additionally, you may know in advance that users with different roles will only be interested in specific sections of articles. In this case, you can choose the Article-type tab template to display the article.

The tab template for article types displays the sections of an article in multiple tabs to allow users to navigate quickly to the section that is most relevant to them.

Finally, if you know users will need to view articles in various languages, you can create translated articles in your knowledge base.

Thinking about Approval Processes

Whether you're importing existing articles or starting with a clean slate, you need to consider how new articles will be created and added to the knowledge base. Think about who will have the ability to create articles. Also, ask yourself how you'll determine if these articles are ready to be published into your knowledge base.

Salesforce Knowledge provides simple, native functionality to control the creation and publication of knowledge articles with approval processes. You may be accustomed to a manual approval process by requiring article or knowledge managers to approve before publication, but Knowledge gives you the additional control of automating this process.

If you choose to create an approval process for articles, you have the option to ensure that multiple people or groups of people review and approve an article prior to publication. You also have the flexibility to designate the order in which those people or groups review the article.

Salesforce Knowledge makes this an easy process to adopt with the ability to create automated reminders and the ability to view an article's approval history directly on the article record detail page in the system.

If your organization opts to create an approval process for articles, refer to Chapter 12 to learn how to set one up.

Designating Article Access and Permissions

When you know the types of articles that you need to create and the way in which users will interact with those articles, you're ready to plan out what actions your users and consumers of your articles will need to perform and ensure they have the necessary permissions and licenses to use your knowledge base successfully.

Here are the various users who may need access to your knowledge base and ways that you can grant them access:

- ✔ **Internal users:** Knowledge users need a Salesforce feature license and must be enabled to access the Article Management tab or the Articles tab via profiles or permission sets.

  Consider creating permission sets for various roles in your knowledge base. For example, you may want to create an Article Manager permission set that you can use to quickly and easily assign article managers all the necessary permissions. This will be particularly helpful to differentiate your article managers from other users who may share the same profile.

- ✔ **Customer Portal users:** In order to grant customers access to your knowledge base, you need to make the Articles tab visible in your Customer Portal or Customer Community.

- ✔ **Partner Portal users:** In order to grant partner access to your knowledge base, you need to make the Articles tab visible in your Partner Portal or Partner Community.

  To see how you can make the Articles tab visible for your Partners and Customers, turn to Chapter 14.

- ✔ **Public knowledge base users:** If you want to make your Salesforce Knowledge articles available to the general public, you can install, configure, and customize a knowledge base using the Public Knowledge Base app from the AppExchange.

Salesforce users with full licenses have the ability to read published articles, but they won't be able to access archived or draft articles unless they have a Knowledge User license. Without a Salesforce Knowledge license, users will also be unable to create, edit, delete, or publish articles.

With Enterprise, Unlimited, and Performance Edition, users with a Service Cloud, Sales Cloud, Community, or Portal license only need to have read access to article types in order to view and leverage the knowledge base. However, in order to create, edit, delete, or publish articles, you will need to purchase Knowledge User licenses for these users in addition to whichever license they already have.

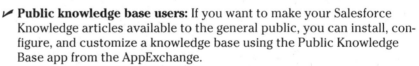

In addition to considering the licenses your users will need, be sure to consider the actions those users will need to perform in your Knowledge base so you can ensure they have the appropriate system permissions to perform their job functions:

- **Manager Salesforce Knowledge permission:** Needed to create article types, manage articles, and modify Knowledge-related settings. At least one member of your Knowledge Management team will need this permission in order to set up and make changes to your organization's Knowledge base. Users with this permission should ideally be certified Salesforce administrators.

- **Manage Articles permission:** Needed to edit draft articles, edit translations, and manage the publication of articles. Your entire Knowledge Management team will need this permission in order to review, edit, approve, and publish articles to the Knowledge base. For example, a Technical Publications Associate may need this permission to create draft articles and submit them for approval. Additionally, be sure to grant this permission for any users who will be responsible for translating articles.

- **Manage Data Categories permission:** Needed to create data categories. The user, or users, with this permission will likely be the same as those with the Manage Salesforce Knowledge permission. This may be reserved for your Knowledge Director and a Knowledge Associate with Salesforce expertise. We recommend that any user with this permission is a certified Salesforce administrator.

- **Read, Create, Edit, and Delete permissions:** All are needed in order to import articles and import or export article translations. Particularly if your organization is moving from an outdated Knowledge base to Salesforce, you may have a need to import articles or translations in bulk. In the event that a Knowledge Associate in your organization needs to import or export articles and article translations, they will need all of the above permissions.

Chapter 11

Setting Up Salesforce Knowledge

In This Chapter

▶ Creating article types

▶ Enabling Salesforce Knowledge

▶ Integrating cases with the knowledge base

*R*emember the days when you had to call a company like IKEA to ask questions about a certain part or how to assemble a product? It seems like a waste of time today, because we have so many other, more efficient tools to quickly get the answers we need.

Today's customer wants answers and wants them now. Salesforce Knowledge gives businesses a powerful tool to enhance customer service. Although not for free, a knowledge base is a fantastic way to create and manage custom articles that you can share with your users, partners, customers, and all visitors to your website.

If you haven't already read Chapter 10, you'll want to do so before setting up Knowledge for your organization. This chapter assumes that you understand the purpose and functionality of this feature, you're familiar with the terms, and you've spent a considerable amount of time planning your Knowledge implementation. The planning phase is ultimately where most of the time should be spent in a Knowledge implementation, because there are numerous considerations depending on your needs.

In this chapter, we show you how to set up Salesforce Knowledge. We take you through creating articles and article types, including how to customize their layouts, templates, and access to fit your specific business requirements. Next, we walk you through the steps to actually turn the feature on in your organization, so that you can follow along and see it for yourself. Finally, we show you how to integrate your articles and knowledge base with your case management system in Service Cloud to expedite case resolution and make everything work seamlessly together for an enhanced customer service experience.

Segmenting Knowledge with Article Types

You can think of article types as similar to record types for articles in Salesforce Knowledge. In other words, as discussed in the previous chapter, article types are essentially a way for us to distill different information on articles. Article types differentiate between articles and the type of content they contain. They can also each have a different look and feel or simply just be intended for different audiences.

Every article in Salesforce Knowledge must have an article type assigned to it. Plus, you can't enable Salesforce Knowledge until you create at least one article type, so this is an obligatory first step before creating articles or turning on Knowledge for your organization.

Before getting started, make sure you're a Salesforce Knowledge user, by following these steps:

1. **Navigate to your username in the top right of your organization's screen and click the down arrow.**

   A drop-down of options appears.

2. **Click My Settings.**

   The My Settings page appears with a left sidebar of options.

3. **Click Personal in the left sidebar, and then Advanced User Details.**

   Your user record appears with a Knowledge User check box in the right-hand column.

   If the Knowledge User check box does not appear on the user detail page, make sure that your organization has purchased enough Knowledge feature licenses. You may also be able to check this yourself in the Setup menu under Administration Setup ➪ Company Profile ➪ Company Information, in the Feature Licenses related list.

4. **Click the Edit button on the user record, check the Knowledge User check box, and click Save.**

   You're now a Knowledge(able) User.

Building article types

After planning your knowledge base design and deciding which article types you need to create that will best serve your user and customer base, create an article type. To create an article type, navigate to the Setup menu again, choose Build ➪ Customize ➪ Knowledge ➪ Article Types, and follow these steps:

1. **Click the New Article Type button.**

   The Article Type edit page appears with some basic information fields to fill out, as shown in Figure 11-1.

New Article Type

Article Type Edit		Save	Save & New	Cancel

Article Type Information

The singular and plural labels are used in tabs, layouts, and reports.

Label	[ ]	Example: Offer
Plural Label	[ ]	Example: Offers
Starts with vowel sound	☐	

The Object name is a unique identifier used for API purposes.

Object Name	[ ]	Example: Offer

Description	[ ]

Deployment Status

☐ In Development
☒ Deployed

Save	Save & New	Cancel

Figure 11-1: Creating an article type in the edit page.

---

2. **Fill out the fields and click Save.**

   The Article Type detail page appears and you have successfully created your first article type.

3. **Follow Steps 1 and 2 to create as many article types as your organization needs, name them intuitively, and continue to the next section when you're done.**

 We know how exhilarating it is to create article types and that you might not be able to contain yourself, but don't get trigger happy here. You need to be methodical in your creation of article types and only build what's necessary to create and maintain a functional and manageable knowledge base.

Identifying article type properties and fields

After you've created at least one article type, you're ready to hit the Article Type detail page. If you aren't currently viewing this page, go back to Setup ⇨ Build ⇨ Customize ⇨ Knowledge ⇨ Article Types and click an article type. You see the basic information you've filled out and the standard fields available, as shown in Figure 11-2.

Figure 11-2: The Article Type detail page.

Article Type Detail			
Singular Label	FAQ	Description	
Plural Label	FAQs	Deployment Status	Deployed
Object Name	FAQ		
API Name	FAQ__kav		
Created By	Mary Matthews, 12/6/2014 9:45 AM	Modified By	Mary Matthews, 12/6/2014 9:45 AM

Fields			
Action	Field Label	API Name	Data Type	Modified By
Edit	Archived By	ArchivedBy	Lookup(User)	
Edit	Archived Date	ArchivedDate	Date/Time	
Edit	Article Number	ArticleNumber	Auto Number	
Edit	Article Type	ArticleType	Picklist	
	Created By	CreatedBy	Lookup(User)	
	Created Date	CreatedDate	Date/Time	
Edit	First Published Date	FirstPublishedDate	Date/Time	
Edit	Is Latest Version	IsLatestVersion	Checkbox	
Edit	Is Master Language	IsMasterLanguage	Checkbox	
Edit	Language	Language	Picklist	
	Last Modified By	LastModifiedBy	Lookup(User)	
	Last Modified Date	LastModifiedDate	Date/Time	
Edit	Last Published Date	LastPublishedDate	Date/Time	
Edit	Master Version	MasterVersion	Lookup(FAQ)	
Edit	Owner	Owner	Lookup(User, Queue)	
Edit	Publication Status	PublishStatus	Picklist	
Edit	Summary	Summary	Text Area(1000)	
	System Modstamp	SystemModstamp	Date/Time	
	Title	Title	Text(255)	
Edit	URL Name	UrlName	Text(255)	
Edit	Version Number	VersionNumber	Number(6, 0)	
Edit	Visible In Internal App	IsVisibleInApp	Checkbox	
Edit	Visible In Public Knowledge Base	IsVisibleInPkb	Checkbox	
Edit	Visible to Customer	IsVisibleInCsp	Checkbox	
Edit	Visible to Partner	IsVisibleInPrm	Checkbox	

The fields displayed are not on the layout, so they won't be visible to anyone until you add them to it. However, these preexisting fields are relevant to a wide variety of article types, so they're available for your use. Let's take a look at a few of the fields of a standard article type in Service Cloud to make sure you really understand them.

- ✔ **Article Type:** A picklist field that lists available article types.

- ✔ **Created Date:** A timestamp field that is populated when the article is created.

- ✔ **First Published Date:** A timestamp field showing the date the article was originally published. This is dependent on your publishing process for an article.

- ✔ **Version Number:** The article's version number.

- ✔ **Is Latest Version:** A check box indicating if the article is the most recent version.

- ✔ **Last Published Date:** A timestamp field showing the date the article was last published.

- ✔ **Publication Status:** A picklist field displaying where in the publication process the article stands.

- ✔ **Title:** A text field for the article's title that the author should fill in.

- ✔ **Summary:** A text field serving as a description for the article that the author should fill in.

- ✔ **URL Name:** A text field used as a hyperlink for the article.

- ✔ **Visible in Internal App:** A check box that indicates whether the article is visible internally in the Articles tab.

- ✔ **Visible in Public Knowledge Base:** A check box that indicates whether the article is visible and published in the public knowledge base.

- ✔ **Visible to Customer:** A check box that indicates article visibility in the customer portal.

- ✔ **Visible to Partner:** A check box that indicates article visibility in the partner portal.

Of course, along with the standard fields that come out of the box, you can also create custom fields on your article type to make it more relevant or to prompt authors to enter custom information.

You'll probably have to create a custom field where article authors can write the body of their article.

To create a custom field for article types, on the Article Type detail page, click the New button in the Fields related list, and follow these steps:

1. **Choose the field type and click Next.**

   The edit details page appears with some required fields, as shown in Figure 11-3.

2. **On the Enter the details page, fill in the fields and click Next.**

   The field-level security page appears.

3. **Establish field-level security and click Next.**

   Select the profiles to which this field will be read-only or editable. Any profiles that do not have a check box checked will not see this custom field.

   If you have a profile for Knowledge, knowledge managers, and/or knowledge users, make sure they have access to these custom fields unless you specifically want them hidden.

4. Add the field to the article type layout and click Save.

Alternatively, click Save & New to create another custom field.

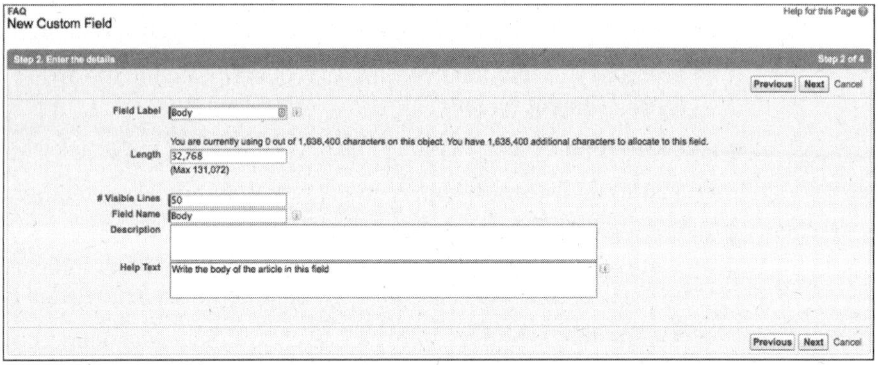

Figure 11-3:
Creating
a custom
field for the
article body.

[Screenshot: FAQ — New Custom Field — Step 2. Enter the details — Step 2 of 4, showing fields for Field Label (Body), Length (32,768, Max 131,072), # Visible Lines (50), Field Name (Body), Description, Help Text (Write the body of the article in this field)]

The custom field now appears in the fields related list on the Article Type detail page.

If you already have an existing knowledge base with articles types that have custom fields, don't change the field type of the custom field unless you don't have data you need captured in those fields. You'll lose this data once you change the field type of a custom field on the article type.

Modifying article-type layouts and templates

You can modify and customize your article-type layout and format in two ways, using article-type layouts and article-type templates. What's the difference?

Think of it like this: You use article-type layouts to set up the placement of different sections of an article, as well as to control the fields users see and edit when inputting article information. You use article-type templates to control the format, or *how* this appears and *for whom* when the article information is entered.

For example, you can modify the article-type layout of an FAQ article to have a Question section with fields pertaining to the question at the top of the page, and an Answer section with the relevant fields beneath the Question section. That way, the author of the article is guided to fill out the question and its information first, followed by the response details. Then, modify the FAQ article-type template to determine how (not where) the Question and the Answer sections display for each channel or audience.

While you can choose a distinct article-type template for each of the article type's four channels, you can have only one article-type layout.

What the reminder above also means is that if you publish the same article internally for your colleagues and externally for your customers, you must display the same layout. If you don't want certain internal-only fields to be visible to your customers, you shouldn't hide them on the layout but rather use field-level security when creating the field (available in Enterprise, Unlimited, Performance, and Developer editions only).

Customizing layouts for your article types

To modify the article-type layout, go back to the Article Type detail page, and follow these steps:

1. **Scroll down to the Fields related list and click the Edit Layout button.**

   The layout editor appears with the palette at the top, holding a Section creator and the available fields for the layout, and the layout preview below. Your custom fields automatically appear in the Information section of your layout if you selected that option when creating the custom field(s).

2. **Drag and drop the fields you want on your article type layout and/or Sections to segment the layout into logical components.**

   The layout preview contains the sections and fields, with the selected fields grayed out in the palette, as shown in Figure 11-4.

   To save some time, select multiple fields to drag and drop onto the layout by Ctrl+clicking and then dragging them down.

3. **Click Save when you're done.**

   The Article Type detail page reappears.

Assigning article-type templates

Service Cloud comes with two standard templates but also gives you the option to use Visualforce to create custom ones for your business. The two article-type templates that come out of the box are

- ✔ **Tab:** This template renders each section defined in your layout as a separate tab. It looks similar to a browser tab, but it's within the article.

- ✔ **Table of Contents:** This template renders each section defined in your layout in a sidebar on the left side with hyperlinks to each section.

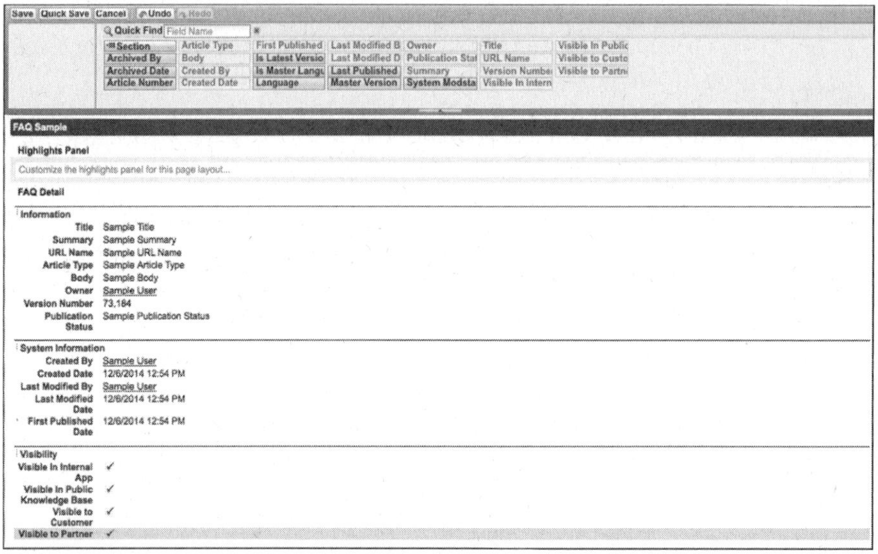

Figure 11-4:
Modifying
the article-
type layout.

Article types require a template to be assigned for each channel. The default is using the Tab template for all channels except the Public Knowledge Base, which defaults to the Table of Contents template.

To change article-type templates for each channel, on the Article Type detail page, scroll to the bottom of the page and follow these steps:

1. Click the Edit button in the Channel Displays related list.

The Channel Display edit page appears, as shown in Figure 11-5.

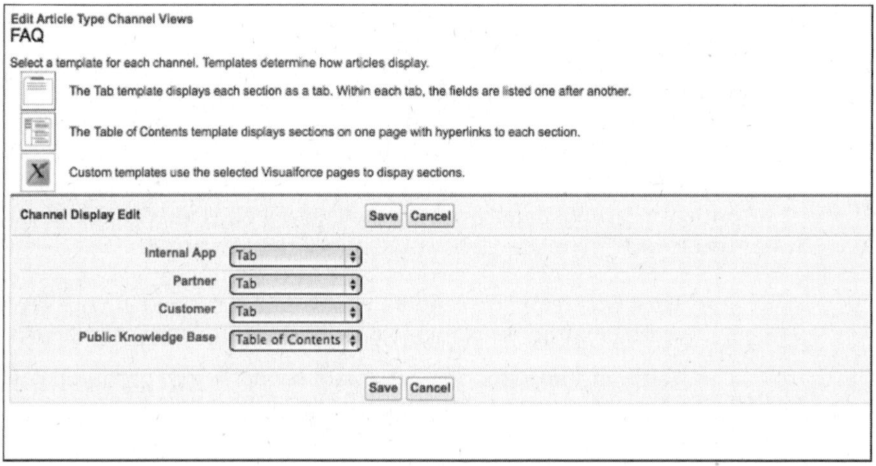

Figure 11-5
Assigning
article-type
templates
to your
channels.

2. **For each channel, choose a template from the picklist and click Save when you're done.**

The Article Type detail page reappears.

Designating article access

Permissions for each article type object (yes, they are strange objects, but they're objects in Salesforce nonetheless) are disabled for all profiles by default. This is intentional so that administrators or Knowledge managers can set up and customize a comprehensive knowledge base "behind the scenes" before making it accessible to anyone.

After you've set up your article types in Service Cloud, you can designate access to each in permission sets or by editing custom profiles. It's imperative that you understand the types of articles your organization is implementing, as well as how users and others will interact with these articles types. This and this alone will determine the level of access, article-type permissions, and article actions that you'll assign your Knowledge users.

Reading a Knowledge article

As an introduction to article permissions, it's important to note that all Salesforce users with a full license can read or see all *published* articles (not drafts or archived articles). The only users who can access drafts or archives are those that also have a Knowledge feature license (check that Knowledge User check box we discuss earlier in this the chapter).

Taking action on an article

Anything beyond reading an article — such as creating, editing, deleting, or publishing one — requires three things:

- Knowledge User license
- Manage Articles permission, at the profile level
- Article action on the article type

You can grant users these permissions in one of two ways:

- **Profiles:** Add these permissions to a profile, but remember that all users in that profile will have this access.

- **Permission sets:** Create Knowledge-specific permission sets with specific permissions that you can assign to individual users. Choose this option if only a couple of users need this access.

Don't fall into the trap of creating many different permission sets. These can get unwieldy and become a nightmare to maintain for your administrator. In the same vein, too many profiles with only slight nuances can also quickly become cumbersome. Find a middle ground and consolidate where possible.

Turning on Salesforce Knowledge

Now that you've created and refined your article types and ensured that the right people in your organization can use them, it's time to turn on Salesforce Knowledge for your instance.

Enabling Knowledge

To turn on Knowledge, go to the Setup menu and follow these steps:

1. **Choose Build ➪ Customize ➪ Knowledge ➪ Settings.**

   The Knowledge Settings page appears, with some important information to consider before enabling the feature.

2. **Click the check box to confirm that you understand the impact of enabling Knowledge and click the Enable Salesforce Knowledge button, as shown in Figure 11-6. If a pop-up appears, click OK.**

   The Knowledge Settings page appears in its expanded form.

3. **Click the Edit button.**

   The Knowledge Settings page appears in edit mode.

4. **Select the settings according to your business needs.**

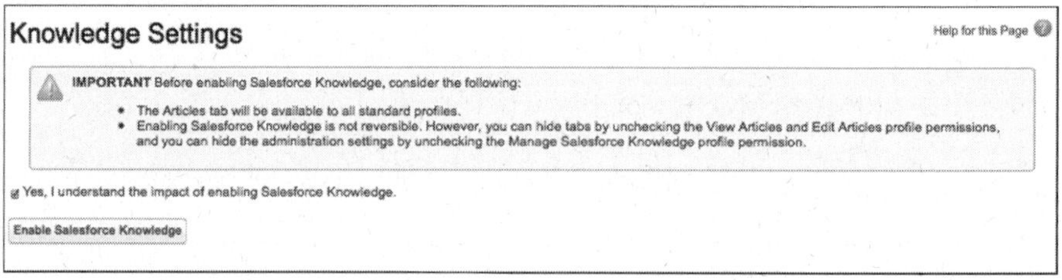

Figure 11-6:
Enabling
Salesforce
Knowledge
for an orga-
nization.

Knowledge Settings

Help for this Page

⚠ **IMPORTANT** Before enabling Salesforce Knowledge, consider the following:

- The Articles tab will be available to all standard profiles.
- Enabling Salesforce Knowledge is not reversible. However, you can hide tabs by unchecking the View Articles and Edit Articles profile permissions, and you can hide the administration settings by unchecking the Manage Salesforce Knowledge profile permission.

☑ Yes, I understand the impact of enabling Salesforce Knowledge.

[Enable Salesforce Knowledge]

Here's what some of the general settings mean:

- *Allow users to create and edit articles from the Articles tab:* Select this setting to enable your users to edit articles straight from the Articles tab (or the Knowledge tab, depending on your settings), without having to go to the Article Management tab.

- *Activate Validation Status field:* Select this setting to add the Validation Status field to your knowledge base articles and track the state of an article in the publication lifecycle.

- *Allow users to add external multimedia content to HTML in the standard editor:* This setting allows users to copy and paste `<iframe>` elements in the standard editor to embed multimedia content in articles, such as videos from Vimeo or YouTube that can "show, not tell" a solution for your customers or internal staff.

- *Article Summaries Settings:* Select at least one channel from the list to have the Summary field for each article appear in article list views there.

- *Knowledge One Settings:* Here you can customize search settings within the Knowledge tab.

- *Language Settings:* Select a default knowledge base language for your organization. This language should probably be the same as your organization's language.

- *Case Settings:* Here you can allow your users to create an article from a case (for instance, if it reflects a common problem).

- *Answers Settings:* Click the Allow Users to Create an Article from a Reply check box to create articles from replies in Answers, if you use them.

5. Click Save when you're done.

The Knowledge Settings page appears with your selected settings.

Congratulations! You now have Salesforce Knowledge enabled in your organization.

Opening up Knowledge access to users and public groups

Give your internal users access to Salesforce Knowledge. If a user needs permissions that go beyond reading articles, go to the individual's user record and click the Knowledge User check box.

The next step is to make the Article Management and Knowledge tabs visible in your organization by creating a custom app and adding the tabs to it. To do this, go to the Setup menu and follow these steps:

1. **Choose Build ⇨ Create ⇨ Apps, then click the New button in the Apps list.**

   The New Custom App page appears.

2. **Select the Custom App option from the list and click Next.**

3. **Type in the label for the app, such as** Knowledge, **and then press Tab and Next.**

   The App Name automatically populates the same name.

4. **(Optional) Upload an image or logo for the custom app, and click Next.**

5. **Select the tabs in the app, such as Articles (or Knowledge) and Article Management, as well as the default landing tab, and click Next.**

6. **Select the profiles that should be able to see and access this app.**

   You can click the Default check box to make the Knowledge app the default app for the profile when a user of that profile logs onto Service Cloud. This is a good idea if you have a Knowledge Manager or Knowledge User profile.

7. **Click Save when you're done.**

   The list of apps appears with your new custom app.

8. **Navigate to the blue app picker at the top right of your screen and click it.**

   You should see your new custom Knowledge app.

Now, just because you've created the app to access Article Management and Knowledge, doesn't mean everyone can access them. Even if you made the app visible to every profile in your organization, not everyone should manage articles, so they won't automatically see the Article Management tab without the Manage Articles permission on their profiles.

A custom profile still needs to have visibility into each tab in order to see it, as well as at least Read access on at least one article type to view the Knowledge tab. To give a custom profile access to the tab, go to the Setup menu and follow these steps:

1. **Choose Administer ⇨ Manage Users ⇨ Profiles, and select the profile.**

   The profile page appears.

2. **Click Edit.**

   The profile page appears in edit mode.

3. **Under Tab Settings, make sure that Article Management and Knowledge are set to anything but Hidden.**

4. **To give the profile Read access to an article type, scroll down to Article Type Permissions and click the Read check box.**

   You can also give the profile Create, Edit, and Delete for that article type, but this won't take effect until you enable the Manage Articles permission on the profile as well.

5. **Click Save when you're done.**

If a user still doesn't see the Knowledge tab at this point, it's because his profile doesn't have the Knowledge One permission enabled. This means that the tab is called Articles instead of Knowledge, and you can grant them this permission to change that on the profile.

Article actions are a way to further refine permissions around article management. Article actions work in concert with article-type permissions (Create, Read, Edit, and Delete) to fine-tune what users or groups of users can do in the publishing or translating process.

Service Cloud provides four article actions:

- ✔ Publish articles
- ✔ Archive articles
- ✔ Edit published and archived articles
- ✔ Delete articles

By default, all users in a profile that has the Manage Articles permissions will be able to perform all four of these article actions. Service Cloud enables you to limit this and add nuance to article management permissions using public groups. For example, you can create a public group called Knowledge Publishers and assign it to the Publish Articles action. Now, only article managers who belong to the Knowledge Publishers group can publish articles.

To do this, create your public group (see Chapter 6) and then, in the Setup menu, follow these steps:

1. **Choose Build ➪ Customize ➪ Knowledge ➪ Article Actions, and click the Edit button.**

   The Article Actions page appears in edit mode.

2. **Under the desired action, click the Only Article Managers in the Following Public Groups radio button.**

   A Select Public Groups pop-up window appears.

3. **Search for and select the appropriate public group and click OK (see Figure 11-7).**

   The Article Actions page reappears in edit mode, with your selection.

4. **Click Save when you're done.**

   The Article Actions page appears with your selection.

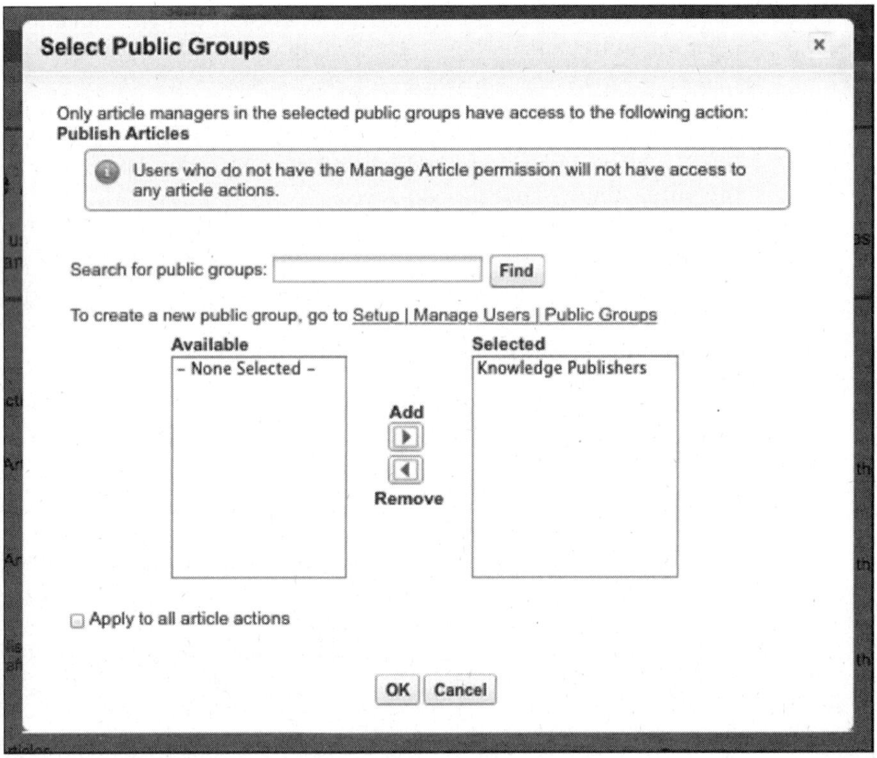

Select Public Groups   ✕

Only article managers in the selected public groups have access to the following action:
Publish Articles

> ⓘ Users who do not have the Manage Article permission will not have access to any article actions.

Search for public groups: [   ] [Find]

To create a new public group, go to Setup | Manage Users | Public Groups

Available   **Selected**
– None Selected –   Knowledge Publishers

                          Add
                          [▶]
                          [◀]
                          Remove

☐ Apply to all article actions

[OK] [Cancel]

Figure 11-7: Assigning a public group to an article action.

Using Cases with the Knowledge Base

This is where we get fancy. If you've already invested in a knowledge base, you probably want it to be as integrated and as easy-to-use as possible. Salesforce Knowledge gives you a few neat tools to integrate your knowledge base with case management, saving you clicks, time, and frustration.

Suggesting articles on new cases

One of the first features that comes standard is the auto-search function. Why reactively research an answer when it can proactively be pushed to you? This Service Cloud feature suggests relevant articles to an agent when she hits Save on a newly created case. The search engine looks for articles based on keywords in the title or subject of the case.

To set this up for your organization, go to the Setup menu and then follow these steps:

1. **Choose Build ⇨ Customize ⇨ Cases ⇨ Support Settings.**

    The Support Settings page appears.

2. **Click the Edit button.**

    The Support Settings page appears in edit mode.

3. **Select the Enable Suggested Articles radio button.**

    This automatically deselects Enable Suggested Solutions, because they can't both be enabled simultaneously.

4. **Select the channel that will have articles suggested when submitting a case, as shown in Figure 11-8, and then click Save.**

    The Support Settings page appears with your selection.

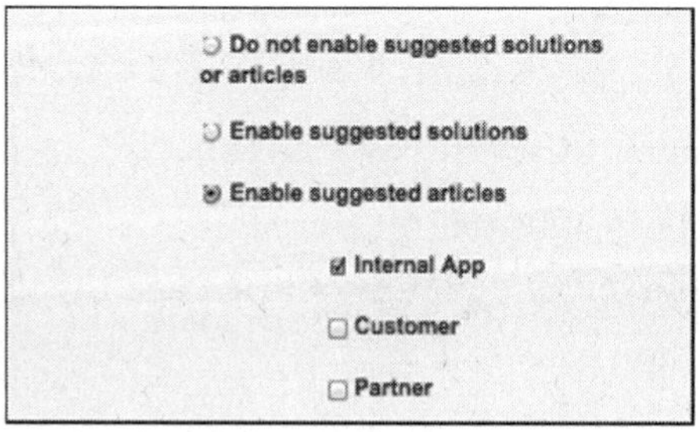

Figure 11-8: Enabling suggested articles.

Enabling article submission upon case closure

If you want your agents to get in the habit of creating draft articles after they close a case and capture the information that helped solved it, enable the Save and Create Article feature. You can turn this on by navigating to the Setup menu and following these steps:

1. **Choose Build ⇨ Customize ⇨ Knowledge ⇨ Settings.**

   The Knowledge Settings page appears.

2. **Click the Edit button.**

   The Knowledge Settings page appears in edit mode.

3. **In the Case Settings section, check the Allow Users to Create an Article from a Case button.**

   The simple editor option is automatically selected by default.

4. **Select a default article type.**

   This determines the fields that appear in the draft article that displays.

   You can create a Problem Resolution article type and assign it as the default for close case draft articles.

5. **Click the lookup icon and select a user to assign the new draft article to.**

   The draft article created from a closed case is sent to this user for review. Make sure this user has the ability to read, edit, delete, and publish articles.

   After the article is published, it's automatically associated to the case from which it was created.

   You can use Apex customization to prepopulate fields in the draft article from the case by creating an Apex class and selecting it in the field.

6. **Click Save when you're done.**

   The Knowledge Settings page reappears.

7. **Choose Build ⇨ Customize ⇨ Cases ⇨ Page Layouts.**

   The Case Page Layout page appears.

8. **Click the Edit link to the left of your Case Close Page Layout.**

   The page layout editor appears.

9. **Click Layout Properties at the top bar of the palette.**

   The Layout Properties pop-up appears.

10. **Click Enable Submissions During Case Close and select Submit Articles, and then click OK and Save.**

    The Case Page Layout page reappears.

Now, when you hit the Close Case button on a case, it will take you to the Close Case edit page and display a Save and Create Article button, as shown in Figure 11-9.

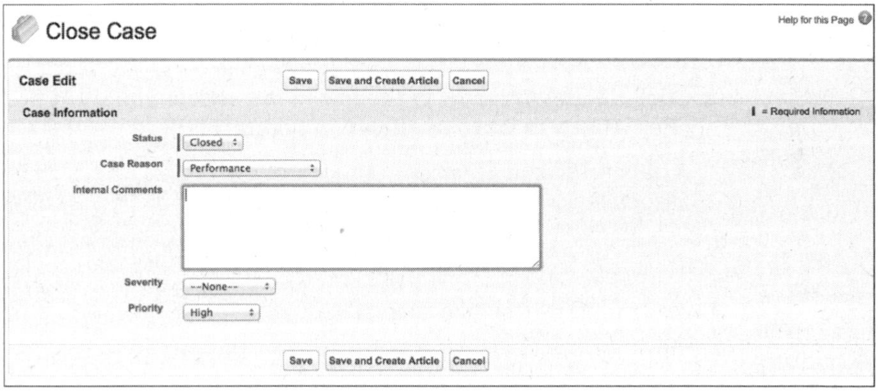

Figure 11-9: The Close Case edit page with the Save and Create Article button.

Attaching articles to a case

The first thing you want to do in order to attach and view articles on a case is to add a related list for them to the case page layout. To do this, from the Setup menu choose Build ⇨ Customize ⇨ Cases ⇨ Page Layouts, and follow these steps:

1. **Click Edit to the left of the layouts you want to add articles to.**

    The page layout editor appears.

2. **Click Related Lists on the left section of the palette.**

    The page scrolls to the case's related lists.

3. **Choose the Articles related list and drag it wherever in the related list section you want it to be.**

    If a Solutions related list appears there and you're no longer using them, remove it.

4. **Click Save or Quick Save and do the same for all the page layouts necessary.**

Now that your cases have the Articles related list on them, you can attach articles to them.

1. **Navigate to a case.**

   The case detail page appears.

2. **Scroll down to the Articles related list and click the Find Articles button.**

   A list of relevant articles appears. From here, you can always click Back to Case to return to it or clear out the search criteria and enter something different.

3. **Click the down arrow to the left of the article you want to attach, and click Attach to Case, as shown in Figure 11-10.**

   A paperclip icon appears to the left of the article title, signifying that it's associated with one or more cases.

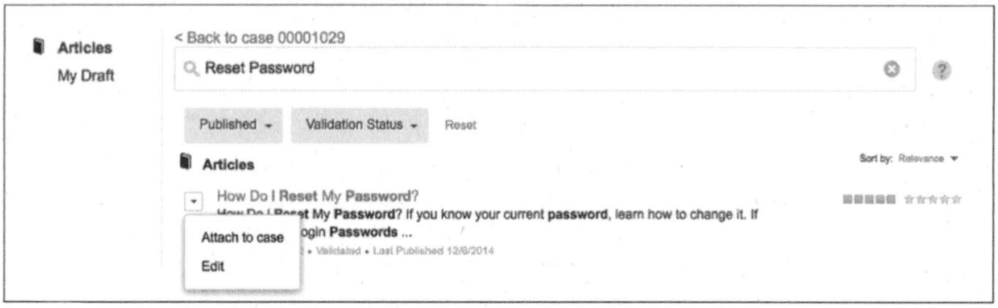

Figure 11-10:
Attaching
an article
to a case
in Service
Cloud.

Chapter 12

Managing and Categorizing Articles

In This Chapter

▶ Managing the article publication process

▶ Understanding article actions

▶ Categorizing and finding articles

▶ Automating the article lifecycle

*W*ith Articles, harnessing your organization's knowledge has never been easier. Your service organization can fine-tune every aspect of the knowledge management lifecycle to the level of detail that suits the team and the organization's culture. The ability to categorize your articles hierarchically will allow your support agents to quickly search an entire catalogue of knowledge articles and find the result they, and the customer, are looking for in a matter of moments.

In this chapter, we lay the foundation for managing and categorizing the articles in your knowledge base. We walk you through each phase of the article lifecycle and explain the configuration steps needed along the way. Then we explain how you can leverage powerful categorization tools available natively with Salesforce to organize your articles in a manner that allows your agents to most easily locate relevant information. Finally, we help you figure out how to automate specific steps and actions that need to take place in your articles' lifecycle using simple workflow rules and approval processes in Salesforce.

Note: This chapter contains many administrative processes that assume your organization has already enabled Salesforce Knowledge. That said, this chapter can serve as an excellent course in the key benefits and intricacies of article management if you and your colleagues are evaluating a potential Knowledge implementation.

Managing Articles

Let's take a few moments to review some of the key knowledge terms you needed to understand managing articles.

First things first, an *article* contains information that you want to make available in your organization's knowledge base (for example, product information). Articles may contain information meant for your own customer support agents or information intended for direct consumption by customers, partners, or the public.

Users assigned to the Manage Articles user permission are *Article Managers.* Article Managers gain access to the Article Management tab and will have the ability to create, edit, assign, publish, archive, and delete any article in your system.

Articles can exist in the following statuses:

- ✔ **Draft:** In-progress articles that are not visible via any channel.
- ✔ **Published:** Available via the Articles tab and any other channel where you choose to expose articles. Published articles can be archived or changed back to draft status to ensure users and visitors no longer have access to them.
- ✔ **Archived:** Articles withdrawn from public visibility after being published. Articles can be archived manually or automatically using an expiration date.

By default, all Article Managers can complete the following Article Actions:

- ✔ Publish articles.
- ✔ Archive articles.
- ✔ Edit published and archived articles.
- ✔ Delete articles.

In order to restrict Article Managers to specific actions, follow these steps:

1. **From the Setup menu, under the Build section, choose Customize ➪ Knowledge ➪ Article Actions.**

   The Article Actions page displays. Here, you see a list of actions that Article Managers can perform, and the associated groups of Article Managers who have access to perform those actions in your organization. The default group of Article Managers enabled for each action will be All.

2. **Click Edit.**

   The edit page for Article Actions appears, as shown in Figure 12-1.

3. **Select the Article Managers in your organization to enable for each action (Publish, Archive, Edit, or Delete).**

   On the Article Actions edit page, you can choose whether to allow all Article Managers to complete each action or only a subset of Article Managers by selecting specific public groups. You can choose between these options using the radio buttons on the page. If you choose to enable an action for Article Managers in public groups, a new window displays where you can choose specific public groups. Not all members of the public group you select will automatically be able to complete the action. Only users with the Manage Articles permission enabled on their profile who are also members of the group you select will be able to perform the associated action.

   If you select to allow only Article Managers in certain public groups to perform specific article actions, you need to have public groups in place in order to select them. If you're unfamiliar with creating public groups, you can refer to Chapter 5 or Chapter 19 to learn more.

4. **Click Save.**

   The saved Article Actions page displays with your preferences recorded.

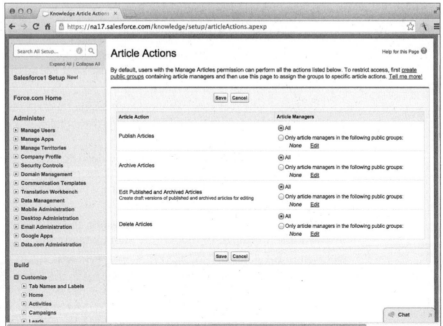

Figure 12-1:
The Article
Actions edit
page.

Creating a draft article

To create draft articles, follow these steps:

1. **From the Article Management tab, as shown in Figure 12-2, click New.**

   The new article pop-up window displays. Select your article type and enter a title for your article.

2. **Click OK.**

   The article edit page displays, as shown in Figure 12-3.

3. **Populate the fields on the article edit page.**

   You need to populate the following fields:

   - *Title*

   - *URL Name:* The URL Name is used to make it easier for people and search engines to find your article.

   - *Summary:* The Summary field houses the actual content of your article. This is where the magic — er, knowledge — happens.

4. **Choose the channels where you want to eventually publish your article in the Article Properties section, as shown in Figure 12-3.**

   Salesforce has the following channels as options:

   - *Internal App:* Articles are available to users via the Articles tab in your organization.

   - *Customer:* Your customers can view articles via the Articles tab if it's available to them in either your Customer Portal or Customer Community.

   - *Partner:* Your partners can view articles via the Articles tab if it's available to them in either your Partner Portal or Partner Community.

   - *Public Knowledge Base:* You can provide articles to the public by using the Sample Public Knowledge Base for Salesforce Knowledge app. This app is available on the AppExchange and will allow you to create a public knowledge base to share your articles.

5. **Click Save to save your article and remain on the edit page or click Save & Close to return to the Article Management tab.**

   The Article Management tab displays with a list of My Draft Articles. Your newly saved draft article displays in the list. Additionally, a small window appears with the message:
   `Success! "[Article Title]" has been saved as a draft.`

Figure 12-2:
The Article
Management
tab.

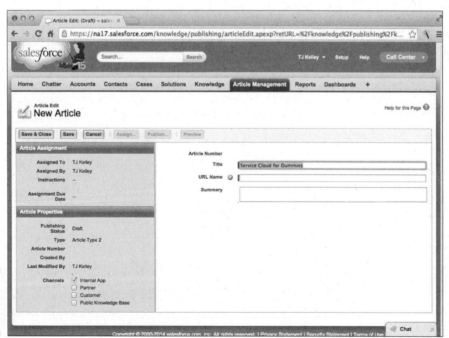

Figure 12-3:
The article
edit page.

Assigning articles and sending them for approval

If your organization intends to stand up a small, tightknit team to manage articles, you may be able to skip this section. However, if multiple users will collaborate on multiple phases of the article lifecycle, from creation to publication, we recommend you spend some time learning about article assignments and approvals.

Article assignments allow users to specify not only what steps need to take place next in the article lifecycle, but also who is responsible for completing those steps. If there are several stages for an article prior to publication — particularly if they're collaborative steps — article assignments are a must for your organization.

Article assignments allow you to specify an assignee and assignment details for the assignee. This helps ensure that a single person, at any given point in time, owns the article's edit. Due to the fact that multiple users are technically able to edit an article at once, this helps ensure that data doesn't get overwritten.

To assign an article to an Article Manager, follow these steps:

1. **Navigate to the Article Management tab.**

   Your draft articles display by default. You can work off of this list, or you can select Anyone in the Assigned To drop-down in the left sidebar to look at all draft articles.

2. **From this page, locate the article you would like to assign to another Article Manager, click the check box next to it, and click Assign.**

A new pop-up window displays with assignment options.

From the Article Management tab, you can also click the Article Title link to navigate to the article detail page, or click the Edit button in the Action column to navigate to the article edit page. The article detail page or the article edit page will display, depending on your choice. In either case, you see an Assign button, as shown in Figure 12-3.

3. Enter assignment details.

   Input the following details in the assignment window:

   • Choose an assignee in the Assign To field.

   • Enter steps for the assignee to complete in the Instructions box.

• Select a Due Date for the assignee.

• Optionally, click the Send Email box to notify the assignee of their new article assignment.

4. Click OK.

The assignee will now see the draft article under "My Draft Articles" on the Article Management tab.

If your organization enables an approval process for specific article types, the article will require approval before publication can take place.

If an article requires approval, follow these steps to submit it.

1. Navigate to the Article Management tab.

Your draft articles display by default. You can work off this list, or you can select Anyone in the Assigned To drop-down in the left sidebar to look at all draft articles.

2. From this page, locate the article you want to submit for approval and click the Article Title link to navigate to the article detail page, or click the Edit button in the Action column to navigate to the article edit page.

The article detail page or the article edit page will display, depending on your choice. In either case, you see a Submit for Approval button.

3. Click Submit for Approval.

A pop-up window appears and warns you that you may not be able to edit the record or recall from approval depending on the setup of the approval process.

4. Click OK.

The article enters the approval process, and the saved page displays. At the bottom of the page, you can view the Approval History related list.

To learn more about approval processes for article management, continue reading this chapter.

Publishing articles

To assign an article to an Article Manager, follow these steps:

1. Navigate to the Article Management tab.

Your draft articles display by default. You can work off this list, or you can select Anyone in the Assigned To drop-down in the left sidebar to look at all draft articles.

2. **From this page, locate the article you want to publish, click the check box next to the article, and click Publish.**

   A new pop-up window displays with publication options.

3. **Select your publication option.**

   You can choose between the following:

   - *Publish now:* Publish the article immediately.

   - *Schedule publication on:* Choose a specific date in the future for publication to happen automatically.

4. **Click OK.**

   The article will publish at the time you choose in Step 3 and will be available to users in your organization via all channels that you selected in the Article Properties section.

If you want to publish an article that has pending assignment details, those details will all be removed from the article. For example, if an article is assigned to an Article Manager with assignment details to review it and reassign back to you for publication, but you choose to publish prior to completion of the review, the assignment details will disappear from the record when it publishes.

Searching for articles

Support agents and knowledge managers with read access to articles can search for articles in the following places:

- ✔ **The Knowledge Tab:** To search for articles using the Knowledge tab, as shown in Figure 12-4, follow these steps.

  1. From the Knowledge tab, choose if you want to search all articles or only your draft articles in the left sidebar.

  2. Optionally, choose to search for Published or Draft articles using the drop-down on the left below the search bar.

  3. Optionally, choose to filter your search results by article type using the All Article Types drop-down.

     If you choose to filter by specific article types, you must click Apply on the drop-down menu for your choices to impact the search results.

  4. Type your search terms into the search bar at the top of the page and press Enter or Return on your keyboard.

  5. Review your search results.

The Knowledge tab is a newer addition to Salesforce. If your organization has not recently started using Salesforce, you may need to enable profiles with the Knowledge One permission to view it. If you do not have the Knowledge One permission enabled, instead of the Knowledge tab, you'll see an Articles tab. To learn more about Knowledge One, go to http://help.salesforce.com and locate an article titled, "Enabling Knowledge One with Profiles."

✔ **The Article Management tab:** To search for articles in the Article Management tab, follow these steps:

   1. From the Article Management tab, use the radio buttons in the View section in the left sidebar to choose between draft, published, or archived articles.

   If you want, you can choose to show your draft articles or draft articles assigned to anyone.

   2. Enter your search terms in the Find in View text box.

   You can also search manually through the list views presented on the page by using the previous and next arrows at the bottom of the list view.

   3. Click Go.

   The Article Management tab displays search results.

   4. Review your search results.

✔ **Case records:** To search for articles directly from case records, follow these steps:

   1. From a case record, scroll down to the bottom of the page and find the articles related list.

   You must enable articles on cases by adding the articles related list to case page layouts.

   2. Click the Find Articles button on the articles related list.

   The Knowledge tab displays with search results.

   The subject of the case will be used automatically in order to provide some initial search results.

   3. Review your search results. If you don't immediately find an article that fits, refine your results using the steps listed for searching in the Knowledge tab.

   4. When you find an article that fits to solve your case, click the drop-down arrow next to the article's title and select Attach to Case.

   Salesforce attaches the article to your case.

5. Click the Back to Case link above the search bar to return to your case.

The case record displays.

6. Scroll down to the bottom of the page, locate the articles related list, and ensure that the article you selected has been attached to the case.

✔ **The global search bar:** Use the global search bar at the top of any page to enter search terms for articles. The global search results do not return archived or draft articles. Global search will exclusively return published articles in search results.

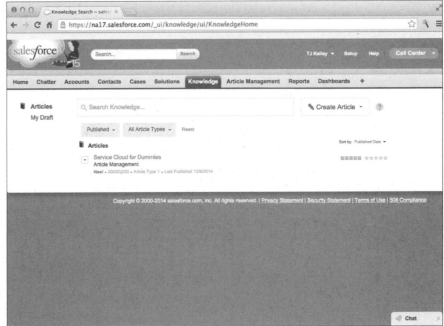

Figure 12-4:
The
Knowledge
tab.

Updating and archiving articles

To make an update to an existing article, follow these steps:

1. **Navigate to the Article Management tab.**

Your draft articles display by default.

2. **In the View sidebar, on the left side of the page, click the radio button for Published Articles.**

The page refreshes, displaying published articles now, in place of Draft articles.

3. **From this page, locate the article you want to update and click Edit in the Action column.**

A new pop-up window displays and prompts you to make a selection for what to do with the article while you're making edits. You can choose to do one of the following:

- *Keep the article published:* This choice allows agents to continue to view the original article while you work on a new draft version of the article. Select this option if the information in the article is accurate, but you're making updates to improve the overall quality of the article, or simply to add a minor detail. This option ensures that agents can still leverage that accurate information during your edits.

- *Remove the article from publication:* This choice does not allow agents to view the original article while you work on your edits. Choose this option if the information in the article is inaccurate. An inaccurate article poses a risk to your organization that agents may share this inaccurate information with your customers. Remove the article from use to prevent this from happening and ensure that your agents only gain access to the article when you correct any errors.

4. **Click OK once you make your selection.**

The article edit page displays and allows you to edit the content of your article.

5. **Make any necessary edits and click Save & Close when finished.**

The article saves and the Article Management tab displays.

If you chose to leave the original article published while working on a draft article, you need to publish your new draft article in order to replace the current version of the article.

If you chose to remove the article from the publication status and make your edits in draft mode, you need to republish the draft to make the article available to agents again.

6. **To publish your revised article, go to the Article Management tab, locate the draft version of your article, click the check box next to it, and click Publish.**

A pop-up window appears with publication options. When you're publishing a new version of an article, you see a Flag as New Version check box in the pop-up window, as shown in Figure 12-5.

If you select to flag your article as a new version, the article will be flagged as new so that agents know an update has been made. The previous version of the article will be archived.

7. Click OK.

The new version of your article saves and publishes.

Salesforce will store up to ten versions of an article. When you create an 11th version of an article, the first, original copy will be lost.

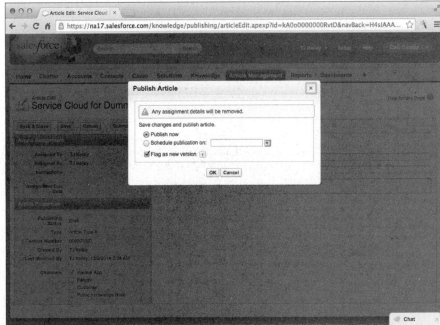

Figure 12-5:
The Flag as New Version check box.

To archive an existing article, follow these steps:

1. Navigate to the Article Management tab.

Your draft articles display by default.

2. In the View sidebar, on the left side of the page, click the Published Articles radio button.

The page refreshes, displaying published articles now, in place of draft articles.

3. From this page, locate the article you want to Archive, click the check box next to it, and click Archive.

A pop-up window appears with archive options. You can choose one of the following:

- *Archive now:* Archive the article immediately.

- *Schedule archive on:* Choose a specific date in the future for archiving to happen automatically.

4. Click OK.

Your article archives at the time you chose in Step 3 and will no longer be available to your organization's agents after archival.

Categorizing Articles into Data Categories

When you organize your closet, are you the type of person who categorizes clothing articles by the following groups only: shirts, pants, sweaters, jackets, or dresses? Or are you the type that defines subcategories for shirts by polos, button-downs, short sleeves, and long sleeves, or dresses by summer, sweater, business, and cocktail? If subcategories are your thing, it's likely that you'll want to define category groups and data categories for your organization's knowledge articles.

Articles can be organized into groups and categories and your users will have the ability to filter by category when searching for relevant articles. Here's what these categories and groups do:

- ✔ **The Data category for articles:** Establishes criteria to differentiate, sort, and categorize articles (for example, Product Families or Sales Regions). Article authors can select categories for their articles, and users can easily find relevant articles via the Knowledge tab by searching in specific data categories.

- ✔ **The Category Group for articles:** Arranges data categories into overarching, hierarchical groups. For example, you may want to create a Products Category Group and organize your product hierarchies within the group using data categories.

We're talking about Knowledge articles now, not clothing articles. Shift your focus from your closet back to your knowledge base and support agents.

Planning your category groups and hierarchy

If you aren't sure whether your organization needs data categories for articles or just needs a quick refresher on data categories to be able to explain them to a coworker, or justify using them for your organization, you can refer to Chapter 10.

If your organization plans to create more than three article types or there is a need to restrict access to articles based on content, data categories are the right option for you.

Data categories and category groups provide two main benefits:

- ✔ **Allow article authors to classify and organize articles proactively.**
  When authors create articles, they have the chance to assign data categories to their articles, which will allow your users, partners, or customers to search for articles by those categories.

- ✔ **Allow administrators to restrict access to specific articles based on categorizations:** Administrators can leverage the data categories to restrict access to articles if needed. For example, you may want to restrict access to specific category groups for users if they aren't allowed to view sensitive product information. Additionally, if the categories contained in the group are irrelevant to a subset of users, you may want to restrict access to refine the possible search results for those users so that they only see articles they may actually leverage when solving customer support cases.

If your organization enables and defines data categories, Article Managers will see categories as an option in the Article Properties section of the article edit page, as shown in Figure 12-6. Additionally, when searching for articles via the Knowledge tab, knowledge agents will have the ability to filter search results by category in the form of a drop-down menu below the search bar, as shown in Figure 12-7 with the Products drop-down.

Setting up data categories

Before setting up data categories, keep in mind that Salesforce enforces the following limits on categories:

- ✔ You can create up to three category groups. A category group, such as Products, is a container for data categories, such as your product families.

✔ Each category group can have up to five hierarchy levels of data categories.

✔ Each category group can house up to 100 categories.

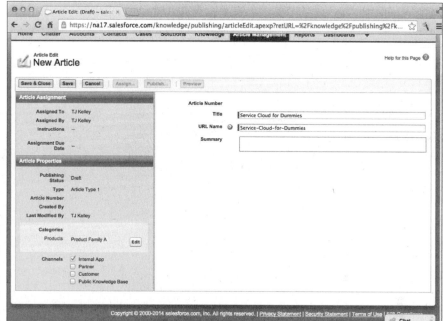

Figure 12-6:
Data cat-
egories on
the article
edit page.

To set up data categories in your organization, follow these steps:

1. **From Setup, under the Build section, choose Customize ⇨ Data Categories ⇨ Data Category Setup.**

   The data category setup page displays, as shown in Figure 12-8.

2. **Enter details for a category group.**

   If this is your organization's first category group, enter a group name, group unique name, and description for a new category group.

   If your organization already has category groups, click Create New and then enter the details.

3. **Click Save.**

   Your new category group will save to the Inactive Category Groups section.

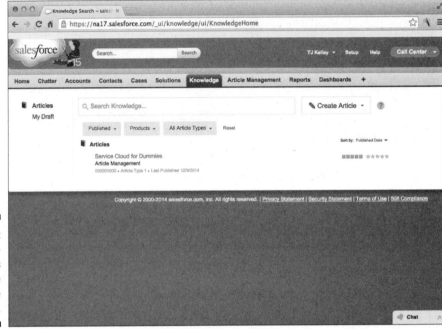

Figure 12-7:
Data cat-
egories
on the
Knowledge
tab.

4. Add categories to your category group.

Add categories and category hierarchies to your category group using
the following actions, as shown in Figure 12-9.

- Add categories using the blue Add link.

- Use the blue Cancel link to cancel any in-progress changes.

- Hover over an existing category and use the Actions drop-down to
  add a sibling category, add a child category, edit the existing category, or delete the category.

- Use the Expand All button to view the entire hierarchy of your category group.

- Use the Collapse All button to collapse the hierarchy and view only
  the first level of categories in your category group.

- Use the Undo button to undo previous edits.

5. Click Save when you're satisfied with your data category hierarchy.

**6. To edit an existing group, hover over the category group in the
Inactive Category Groups section of the page and click the Edit icon,
which looks like a gear.**

7. **To activate your data category group, hover over the group in the Inactive Category Groups section of the page and click the Activate icon, which looks like a flashlight.**

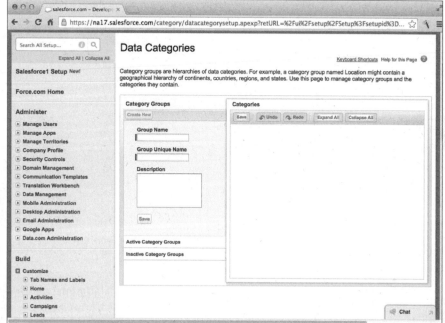

Figure 12-8:
Create a new category group on the data category setup page.

After you've created or updated existing category groups or categories, be sure to set up or update your data category visibility settings. If you fail to assign visibility settings for users, those users will only see uncategorized articles unless default category visibility is set up.

Editing default data category visibility settings

Data category visibility settings are crucial to well-functioning data categories. Default visibility settings allow administrators to set the default category visibility for all users. Additionally, if an administrator chooses, he or she can map categories to specific roles, profiles, and permission sets to ensure that your organization realizes the full potential of data categories by restricting access to specific categories.

Figure 12-9:
Add data
categories
to your
existing
category
group.

Three types of visibility settings are available for administrators to leverage:

✔ **All categories:** Enables assigned roles, profiles, or permission sets to view all data categories.

✔ **None:** Ensures that no data categories are visible for assigned roles, profiles, or permission sets.

✔ **Custom:** Enables assigned roles, profiles, or permission sets to view only selected data categories.

To set the default visibility settings for a particular category group, follow these steps:

1. **From Setup, under the Build section, choose Customize ⇨ Data Categories ⇨ Default Data Category Visibility.**

   A list of data category groups displays.

2. **Locate the category group you would like to set default visibility for and click Edit in the Action column.**

   The default visibility settings edit page appears.

3. **Use the radio buttons, as shown in Figure 12-10, to select the default visibility for all categories in this category group.**

If you choose Custom, you can select categories from the Available Categories box and add them to the Selected Categories to make them visible by default.

4. Click Save.

Map more specific visibility settings by navigating to individual roles, profiles, or permission sets and setting visibility settings on a case-by-case basis.

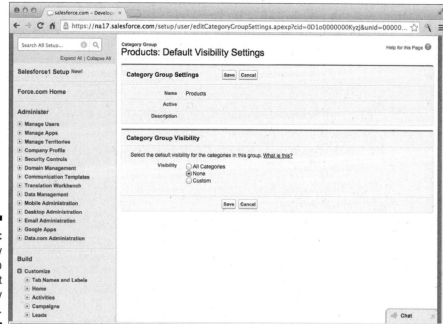

Figure 12-10: Category group default visibility settings.

Automating Article Management

Article management requires many steps and a lot of attention to detail to ensure that accurate, useful information gets published and maintained consistently.

Leverage workflow rules and approval processes in your organization to automate the management of your knowledge base. Workflow rules allow you to create targeted alerts and update fields on articles when specific criteria are met.

An approval process for an article type allows you to automate the approval of articles and ensure consistency for all articles published to your agents. For example, you may want to ensure that product specialists get a chance to review article types about specific products before they go to publication. Additionally, you may want to allow your legal team or management team to review all, or certain, articles prior to publication. An approval process allows you to define when an article becomes eligible for approval and exactly who needs to sign off on the article.

Setting up an approval process for article review and publication

To set up an approval process for articles, follow these steps:

1. **From Setup, under the Build section, choose Create ⇨ Workflow & Approvals ⇨ Approval Processes.**

2. **Select an Article type in the Manage Approval Processes For drop-down list.**

3. **Click Create New Approval Process and select an Approval Process Wizard to use.**

   Use the Jump Start Wizard for very simple approval processes — for example, if you only want to create a single-step approval process to allow a certain group of users to review articles prior to publication. Use the Standard Setup Wizard for more complex approval processes.

   In the following steps, we move forward under the assumption that you've selected the Jump Start Wizard.

   For more information on how to choose a setup wizard, go to `http://help.salesforce.com` and search for an article titled "Choosing an Approval Process Wizard."

4. **Enter Approval Process Information details.**

   Choose a Name, Unique Name, and optionally, an Approval Assignment Email Template to notify approvers when they have a new record to approve.

   Leave the Add the Approval History Related List to All Page Layouts box checked. This allows users to track the approval history directly on article records (for example, Approvals, Rejections, and so on).

5. Specify the Entry Criteria for your approval process.

Entry criteria define the set of criteria that needs to be met before an article can enter the approval process. Follow these steps to set up your entry criteria:

1. In the Field column, select a field to use as criteria (for example, Article Type: Summary).

2. Select an Operator (for example, not equal to).

3. Enter a Value (for example, leave this blank).

In our example, we defined the criterion that the Summary field on our article type cannot be blank. If the summary field of an article is blank, users won't be able to submit the article for approval.

When an article meets the entry criteria for an approval process, the Submit for Approval button can be used on the article record detail page to submit the article to the appropriate approvers.

6. Select an Approver.

In this step, you choose who will approve the article. You can select from the following options without needing any additional configuration:

- *Let the submitter choose the approver manually:* Allows the Article Manager submitting the article to choose who will approve the article.

- *Automatically assign to approver(s):* Choose specific user(s) to set as the approvers for this approval process. If you select this option, two additional radio buttons will appear and allow you to choose whether the first approval or rejection from this group of users will determine the outcome of the approval process or if you'll require unanimous approval from all approvers.

7. Click Save.

You get a pop-up warning that you won't be able to use this approval process until you activate it.

8. Click OK.

9. Review the Approval Process detail page and click Activate if you're satisfied with your new approval process.

A warning appears to inform you that you can't add or remove approval steps after activating this approval process.

10. Click OK.

When you define and activate your approval process, articles for that article type will be required to go through the process and receive approval from all necessary approvers prior to publication.

Creating workflow rules to manage articles

Workflow rules allow you to create email alerts or update fields on articles when an article meets defined criteria. For example, you may want to create workflow rules to execute the following actions for articles:

- Notify a user or group of users when someone archives an article.
- Notify product specialists when an Article Manager creates a draft article associated with their product.
- Notify support agents when a new article publishes.
- Notify the legal team if confidential details appear in an article.
- Add field updates to update information on an article.
- Add an action to automatically publish articles.

You can create workflow rules on specific article types rather than all articles. If you need to create the same rule to apply for all article types, you'll have to create duplicate rules for each article type.

For specific instructions on how to create workflow rules, refer to Chapter 20.

Part V
Recognizing When It Takes a Community

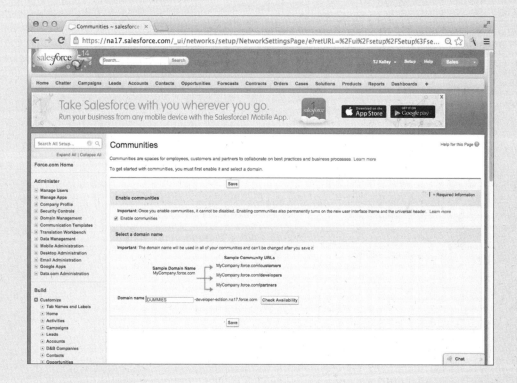

In this part . . .

- Learn the true meaning of *community*.
- See how best to approach and plan for a new community in your organization.
- Leverage communities to engage with your customers and partners.
- Uncover the depth of customizations available with Salesforce communities.

Chapter 13

Understanding Communities

. . . .

In This Chapter

▶ Reviewing the what and why of Communities

▶ Discovering your community needs

▶ Learning the difference between Portals and Communities

▶ Viewing a community from a customer's perspective

. . . .

*U*sing Salesforce Communities, you can quickly create branded environments for your employees, partners, and customers to collaborate and connect with each other to drive business. Driving customer engagement within your organization can lead to increased sales and lasting relationships with your customers and partners. Salesforce Communities empowers your organization to drive that engagement with customizable, collaborative spaces within your Salesforce organization. Communities allows customers, partners, and employees to post updates via Chatter, view activity streams, share documents, and collaborate directly on system records such as Accounts, Opportunities, and Contacts.

In this chapter, we illuminate the power of Communities, walk you through the various use cases for Communities, guide you through the transition process if you have existing Customer or Partner Portals in your organization, and finally, show you what a community looks like from a customer's perspective.

Distinguishing Use Cases for Community Types

Salesforce Communities can display a subset of the features and the records available in your organization and you can selectively choose which of your employees, customers, partners, or other external people you want to add to your communities. You can empower your customers and partners by providing a social forum directly related to your internal business processes so that they can connect with the right information and the right people at the right moments.

Here are the use cases and advantages of Communities:

- ✓ **Customer Communities:** Best for service and marketing purposes.

  Create a community and grant access to your customers to allow them to connect with each other, collaborate with your employees, and access relevant records. Reduce support costs by giving customers access to the following features:

  - Access to support cases, accounts, contacts, knowledge articles, and more

  - Collaboration between customers and your employees

  - Branding options with customizable pages

  - Mobile access

  - Empowerment of customers with self-service options to post questions or search for existing answers to their questions

  - Ten custom objects

  - Salesforce Identity

- ✓ **Partner Communities:** Best for partner and channel management purposes.

  Increase and drive sales with partners. Create a community and grant access to your distributors, resellers, and suppliers to allow them to connect directly with your channel managers and collaborate in real time on deals and leads, while sharing tips and best practices and increasing pipeline velocity.

  Partner communities include all the Customer Community features, plus the following:

  - Collaboration with partners directly on deals and leads

  - Role-based sharing rules

  - Delegated administration

  - The ability to run and export reports

  - Dashboard viewing

  - Salesforce Identity

- ✓ **Employee Communities:** Best used for intranets for mobile, social employees.

  Create an Employee Community to connect your workers to business-critical information, people, and modules necessary to make them successful from anywhere in the world. Empower your employees with the information they need and the ability to quickly communicate and collaborate with their counterparts around the globe.

Employee communities include the following features:

- Accounts (read-only)
- Contacts (read-only)
- Chatter
- Salesforce Knowledge (read-only)
- Cases (create, read, comment only)
- Reports and Dashboards
- Answers and Ideas
- Workflow rules
- Tasks and Events
- Advanced sharing

Determining your community type

If you can answer the following basic questions, you're ready to begin creating communities in your organization:

- ✔ What is the end purpose of your community?
- ✔ Who do you want to be able to access your community?
- ✔ What information do you want to give community members access to?

If you know the answers to the three questions above, proceed to the following sections on customer and partner communities to determine the type that meets your organization's business objectives.

Exploring customer communities

Here are some of the achievable goals for a Customer Community:

- ✔ To provide top-notch customer service
- ✔ To allow employees and brand advocates to interact directly with customers and prospects to increase the impact of your marketing campaigns

✔ To engage customers and prospects in ongoing conversations to strengthen relationships and improve business processes

✔ To gain greater visibility into the conversations taking place with your customers

Salesforce Communities allows you to pursue your business goals with the following features:

✔ **Business integration:** Integrate your business processes with your community to allow customers and employees to collaborate on the same records in the same space.

✔ **Social feed:** Follow the records you care about most and work together with subject matter experts to resolve customer issues and close deals.

✔ **Branding and customization:** Customize your communities to align with company branding and messaging. Create a community that will promote your brand and give your customers and employees a seamless experience.

✔ **Mobile:** Access Communities from any of your devices.

✔ **Social intelligence:** Receive recommendations and content tailored for your interests and business needs within your communities.

✔ **Security and scalability:** Know that your data and user information is safe with the Salesforce platform as the community is an extension of your internal organization.

✔ **Self-service:** Empower your customers to help themselves to take the load off of your support staff and allow them to focus on your most complex customer issues.

Understanding partner communities

The following are some of the achievable goals with partner communities:

✔ Drive more revenue from your partners

✔ Empower your partners to collaborate directly with your employees

✔ Track partner activity and collaboration with your workers

Salesforce Communities for partner communities allows you to pursue your business goals with all the same features as customer communities.

Comparing Communities with Portals

Salesforce Communities are upgraded Portals. With the power and capabilities of Portals, plus new and improved features, switching from Portals to Communities is a no-brainer. In this section, we explain the differences between Portals and Communities so that you can make educated decisions about your transition.

Even after enabling Communities and beginning the transition from Portals, your Customer and Partner Portals are still available for your use. This allows you the flexibility to create a new community as a test or a pilot before making the transition complete and sunsetting your portals.

Identifying what has carried over from Portals

If you're migrating from Portals to Communities in Salesforce, you have the ability to repurpose many features that you may have already set up. You can reuse the following features:

- ✔ **Branding assets**
- ✔ **Reports**
- ✔ **Sharing rules**
- ✔ **Workflow rules**
- ✔ **Knowledge articles:** If your organization uses Salesforce Knowledge, external users will be able to see articles as long as they've been made available in your communities. Refer to Chapter 15 to see how to expose Chatter Answers and/or Salesforce Knowledge in your communities.

Articles that were available in a Customer Portal or Partner Portal will be available to users with the Customer Community license and Partner Community license respectively when you migrate to Communities.

Similar to Partner Portals, you can't use person accounts as partner accounts or create community users that are associated to those person accounts. There is no need to purchase new community licenses if you already have Portal users. And users who are assigned Portal licenses will have the ability to access your communities as long as you add them as members using either profiles or permission sets.

If you want to reassign licenses, Portal licenses correspond to new Communities licenses as follows:

Portal License	*Communities License*
High-Volume Portal User	Customer Community
Authenticated Website	Customer Community
Gold Partner	Partner Community
Customer Portal Manager Standard	Partner Community
Customer Portal Manager Custom	Partner Community

Refer to Chapter 14 to see how to add users as members of a community using either profiles or permission sets.

Getting familiar with what's new in Communities

Whether you're using Portals and want to migrate to Communities, have already migrated to Communities, or are brand new to Communities, you need to be aware of how features work differently in Communities.

The following features function differently in Communities than they did with Portals:

- ✔ **Membership, user management, and delegated administration:** The following changes should be noted for Communities:

  - You can grant access to Communities to any type of user using profiles and permission sets.

  - Internal users with the Manage External Users permission have the ability to manage both partner and customer users.

  - Self-registration is available to both partner users and customer users.

- ✔ **Email, notifications, and templates:** Changes to communication in Communities are as follows:

  - *Reset password email:* The email contains a link to reset password instead of a temporary password.

  - *Case Comment notification:* The notification is available for both partner and customer users.

- *Email templates:* Templates are set up within Communities rather than at the organization level.

- *Change owner to portal user template:* This is no longer used in Communities.

✔ **Custom Objects:** The check box to make custom objects available for the Customer Portal doesn't exist on custom objects once you've enabled Communities. You must select custom objects to make available in your community as described in Chapter 14.

✔ **Tasks:** The Public check box on tasks applies to users with Partner Portal licenses. If a task is marked as Public, it will be visible to users with access to the parent record; otherwise, it's visible by internal users and the task owner.

✔ **Search (with Chatter enabled):** A global search bar appears at the top of the page in place of the sidebar search available in Portals.

✔ **Login:** Portal ID is not required for logging in to a community. Users simply need the URL for the community.

✔ **Visualforce and Apex pages:** Existing hard-coded paths won't work for Visualforce and Apex pages. These need to be updated with the community URL.

✔ **Apex triggers:** If your company has Apex triggers for Chatter, they'll function for all communities automatically. If you want to use the triggers only for certain communities or no communities, you must update the code.

If you're not sure whether your organization uses Visualforce and Apex pages or Apex triggers, contact a developer within your company.

In addition to features that have changed or are brand new in Communities, there are a number of features from Portals that are no longer available with Communities.

The following features are no longer available in Communities:

✔ **Documents tab**

✔ **Old Questions tab**

✔ **Logout page settings per individual community:** The Active Landing page in each community is used instead.

Refer to Chapter 14 for more information on setting up Active Landing pages.

✔ **Custom help settings per community**

✔ **Any existing self-registration settings for your portals:** They won't carry over to your communities. If you want to enable self-registration in your communities, you can do so by enabling the feature for each individual community.

Refer to Chapter 15 to see how to set up self-registration for your communities.

✔ **Top-level solution category and enable self-close from solutions:** The solution hierarchy is not supported for Communities.

If your organization requires similar functionality, you should consider enabling Salesforce Knowledge and exposing Knowledge articles in your communities. Refer to Chapter 10 to see if Salesforce Knowledge is right for your organization.

Glimpsing a Customer Community for New Members

In Chapters 14 and 15, you get the ins and outs of Communities and how to best set them up for your company's purposes. But first, take a moment to review the rest of this section to see how your customers, partners, resellers, or distributors would access a community for the first time.

You'll see that the process is simple and efficient. Your external members can gain access to your organization and begin leveraging the Salesforce Platform to collaborate with your employees in just three simple steps.

After you have a community set up and published, you can send a link to your customers and they'll follow these steps to access the community for the first time:

1. **Click the link sent to the customer to navigate to the Community Login page.**

   The login page (shown in Figure 13-1) appears.

2. **Click the Not a Member? link.**

   The registration page (shown in Figure 13-2) appears.

3. **Fill out the fields shown in Figure 13-2 and click Submit.**

   The landing page of your community will display, as shown in Figure 13-3.

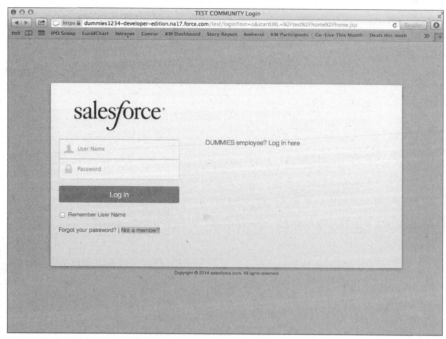

Figure 13-1:
The login
page for
customers.

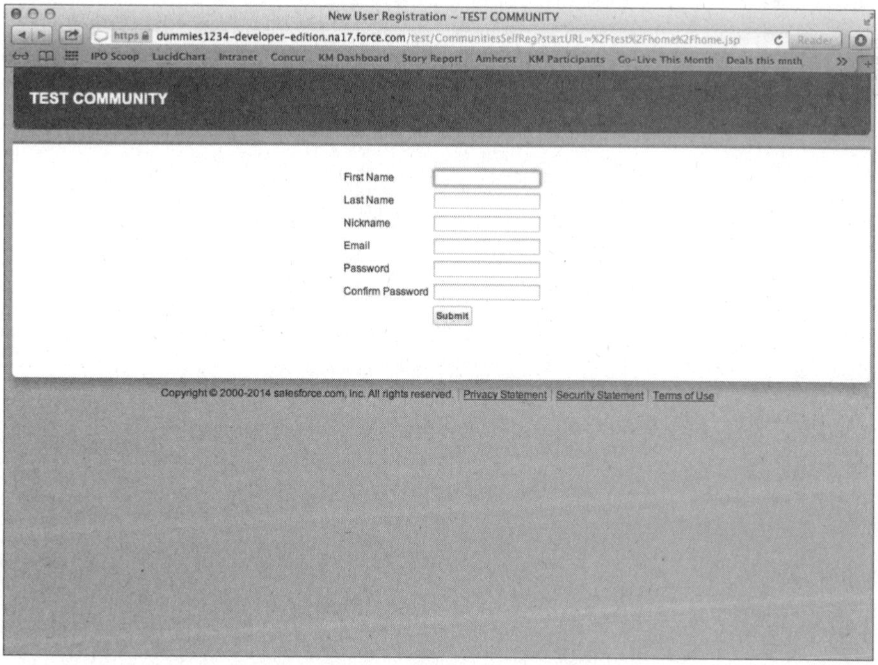

Figure 13-2:
The regis-
tration page
for new
community
users.

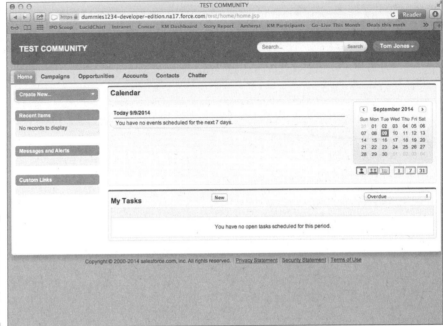

Figure 13-3:
An example
of a landing
page for a
Customer
Community.

Your customer is now registered and admitted to the community you've created. Customers can collaborate directly with your support staff and your subject matter experts on their issues. They can also interact with your other customers and share their experiences with your prospects.

Chapter 14

Creating a Community

. . . .

In This Chapter

▶ Setting up Communities

▶ Understanding how to add members to communities

▶ Determining the right information to display for community members

▶ Sharing and validating communities

. . . .

*W*ith Salesforce Communities, building powerfully collaborative spaces for your employees, customers, and partners is easier than ever before. Your organization can now strengthen the trust in your customer relationships and improve the performance and value of your partner relationships in just a few minutes. Salesforce Communities empowers your employees to drive more sales and provide excellent customer service by enabling transparency and consistency with one set of data for all parties.

In this chapter, we reveal the foundational steps that every system administrator must understand to prepare to deploy Communities from their organization. Then we explain how you can create your very first community. Finally, we help you figure out how to build your community by adding members and displaying important data for them.

Planning Your Community

City planners may not end up in the headlines, but they're critical to the efficiency and success of any metropolis. The same holds true for administrators of Salesforce Communities.

Salesforce Communities allows you to set up a collaborative space where you get to choose how members will navigate to your community, exactly who those members will be, and what those members will find and be able to achieve in the community. Finally, after the community is set up, you have the benefit of sharing it with others and making any necessary changes before opening the space to the public.

These are all important decisions that you need to make as you begin creating your community. Refer to Chapter 13 for help in this process.

Setting Up Communities

Before you begin setting up a community, make sure that your organization has Salesforce Communities licenses. Choose Setup ⇨ Company Profile ⇨ Company Information and view your licenses at the bottom of the page.

Enabling Salesforce Communities in your organization

The first step is to enable Communities in your organization. To do so, follow these steps:

1. **From Setup, choose Customize ⇨ Communities ⇨ Settings.**

2. **Click the Enable Communities check box, shown in Figure 14-1.**

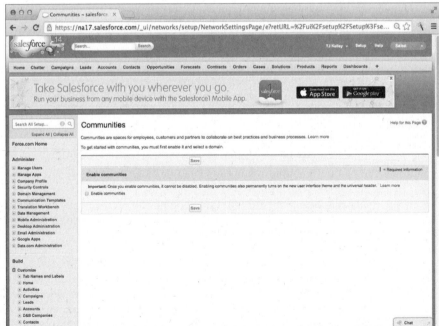

Figure 14-1:
Enabling
Salesforce
Communities.

After you enable Salesforce Communities in your organization, you won't be able to disable it.

Selecting a domain name for your community

After you've enabled Salesforce Communities, select a domain name for your communities and click the Check Availability button to ensure that it isn't already in use (see Figure 14-2).

Select a domain name that will be familiar and recognizable to your users, like your company name or a company slogan.

You can't change the domain name after you've selected it and saved it.

After you've confirmed the availability of your chosen domain name, click Save at the bottom of the page.

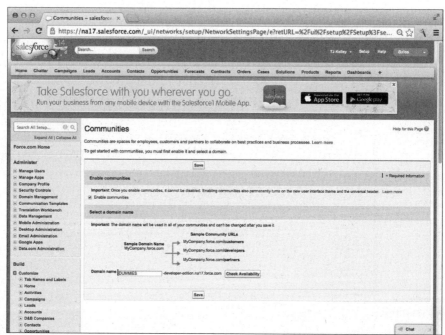

Figure 14-2: Selecting a domain name.

Creating Your Community

After selecting a domain name, you're taken to the Manage Communities page (see Figure 14-3).

If you had previously enabled Communities and you're returning to create your first community, choose Setup ➪ Customize ➪ Communities ➪ Manage Communities to find this page.

To create your community, follow these steps:

1. **Click New Community.**

2. **Choose a Name for your new community.**

3. **Enter a description of your new community.**

   For example, "This is a Customer Community to communicate and collaborate with customers on their open cases."

4. **Fill in the empty box at the end of the URL to create a unique URL for your new community.**

5. **Click Create.**

   You see the message shown in Figure 14-4.

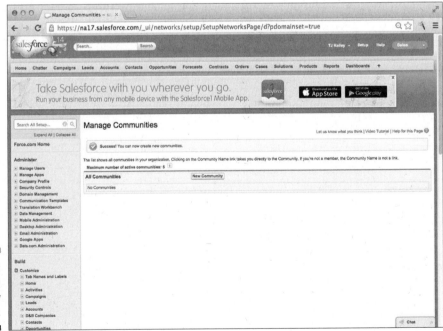

Figure 14-3:
Creating
a new
community.

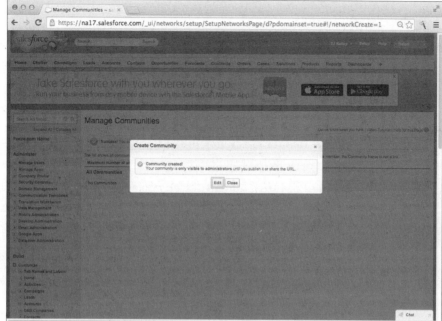

Figure 14-4:
The commu-
nity is only
visible to
administra-
tors.

To find out how to make your community visible to additional users, check out Chapter 15.

Turning on the Global Header for Communities

After enabling Communities in your organization, selecting a domain name, and creating your first community, the next step is to turn on the Global Header for Communities. The Global Header only becomes available after you enable Communities. It lets your users switch easily between your internal organization and any communities that they're members of.

In order to view the Global Header, users must be assigned the View Global Header permission. You must enable the View Global Header permission for all profiles that you want to have access to the Global Header and your communities.

You can start by enabling the View Global Header permission for System Administrators:

1. **Choose Setup ⇨ Manage Users ⇨ Profiles**

2. **Locate the System Administrator Profile and click the Edit link to the left of the profile's name.**

   The Profile page appears for System Administrator Profile.

3. **Scroll to the Administrative Permissions section, and click the View Global Header check box in the right column.**

4. **Scroll back to the top of the page and click Save.**

   If you're a System Administrator, you see the Global Header at the top of your page.

See Adding Members later in this chapter to find out how you can easily assign the View Global Header permission to a large set of users.

If users have the View Global Header permission, they automatically see the Global Header at the top of the page when they login (see Figure 14-5).

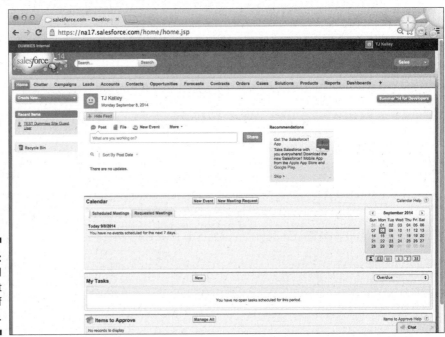

Figure 14-5:
The Global Header at the top of the page.

On the left side of the header, you find the title of your organization followed by an Internal drop-down list. The drop-down allows users to quickly switch between the internal organization and any communities that they're members of.

On the right side of the header, you see your name. Your name is also a drop-down list that now contains the Setup menu and your personal settings.

Understanding Communities statuses

A community can have various statuses in your organization. There are three statuses in which a community can exist:

✔ **Preview:** The community is not yet complete and has never been published.

Users with the Create and Set Up Communities permission can view communities in Preview status if they have access to the community. Refer to the "Adding Members to Your Community" section, later in this chapter, to see how to grant users access to a community. Members of a community can share a link to a community in Preview status with other users who have access. When they have the preview link, members of the community can preview the community regardless of whether they have the Create and Set Up Communities permission or not. This allows key members to view the community before it's published. After a community is published, it cannot be returned to the Preview status.

✔ **Offline:** The community was published but has since been taken offline.

You can use the Offline status if you want to make changes to your community and then republish it for your users. When a community is in Offline status, it won't appear in the drop-down menu of the Global Header and only community members with the Create and Set Up Communities permission will be able to access it. If members without the Create and Set Up Communities permission try to access the community using the URL, they'll get an error message.

✔ **Published:** The community is published and fully available for members.

If your organization fails to pay fees due to Salesforce, your communities will be taken offline. When Salesforce Communities is enabled again, all existing communities will be in Offline status and cannot be returned to Preview status. Your only options are to publish them or leave them offline.

Adding Members to Your Community

To add members to your community, follow these steps:

1. **Choose Setup➪Customize➪Communities➪Manage Communities.**

2. **Click Edit next to the community you want to add members to.**

   The Community Settings page for your community appears.

3. **Click Members.**

   The Members page for your community appears.

4. **Click Save.**

   You're taken back to the Community Settings page. You can now add users using profiles or permission sets.

Profiles and permission sets associated with communities cannot be deleted from Salesforce. They must be removed from the communities before they can be deleted.

Adding members using profiles

Your first option for adding users to your community is using profiles to extend access to groups of users based on the profile they're assigned. Figure 14-6 shows how you can add members using profiles.

The first box you see is the Search box. You can search profiles of the following types:

- ✔ **Internal:** Only internal profiles, which includes profiles corresponding to all internal Salesforce Licenses (including Chatter and Chatter Free).

- ✔ **Chatter:** Only Chatter profiles, which includes the Chatter Free and Chatter Moderator profiles.

- ✔ **Portal:** Only external member profiles, which includes profiles corresponding to external Salesforce Licenses (including Customer Portal, Partner Portal, Partner Community, or Customer Community license).

- ✔ **All:** All profiles.

When you determine the type of profiles you'd like to add as members to your community, select the profiles you want to include from the Available Profiles box and click the arrow pointing to the right called Add. This adds all users assigned to those profiles as members to your community.

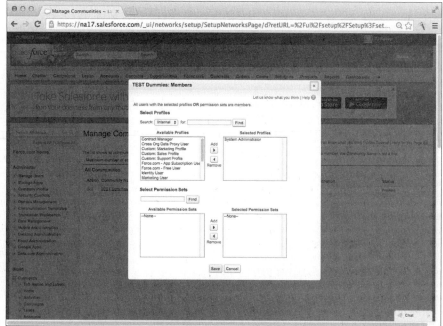

Figure 14-6:
Adding
members
using
profiles.

You can also remove members in the same way by selecting profiles from the Selected Profiles box and clicking the arrow pointing to the left to remove members.

Enable the Global Header for all the profiles you want to add as members to your community. This will allow users to easily switch between the internal organization and any community that they're members of.

Adding members with permission sets

Your second option for adding members to your community is using permission sets. A *permission set* is a collection of settings and permissions that grant users access to tools and functions in your organization. The settings and permissions in permission sets are the same as they are in profiles, but permission sets allow you to extend users' permissions in the system without worrying about which profile they're assigned to.

If you haven't created any permission sets, the Available Permission Sets and Selected Permission Sets boxes will appear with no options to select. Figure 14-7 shows the Available and Selected Permission Sets boxes.

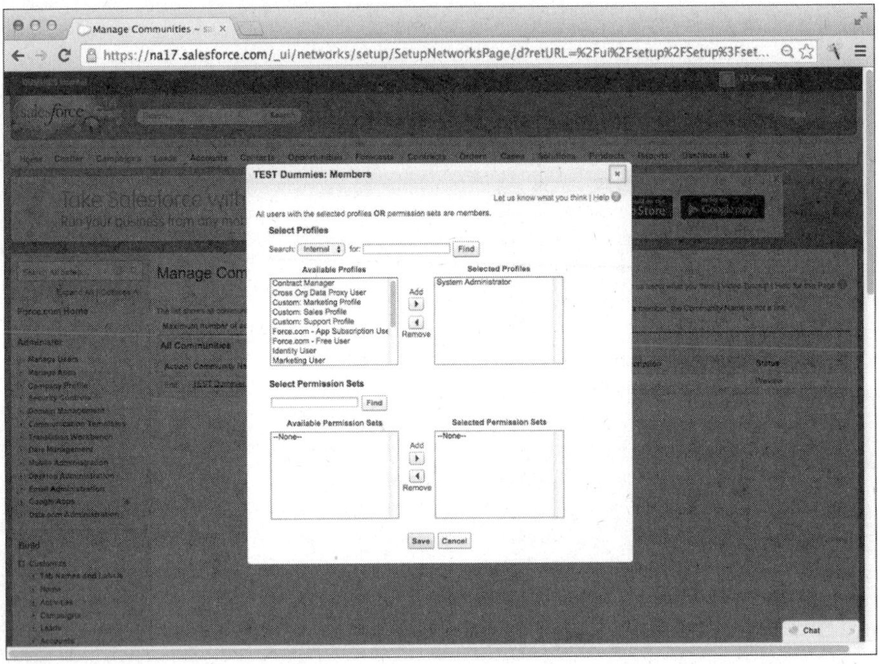

Figure 14-7:
Available
and
Selected
Permission
Sets boxes.

If you want to add users as members to your community without worrying about what profile they're assigned to, you can create a permission set to be assigned to users instead.

Follow these steps to create a permission set for community access:

1. **Choose Setup⇨Manage Users⇨Permission Sets.**

2. **Click New.**

3. **Enter a Label for your permission set.**

   For example, you could call it Community Access.

4. **Enter a description for your permission set.**

5. **Leave User License as None if you want users with multiple different types of licenses to use the permission set.**

6. **Click Save.**

7. **On the new page that loads for your permission set, scroll to the System section and click System Permissions.**

   The System Permissions page appears.

8. **Click Edit at the top of the System Permissions page.**

9. **Click the View Global Header Permission check box.**

10. **Click Save.**

Now that you've created a permission set, you can add members to your community using the permission set in addition to using profiles.

Users still need to be assigned to permission sets in order to be granted access to the community.

You can assign users to permission sets in two different ways:

✔ Go to their user records and click Edit Assignments in the Permission Set Assignments section.

✔ Navigate to the permission set from the Setup menu and click Manage Assignments.

Creating partner and customer users

You can also create community members by granting external users access to Communities directly from Contact records in Salesforce.

To turn partners and customers into community members individually, follow these steps:

1. **Navigate to the Contact record for the person you want to create as a community user.**

2. **On the Contact record, click the Manage External User button and select Enable Customer or Partner User.**

3. **Edit the user record page, selecting the appropriate profile.**

   Remember to ensure that the profile you select has been granted access to the community to which you want to add this contact as a member.

4. **Click Save.**

External users can't be deleted. If you don't want external users to have access to a community anymore, you must deactivate them from their user records.

Adding Tabs to Your Community

After adding members to your community, you need to decide what type of information and actions to make available for them. Community tabs work in the same manner as tabs in your internal Salesforce organization. For example, if a sales rep logs in to your organization, they probably see tabs for Leads, Accounts, Contacts, and Opportunities displayed prominently.

Figure 14-8 shows the window to select tabs for your community.

Select tabs that will display all the information you want your community to interact with.

Displaying tabs in your community

You can customize the appearance and function of your community by selecting the features that display for members. For example, if you create a Partner Community, you may choose to display Opportunities and Accounts in your community. Try to limit the tabs that you include to only those that your community members need access to. This will help to keep the community user friendly and easy to navigate by confining the available options.

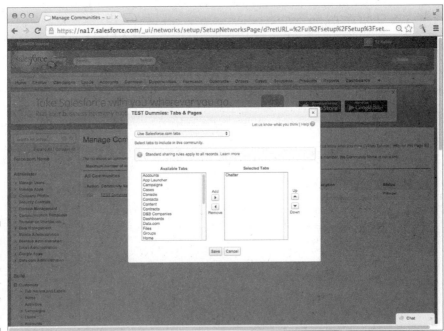

Figure 14-8:
Tabs to display for your community members.

Even though you're selecting tabs to be displayed in your community, profiles still control access to these tabs. This means that in order to view these tabs in the community, users need to be assigned to a profile that will grant them access to those objects.

To choose tabs to display in your community, follow these steps:

1. **Choose Setup ➪ Customize ➪ Communities ➪ Manage Communities.**

2. **Click Edit next to the community you want to add tabs for.**

    The Community Settings page appears.

3. **Click Tabs & Pages.**

    The Tabs & Pages page appears.

4. **Choose the tabs you want to include in your community.**

    You can choose multiple tabs at once by pressing Ctrl while you select the tabs.

5. **Use the Up and Down arrows next to the Selected Tabs box to reorder your tabs.**

6. **Click Save after you've selected all desired tabs and put them in your desired order.**

    You're returned to the Community Settings page.

7. **Click Close.**

8. **Use the Global Header drop-down menu and switch to your community to verify that the tabs you selected are displaying and are in the correct order.**

Choosing a landing tab for your community members

When choosing tabs to display in your community, you can select a landing tab, which will be the first page users land on when they login to the community. The landing tab will be the tab at the very top of your list of selected tabs. In the example shown in Figure 14-9, Chatter is the landing tab.

You can select many different tabs as the landing tab for your community. Just think about how users will be using the community and what would be the best place for them to start when they login.

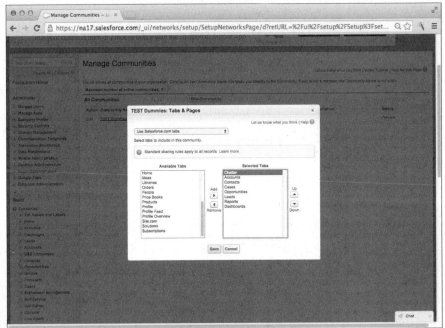

Figure 14-9:
Chatter as
a landing
tab for a
community.

Here are a few examples you could use as landing tabs:

- ✔ **Chatter:** The Chatter tab is a good option to use as a landing tab for your community if members will be frequently collaborating with each other or commenting on Opportunities, Cases, Accounts, and so on. The Chatter tab allows users to land on a feed of items that they follow when they first login.

- ✔ **Home:** The Home tab is a great second option if your organization isn't using Chatter or doesn't want members to land on the Chatter feed when they login. The Home tab will display components added by your system administrator. Some examples may be a calendar of tasks and events or dashboard graphs.

- ✔ **Opportunities:** Opportunities would be a good landing tab if you've created a Partner Community and partners will be frequently logging in to check the status of opportunities.

- ✔ **Cases:** The Cases tab might be a good fit for a Customer Community where you have customers logging in to check on cases that they've logged with your organization.

Enabling cases in your community

You can enable cases for external users in your community. To enable cases for external users, you need to make the Cases tab available in your community and ensure that the users have Read, Create, and Edit permissions on the case object. You can apply these permission settings on profiles or permission sets.

When you enable cases for external users, you can allow them to do the following in your communities:

- ✔ Create new cases.
- ✔ Own cases in your communities.
- ✔ Edit existing cases.
- ✔ Add case comments.
- ✔ Reassign cases.
- ✔ Find case solutions.
- ✔ Create case teams.

External users cannot edit case comments, associate assets with cases, or delete cases.

Previewing Your Community

After you've created your community, added the appropriate members, and selected the tabs that you want to display in your community, you may want to preview your community and share it with other key decision makers in order to validate the initial design and configuration and discuss community membership.

At this point, your community should still be in Preview status.

While the community is in Preview status only members or the community with the Create and Set Up Communities permission will be able to access and view it.

If you want to share the community with key decision makers, you can do so in three ways:

- ✔ If you've enabled the Global Header, instruct them to use the Global Header to switch from the internal organization to the community.

- ✔ If you haven't enabled the Global Header for these users, you can instruct them to access the community via the Setup menu by choosing Setup ➪ Customize ➪ Communities ➪ Manage Communities and clicking the community you want them to review.

- ✔ Share the link to the community with key users directly. You can find the link by choosing Setup ➪ Customize ➪ Communities ➪ Manage Communities and clicking Edit next to the community. You can copy and paste the URL from the Community Settings popup, as shown in Figure 14-10.

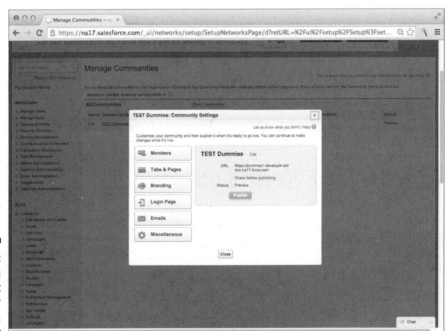

Figure 14-10:
Sharing
the direct
link to your
community.

Chapter 15

Optimizing Your Community

In This Chapter

▶ Customizing your communities

▶ Keeping your company's brand consistent in your communities

▶ Improving the login experience for your community members

▶ Keeping communications consistent in your communities

▶ Opening your communities to your members

▶ Moderating and governing community usage

▶ Integrating your communities

*W*ith the foundation and groundwork complete, it's time to put a fresh paint job on the structures and ensure that navigation and communication processes are fine-tuned before opening up your community to the masses. You also need to put regulations in place and elect leaders to control and shape your community.

Salesforce Communities empowers you to customize the user experience for your partners, customers, and employees, and provides all the tools necessary to control and preside over the populace.

In this chapter, we show you how to polish your community's appearance and ensure members can gain access efficiently. Then we present the steps every organizer should take to govern and moderate an active community. Finally, we show you how to truly take your community to the next level.

Customizing and Branding Your Communities

Salesforce Communities provides flexible design options so you can tailor the appearance of your community to match your company's branding. Adding your company's logo and colors will ensure that your employees, customers, and partners can immediately identify with their experience in the community. Plus, administrators can enhance the login page and registration process for external users. Finally, you can select and customize email templates for your community to ensure consistency in your company's communications.

In order to begin customizing and branding your communities, you need to create them first. Refer to Chapter 14 to find out how to set up Communities.

Customizing your community's look and feel

The most basic steps you can take to customize your community are to select a header and footer, as well as a color scheme. These elements will remain constant as your members navigate through the community.

You must have the Create and Customize Communities permission enabled on your profile in order to make customizations to your community.

Changing your header and footer

Choosing a consistent header and footer for your community will keep your company's branding visible at all times in your community.

To choose a header and footer, follow these steps:

1. **From Setup, choose Customize ⇨ Communities ⇨ Manage Communities.**

2. **Click Edit next to the Community you want to customize.**

   The Community Settings page appears.

3. **Click the Branding tab.**

   The Branding page appears.

4. **Use the lookup fields for Header and Footer to make your selections.**

   The header will replace the Salesforce logo just below the global header, and the footer replaces the Salesforce copyright and privacy footer (as shown in Figure 15-1).

5. **Click Save.**

You have to upload the files you want to use as a header and footer to the Documents tab and make them publicly available before you can add a header and footer. The header file can be HTML, GIF, JPG, or PNG. The footer needs to be an HTML file.

This is the header

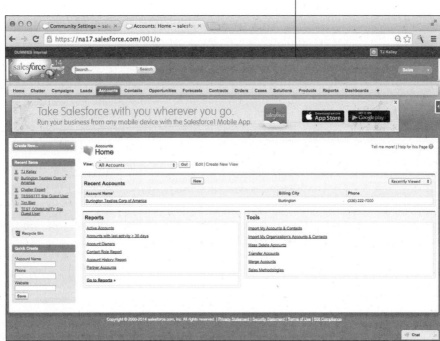

Figure 15-1:
Community
header and
footer.

This is the footer

Choosing a color scheme

Branding your community with your company's color scheme will give your employees a familiar look and feel and ensure that your partners and customers are engaging with your company's brand at all times. You have the following options for your color scheme:

✔ **Header Background:** Appears at the top of the page under the global header.

If you chose an HTML file for your header, the color you select in the Header Background section will override the color choice in your HTML file.

✔ **Page Background:** Appears as the background color for all pages in your community.

✔ **Primary:** Appears as the color of a selected tab.

✓ **Secondary:** Appears as the color of lists and tables, as well as the button on the login page.

✓ **Tertiary:** Appears as the background color for section headers on record edit and detail pages.

To customize your color scheme, follow these steps:

1. From Setup, choose Customize ➪ Communities ➪ Manage Communities.

2. Click Edit next to the Community you want to customize.

3. Click the Branding tab.

4. Click Select Color Scheme to choose from preset options.

Alternatively, you can click the color box, or the text box, next to each section to select a different color.

5. Preview your selections in the preview section at the bottom of the window, as shown in Figure 15-2.

6. Click Save.

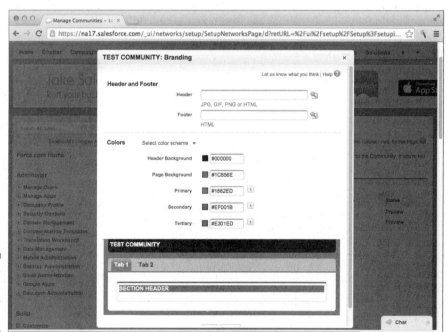

Figure 15-2:
Previewing a color scheme.

Enhancing the login page for your community

Salesforce Communities allow you to improve your community login page both aesthetically and functionally. You can customize the appearance of your login page in order to keep your brand consistent. And you can select the manner in which *external users* (people with Community, Customer Portal, or Partner Portal licenses) can access your community.

Uploading a logo

You can upload a logo to keep your brand visible to external users as they access your community. Follow these steps to upload a logo on your login page:

1. **From Setup, choose Customize ➪ Communities ➪ Manage Communities.**
2. **Click Edit next to the Community you want to customize.**
3. **Click the Login Page tab.**

   The Login Page edit page appears (see Figure 15-3).

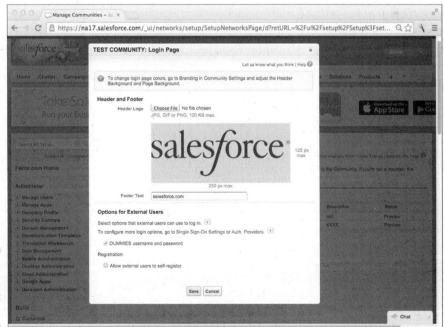

Figure 15-3: The Login Page edit page.

4. **Click Choose File next to Header Logo and select a logo to display as your header.**

Uploading a logo for a community creates a Communities Shared Document Folder in the Documents tab where the logo will be saved. Users can't delete this folder.

Your Header Logo will display at the top left of the login page within a browser, as well as within the Salesforce application.

5. **Enter up to 120 characters for your Footer Text.**

The footer text will display at the bottom of the login page.

6. **Click Save.**

 You can control the colors displayed on the login page by selecting a Header Background and Page Background in the Branding tab of your Community Settings. Refer to the "Choosing a color scheme" section, earlier in this chapter, for more detail.

Setting up self-registration for external users

The default login option for external users is a username and password that each user was assigned. This option requires a system administrator to create each individual external community member. You can reduce the workload for your administrator by setting up self-registration for external users.

In order to set up self-registration for users, you must enable the feature in your community- and edit-related Visualforce pages and Apex controllers.

 When you enable Communities in your organization, related Visualforce pages and Apex controllers are created automatically for the self-registration feature. In this section, we show you how to edit one of the Apex controllers to enable the self-registration feature. If you want to make additional edits to the self-registration process, contact a developer within your organization to make the changes.

Follow these steps to set up self-registration to your community:

1. **From Setup, choose Customize ➪ Communities ➪ Manage Communities.**

2. **Click Edit next to the community you want to customize.**

3. **Click the Login Page tab.**

The Login Page settings window opens.

4. **In the Options for External Users section, click the box to allow external users to self-register.**

5. Select a default profile for users who self-register.

You can only select Portal Profiles that have been made available within the community. Refer to Chapter 14 for more information on adding profiles to your community.

If a profile is selected as the default for self-registration users, and you remove it from the available profiles for the community, the default profile will be reset to None.

6. Click Save.

7. Specify an Account for self-registration users in the default Apex controller following these steps:

    1. From Setup, choose Develop⇨Apex Classes.

    2. Click Edit next to CommunitiesSelfRegController.

    3. As shown in Figure 15-4, input the Salesforce ID of a partner or customer account that you want to assign self-registered users to on line 30.

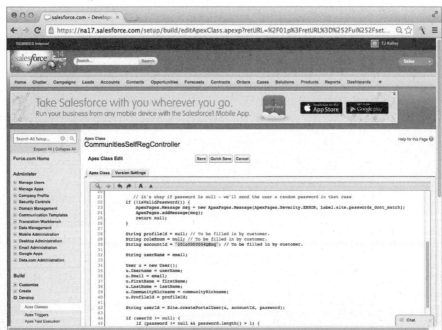

Figure 15-4:
Edit
Communities
SelfReg
Controller.

In order to find an Account's Salesforce ID, create an Accounts report and drag the Account ID field into the report as a column. Find the Account you'd like to add self-registered users to, and copy the associated Account ID. For more information on how to create an Accounts report, turn to Chapter 17. You can also refer to *Salesforce.com For Dummies,* 5th Edition, by Tom Wong, Liz Kao, and Matt Kaufman (Wiley).

The self-registration feature for your community won't work until you've edited the CommunitiesSelfRegController to include an Account ID.

4. Click Save.

8. **Enable access to accounts and contacts for self-register users.**

   This allows users to self-register. To enable access, follow these steps:

   1. From Setup, choose Customize ➪ Communities ➪ Manage Communities.

   2. Click the Force.com link for your community.

   3. Click the Public Access Settings button.

   4. Click Edit.

   5. Select Read and Create next to Accounts and Contacts in the Standard Object Permissions section.

   6. Click Save.

   7. In the Enabled Apex Class Access section, click Edit.

   8. Add CommunitiesSelfRegController and click Save.

   9. In the Enabled Visualforce Page Access related list, click Edit.

   10. Add CommunitiesSelfReg and click Save.

Selected login options for external users, such as self-registration, will show up for all users on the login page, but they'll only function properly for external users. If internal users try to use the self-registration feature, they'll get a login error. Internal users need to click the Log In Here link and log in using their Salesforce usernames and passwords.

Selecting email templates and settings for your community

Salesforce Communities allows you to customize email sender information, Chatter email branding, and templates in emails sent from your community.

Follow these steps to customize email settings for your community:

1. **From Setup, choose Customize ⇨ Communities ⇨ Manage Communities.**

2. **Click Edit next to the community you want to customize email settings for.**

3. **Click Emails.**

4. **Choose values for the email sender's name and address to replace the default values.**

   When you change these values, an email will be sent to the new address with a verification link. The old address will be used until the new one has been verified. You have 72 hours to confirm the new email address.

5. **Select a logo and footer text for Chatter emails.**

   All Chatter emails display the Chatter logo and Salesforce information in the footer by default until you customize this information.

   The logo you select must be an existing document in the Documents tab and must be marked Externally Available Image.

6. **Select Send Welcome Email if you want to send an email to users when they're added to the community.**

   Welcome emails are sent under the following circumstances:

   - A community moves from Preview to Published status.

   - A new profile or permission set is added to a Published community.

   - A user is assigned to a profile or permission set that is already part of a Published community.

     Welcome emails contain login information for external members. If you don't select to send welcome emails, you need to send external members their usernames and passwords manually.

7. **Use the default email templates.**

   You can select a template for Case Comments if your organization uses email templates to submit case comments. Otherwise, leave this blank.

   You can customize the default templates if you need to. In order to do, from Setup, choose Communication Templates ⇨ Email Templates and click Edit next to the template you want to modify.

8. **Click Save.**

Publishing and Governing Your Communities

After preparing your community for the public, you can move it from the Preview status to the Published status. After you've moved a community into Published status, it will be visible to all members.

After publishing, Salesforce Communities provides many options for you to manage your community proactively, monitor the activity of your members, and view the overall health of the community.

Complete any customizations you want to make while your community is still in Preview status. This way, you can ensure that your community is completely ready for users before allowing them access. However, if you want to make customizations after a community has been published, you can still do so. You can leave the community in Published status and make your customizations on the fly, or you can take the community offline to make your edits.

Publishing your community and welcoming members

After you've completed all customizations, follow these steps to publish your community and welcome your users:

1. **From Setup, choose Customize ⇨ Communities ⇨ Manage Communities.**

2. **Click Edit next to the community you want to publish.**

3. **Click the green Publish button.**

   A popup window appears (see Figure 15-5).

4. **Click OK.**

   The Community Settings window displays with a message letting you know the community has been published.

5. **Click Close.**

The welcome emails need to be enabled for your community first. If the Send Welcome Email option is selected for your community, each community member will receive an email with a link to navigate to the newly published community.

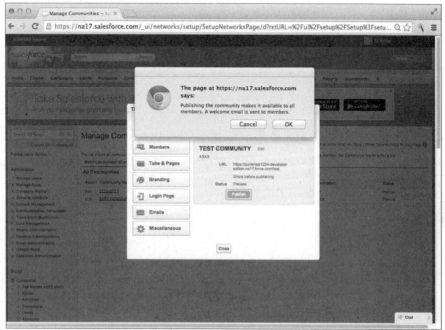

Figure 15-5:
The popup notification for publishing your community.

External users who are members of multiple communities within your organization will be able to use the same login credentials for each and every community they're added to.

Selecting a Community Manager

Just like any organized group or population, a Salesforce community needs a leader to step up and take responsibility for the health of the community. A Community Manager is a member of the community who has the added responsibility of monitoring members and their participation, spurring and augmenting conversations in the community, and giving members recognition for their participation to encourage and ensure a flourishing community.

Community managers must be members of the community and employees of your organization. They cannot be external community members.

To select a user as a community manager, you need to assign them the Manage Communities system permission. You can assign users the Manage Communities permission in two ways:

- ✔ **Profiles:** Enable the Manage Communities permission at the profile level for the user you want to choose as the Community Manager. From Setup, choose Manage Users ➪ Profiles and click Edit next to the Profile you want to enable Manage Communities for.

- ✔ If you enable the Manage Communities permission at the profile level, this enables all users who are assigned that profile and are members of your community to manage that community. If you want to limit the number of users who can manage your community further, you should use Permission Sets.

- ✔ **Permission Sets:** Enable the Manage Communities permission for a Permission Set that you can then assign to the individual user. From Setup, choose Manage Users ➪ Permission Sets and click Edit next to the Permission Set you want to enable Manage Communities for.

You should consider creating a Community Manager permission set so that you can have a unique permission set to assign to all Community Managers. This will not only allow you to limit the number of users who have the ability to manage communities, but also ensure that you can tailor the permissions and settings for Community Managers specifically.

Leveraging the Community Engagement Console

One of the key tools available to community managers is the Community Engagement Console, which they can leverage to keep tabs on activity within the community.

To access the Community Engagement Console, follow these steps:

1. **Log in to your community.**

2. **From your community page, click the gear symbol shown in Figure 15-6.**

3. **Choose the part of the community you want to manage:**

   - *Overview:* Choose overview to use dashboards set up for this community. If you're a Community Manager and no dashboards appear, work with your administrator to have dashboards enabled.

   - If you're an administrator, read the next section, "Utilizing Communities analytics," to learn how to set up these dashboards.

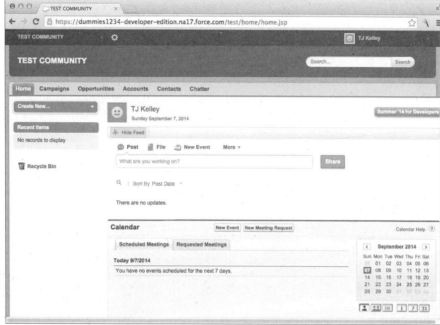

Figure 15-6:
Access your
Community
Engagement
Console.

- *Reputation Levels:* Reputation points allow community members to collect points based on the point system set up by Community Managers.

- *Point System:* Community Managers can set the number of points members will gain or lose based on the activities they complete in the community.

To enable Reputation Levels and the corresponding Point System, follow these steps:

1. **From Setup, choose Customize⇨Communities⇨Manage Communities.**

2. **Click Edit next to the community you want to enable Reputation Levels for.**

3. **Click the Miscellaneous tab.**

   The Miscellaneous Community Settings window appears.

4. **Click the check box to enable setup and display of reputation levels (see Figure 15-7) and click Save.**

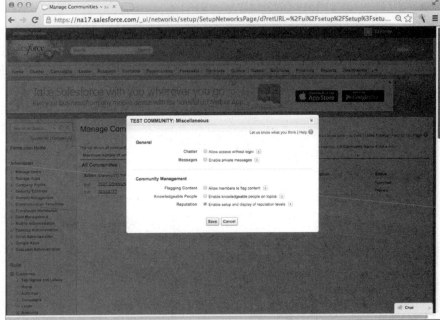

Utilizing Communities analytics

A Community Manager will be a more effective leader with useful information and analytics at his or her fingertips. Salesforce Communities provides
multiple ways for administrators and users to access community-specific
information.

Reporting on Communities usage

As a Community Manager or an administrator, you'll want to report on
community usage to understand how frequently users are engaging in your
communities.

To build and run a report for Communities usage, you must have the following permissions:

✔ Run Reports

✔ Create and Customize Reports

✔ Report Builder

Follow these steps to report on community usage:

1. **From Setup, choose Create ⇨ Report Types.**

2. **Click Continue.**

3. **Click New Custom Report Type.**

4. **Select Users as the Primary Object.**

5. **Enter** Community User Report **as the report type label,** Community_ User_Report **as the report type name,** Report on Community Usage **as the description, and** Administrative Reports **as the category to store your report type in.**

6. **Select Deployed.**

7. **Click Next.**

8. **Click to relate another object and select Networks {Created By} as object B in the relationship. Leave the A to B relationship selected as "Each 'A' record must have at least one related 'B' record."**

9. **Click to relate another object and select Network Activity Daily Metrics as object C in the relationship. Leave the B to C relationship selected as "Each 'B' record must have at least one related 'C' record."**

10. **Click Save.**

11. **Click the Reports tab and create a new report using your recently created report type.**

12. **Optionally include the following fields:**

    - *Network ID:* Shows which community activity has happened in.

    - *User Type, Profile, and Role:* Shows what type of user completed the activity.

    - *Comment Count and Post Count:* Shows the counts of comments and posts by members of the community.

Enabling dashboards to measure success in your community

To select dashboards for your community managers to leverage, follow these steps:

1. **From Setup, choose Customize ⇨ Communities ⇨ Settings.**

2. **For each page, under the Dashboard Settings section, select a corresponding dashboard that you want to display for community managers.**

3. Click Save.

You can verify that the dashboards have been selected properly by navigating to the Community Engagement Console in each of your existing communities.

Salesforce Communities offers the Salesforce Communities Analytics package. You can install the package in your organization, and you get a default dashboard for each of the pages listed in Community Settings.

Start out your Communities Analytics by installing the Salesforce Communities Analytics package. If you want to change or expand upon the default dashboards provided in the package, you can always create new dashboards and override the default values in Community Settings.

Moderating your community

Enabling moderation within your Salesforce Communities can lighten the load on your community managers by empowering other members of the community to monitor activity and content to make sure that only relevant and helpful information is posted within the community.

Salesforce Communities allows you to achieve the following with Moderation:

- ✔ Select individual users as moderators.
- ✔ Allow all members to flag inappropriate posts, comments, or files.
- ✔ Let moderators review all flagged items and take corresponding action.
- ✔ Allow managers and owners of groups within your community to moderate their own groups.
- ✔ Automatically flag inappropriate posts, comments, or files with triggers. You can set up triggers with predefined criteria to flag posts based on various words included, and so on.
- ✔ Report on flagging and moderation activity.

Flagging items in your community

To allow your community members to manually flag posts, comments, and files, and also allow your group owners and managers to moderate their own groups, follow these steps:

1. From Setup, choose Customize ➪ Communities ➪ Manage Communities.

2. Click Edit next to the community you want to enable flagging for.

3. **Click the Miscellaneous tab.**

4. **Click the Allow Members to Flag Content check box.**

5. **Click Save.**

Selecting a community moderator

To select individual users as moderators for your communities, you need to assign one or both of the moderation permissions for those users. Here are the moderation permissions available:

- ✔ **Moderate Communities Feeds:** Allows moderators to review flagged posts and comments and take subsequent action. Gives users access to a filter and list view for flagged items.

- ✔ **Moderate Communities Files:** Allows moderators to review flagged files that they have access to and take subsequent action.

Moderators can be employees within your organization or external users who are members of your community. Regardless of whether the Allow Members to Flag Content feature is enabled, moderators will have the ability to flag inappropriate content and take action to delete that content.

You can assign these permissions in two ways:

- ✔ **Profiles:** Enable the moderation permissions at the profile level for the users you want to select as community moderators. From Setup, choose Manage Users ➪ Profiles and click Edit next to the profile you want to enable the permissions for.

  If you enable the permissions at the profile level, this will enable all users who are assigned that profile and are members of your community to moderate that community. If you want to limit the number of users who can moderate your community further, you should use Permission Sets.

- ✔ **Permission Sets:** Enable the permissions for a Permission Set that you can then assign to the individual user. From Setup, choose Manage Users ➪ Permission Sets and click Edit next to the Permission Set you want to enable the permissions for.

Educating your users about communities

Whether Communities are brand new to your organization or you already have published communities, educating your users on the basics of Communities is extremely important to ensuring a successful and vibrant community. The bare essentials for your users should include how to navigate to Communities, how to reset passwords, and how to conduct searches in Communities.

Navigating to communities

Navigating in and out of Communities is an important skill for any user to have. All users access Communities using the menu on the left side of the global header, shown in Figure 15-8. This menu provides different options for the following users:

- **Internal users:** Allows users to switch between communities and your internal organization. Internal users who are not members of any communities will simply see your company name displayed.

- **External users:** Allows users to switch between various communities that they're a part of. External users who are only part of one community will see only the name of that community.

Resetting external users' passwords

When you invite partners or customers to a new community, make sure you educate them on how to reset their passwords. You can reduce overhead for your administrators by ensuring that external users can reset their own passwords.

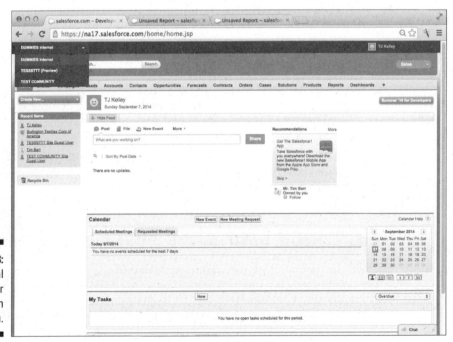

Figure 15-8:
The global header navigation menu.

An external user's password needs to be reset by the administrator or the user. Upon reset, the user will receive an email with their username and a link to your community. The user should navigate to the link where he'll need to reset his password before entering the community.

Searching in communities

Be sure to educate your users on how search behavior in Communities is different from the way it is in your internal organization. The search behavior differs in the following ways:

✔ Searches return matches from within the community you're signed into and not from the entire organization.

✔ Search results display information made available to users by profiles and permission sets even if the information is not set to display in the community.

✔ Searches for records and files display all results the user has access to across the entire organization, including all communities the user is a member of.

✔ Searches with the All Fields option selected only query the following fields:

- Name

- Username

- User ID

- Body

- Email

- Phone

- Custom fields

✔ Administrators must enable search result filters for an object from the internal organization.

Integrating your community

If you've already published communities, consider enabling further integrations in your community to optimize the collaborative space you have set up for your employees, partners, and/or customers.

Using Chatter Answers in your community

If your organization uses Chatter in your communities, Chatter Answers could be a very useful integration to allow users to post questions and receive answers and comments from other members of the community.

Follow these steps to enable Chatter Answers in your community:

1. **From Setup, choose Customize ⇨ Chatter Answers ⇨ Settings.**

2. **Click Edit and click the Chatter Answers check box.**

3. **Click Save.**

4. **Validate that your community members have access to Questions and Data Categories in your organization.**

   You can ensure that users have access to Questions by selecting the Read, Create, Edit, and Delete permissions for the Questions object on their profiles.

   You can ensure that users have access to Data Categories by click the View Data Categories check box at the profiles level.

5. **Create a zone for Chatter Answers in your community by following these steps:**

   1. From Setup, choose Customize ⇨ Chatter Answers ⇨ Zones.

   2. Click New.

   3. Create a new zone by selecting Community in the Show In box and choosing the community you would like to enable Chatter Answers for from the Community box.

   4. Click Save.

6. **Add the Q&A tab to your community.**

   1. From Setup, choose Customize ⇨ Communities ⇨ Manage Communities.

   2. Click Edit next to the community that you want to add Chatter Answers to.

   3. Click Tabs & Pages.

   4. Add the Q&A tab to the Selected Tabs box.

   5. Click Save.

   6. Click Close.

7. **Make the Q&A tab visible for profiles that you want to have access to Chatter Answers.**

   1. From Setup, choose Manage Users ⇨ Profiles and click Edit next to the profile(s) you want to give access to.

   2. Set the Q&A tab to Default On.

   3. Click Save.

Displaying Knowledge in your community

If your organization has already implemented Salesforce Knowledge, you should consider displaying Knowledge articles in your communities to make the collective knowledge of your organization available to external users as well as internal ones.

To enable Salesforce Knowledge in your communities, follow these steps:

1. **Clone the Customer Community User or Partner Community User profile.**

   Creating new profiles for knowledge users will allow you to easily manage your knowledge users separately from other users in your organization.

   1. From Setup, choose Manage Users ⇨ Profiles and click Clone next to the profile you want to clone.

   2. Enter a new Profile Name

   3. Click Save.

      The profile's detail page appears.

   4. Click Edit.

   5. Scroll down to the Article Type Permissions section of the page, and select the Read permission for article types you want to share with your community.

   6. Under the Tab Settings section of the page, ensure that the Articles (or Knowledge) tab is set to Default On.

2. **Add the Articles (or Knowledge) tab to each community.**

   Refer to Chapter 14 to find out how to add the Articles (or Knowledge) tab to each community.

3. **Educate users who create new articles that they need to select Customer Portal or Partner Portal as a channel option when creating or modifying articles.**

   This is the only way to ensure that new articles will be published in communities.

Part VI
Measuring Contact Center Performance

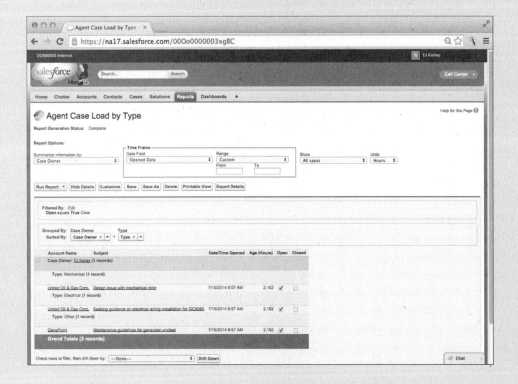

In this part . . .

✔ Measure your support organization's effectiveness.

✔ Create your own custom reporting.

✔ Use custom report features to dig deeper into your data.

✔ Plan, design, and create your dashboards to track key performance indicators for yourself, your team, or your organization.

Chapter 16

Understanding Key Salesforce Contact Center Reports

....

In This Chapter

▶ Finding the Reports home page

▶ Understanding the Reports home page

▶ Reporting on common case and agent metrics

▶ Tracking the success of your knowledge base

....

As any data guru will tell you, what gets tracked gets better, but as any bloodhound will tell you, tracking is hard work! Fortunately for you, Salesforce Service Cloud has standard support reports readily available for your use so that you can begin tracking support activity immediately.

In this chapter, we show you how to navigate reports in Salesforce so you can find what you're looking for. Then we introduce you to some of the most common reports to track your support organization's performance. Finally, we take a quick look at some very helpful reports for Salesforce Knowledge.

Navigating the Reports Home Page

The Reports tab is your starting point whether you want to create a report, view an existing report, or organize your reports. When you click into the Reports tab, as shown in Figure 16-1, you find the following:

> ✔ **A list of recently viewed reports:** The center of the page displays recently viewed reports. You can use the search bar at the top of the page where it says, "Find reports and dashboards . . ." to search for individual reports and dashboards.

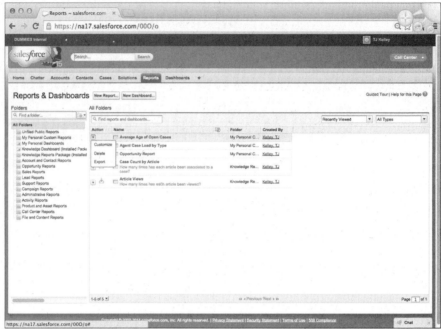

Figure 16-1:
The Reports
home page.

Next to each report name listed, you see a small downward-facing arrow. If you click this arrow, you get a drop-down menu, shown in Figure 16-1, which allows you to customize, delete, or export the report.

You also find drop-down filters at the top-right of the page where you can filter the results displayed to show all items, items you created, or recently viewed items. You can also select to see exclusively reports or dashboards if you want.

✔ **A scrolling sidebar on the left side of the page:** This sidebar displays all Report & Dashboard folders visible to you. You can also use the search bar at the top of this sidebar to search for a folder by name. Just to the right of this search bar, you find a small folder icon. This is a drop-down menu that allows you to create new folders for custom reports and dashboards.

Salesforce has a set of standard reports that are commonly used to measure business across sales, marketing, support, and other business functions. For example, you find a folder titled "Support Reports" that contains common reports for service organizations.

✔ **A New Report button at the top of the page:** Click this button to create new reports (see Chapter 17).

✔ **A New Dashboard button at the top of the page:** Click this button to create new dashboards (see Chapter 18).

Leveraging Common Support Reports

You can use reports within Salesforce to track innumerable support metrics such as the number of cases created, the history of cases (for example, important field changes), case comments, case emails, and many more.

In order to get you jumpstarted using Service Cloud reports, we show you how to quickly leverage some of the most common support reports that already exist so you can begin tracking your agents from day one.

The rest of this chapter explains common support reports and shows how you can create them. If you're unfamiliar with some of the concepts and actions described to create and customize these reports, refer to Chapter 17. For additional information, you can also refer to *Salesforce.com For Dummies*, 5th Edition, by Tom Wong, Liz Kao, and Matt Kaufman (Wiley).

Agent Case Load by Type

Track your team's workload or bandwidth with a simple Agent Case Load by Type report. Whether you're expecting agents to assign themselves to cases from a queue, assigning cases manually to your team, or using assignment logic, you can leverage this report to get a quick understanding of each agent's workload in addition to the types of cases they're working.

To create an Agent Case Load by Case Type report, follow these steps:

1. **Click the Reports tab.**

2. **In the sidebar, click the Support Reports folder.**

   A list of reports in this folder appears in the main panel.

3. **Click Total Open Cases by Agent.**

4. **Click Customize.**

5. **Change the Range filter to All Time or to a different interval to meet your needs.**

6. **Click Show, and select Details.**

7. **Add any columns you want to see in the report and add the Type field as a row.**

   To add columns, you can drag and drop fields into the Report Preview section. For more detailed information on building reports, refer to Chapter 17.

  8. **Click Save in the top-left corner.**

  9. **Select a Report Name and Folder for your report and click Save and Run Report.**

     The report displays.

An Agent Case Load by Type report should ultimately look like the report shown in Figure 16-2.

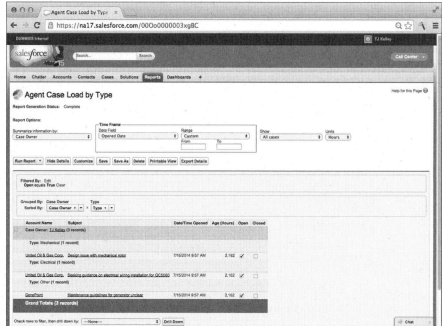

Figure 16-2: An Agent Case Load by Type report.

Average Age of Open Cases

An Average Age of Open Cases report helps you measure how your team is trending against customer service-level agreements (SLAs). Use this report to easily see if your team is meeting, exceeding, or failing to meet expectations on open cases. You can create this report to display by rep, by manager, or by case type, for example, to dig further into the numbers, but let's start with a simple Average Age of Open Cases report.

To create an Average Age of Open Cases report, follow these steps:

1. **Click the Reports tab.**

2. **In the sidebar, click the Support Reports folder.**

3. **Click Total Open Cases by Agent.**

4. **Click Customize.**

5. **Change the Range filter to All Time or to a different interval to meet your needs.**

6. **Click Show, and select Details.**

7. **Add any additional columns you want to see in the report and remove the Case Owner row by clicking the row and dragging it to the sidebar.**

8. **Hover over the right side of the Age column and click the downward-facing arrow shown in Figure 16-3.**

9. **Click Summarize This Field and click the Average check box.**

10. **Click Apply.**

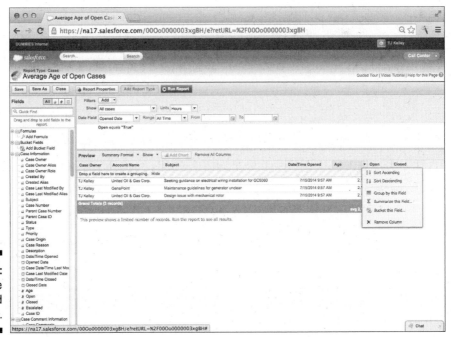

Figure 16-3:
Summarize
the Age field
by Average.

11. Click Save in the top-left corner.

12. Select a Report Name and Folder for your report and click Save and Run Report.

    The report displays.

Average Case Age by Agent (Closed)

Use an Average Case Age by Agent report to understand how productive each agent is. Particularly if you're comparing agents who work on similar cases, this is an excellent way to understand who your fastest agents are.

To create an Average Case Age by Agent for closed cases, follow these steps:

1. Click the Reports tab.

2. In the sidebar, click the Support Reports folder.

3. Click Total Open Cases by Agent.

4. Click Customize.

5. Change the Range filter to All Time or to a different interval to meet your needs.

6. Click Show, and select Details.

7. Add any columns you want to see in the report and add the Type field as a row.

   To add columns, you can drag and drop fields into the Report Preview section. For more detailed information on building reports, refer to Chapter 17.

8. Hover over the Open equals True filter and click Remove.

9. Drag the Closed field into the filter section and set Closed equals True as the new filter.

10. Hover over the right-hand side of the Age column and click the downward-facing arrow (refer to Figure 16-3).

11. Click Summarize This Field and click the Average check box.

12. Click Apply.

13. Click Save in the top-left corner.

14. Select a Report Name and Folder for your report and click Save and Run Report.

    The report displays.

Popular Knowledge Articles

If you've implemented Salesforce Knowledge and are currently leveraging articles in your organization, you can report on the effectiveness of your articles. A Popular Knowledge Articles report can show you the articles that are viewed the most across all your channels. Use this information to help you proactively manage your articles by updating frequently viewed articles with new information and archiving unused articles.

In order to create the following Knowledge reports, you need to download and install the Knowledge Base Dashboards and Reports app from the AppExchange, a marketplace for business applications created for the Salesforce community. You can access the AppExchange at `https://appexchange.salesforce.com`.

To create a Popular Knowledge Articles report, follow these steps:

1. **Download and install the Knowledge Base Dashboards and Reports app from the AppExchange.**

2. **Click the Reports tab.**

3. **In the sidebar, click the Knowledge Reports Package folder.**

4. **Click the Article Views report.**

5. **Click Save As.**

6. **Select a Report Name and Report Folder and click Save & Return to Report.**

   The report displays.

Top Articles Associated with Cases

The Top Articles Associated with Cases report allows you to quickly identify the articles that are used most often by your support agents. Use this data to identify the information, article types, and article-type templates that are used most often. This may indicate that this type of content and format is the most useful for your team and your customers and you can use that information to create similar content or to prioritize popular articles for scheduled updates to ensure the content remains up to date.

To create a Top Articles Associated with Cases report, follow these steps:

1. **Download and install the Knowledge Base Dashboards and Reports app from the AppExchange.**

   Refer to the "Using the Salesforce AppExchange to Measure Your Call Center" web article at www.dummies.com/extras/ salesforceservicecloud for more information on how to use the AppExchange. If you experience any issues or errors while attempting to download and install the app, you should contact your administrator for assistance.

2. **Click the Reports tab.**

3. **In the sidebar, click the Knowledge Reports Package folder.**

4. **Click the Case Count by Article report.**

5. **Click Save As.**

6. **Select a Report Name and Report Folder and click Save & Return to Report.**

   The report displays.

Chapter 17

Customizing Reports

. . . .

In This Chapter

▶ Customizing existing reports

▶ Filtering your dataset

▶ Zooming in or out on your data

▶ Creating your own custom reports

. . . .

A ny Salesforce user — from the CEO with years of experience to the new support agent with one day on the job — should know the basics of Salesforce reports. Becoming familiar with the reporting platform and the various ways you can manipulate report criteria will empower you to get the data you need when you need it. With just a basic tutorial on Salesforce reports, you'll never again be dependent on others to find the data that matters to you.

In this chapter, we take you step-by-step through the process of building your own custom report from scratch. Next, we show you how you can quickly change an existing report to display new data or to change the format. Finally, we show you some of the filtering and display options available for reports that enable you to work with your data on the fly.

Building a Report from Scratch

The first step to becoming self-sufficient with reports is to learn how to build your own with the Report Builder. Don't worry— it's not rocket science. Anyone who takes the time to read this section will be able to create his or her own report in just a few minutes.

To create a new report from scratch, follow these steps:

1. Click the Reports tab and click New Report.

The Create New Report page appears.

2. Select the type of report you want to create, and click Create.

Choose the basic category you want to report on first (for example, Opportunities or Leads) and click the plus sign to expand the menu. Next, select the specific report type you want to create. After you click Create, the Report Builder window appears.

3. Now you can customize your report using the following features as shown in Figure 17-1:

- *Filters pane:* Displays in the top section of the page above the Preview pane. Change the view to show just records you own, ones that you and your team own, or all records you're able to see in the system. Set the time frame of the report. Add any custom filters using the Add drop-down menu.

- *Fields pane:* Displays in the sidebar on the side of the page. Drag and drop fields into the Preview pane, and place them where you want to create a new report column. Additionally, you can drag fields from the Fields pane into the Filter pane to further filter the types of records you want to return.

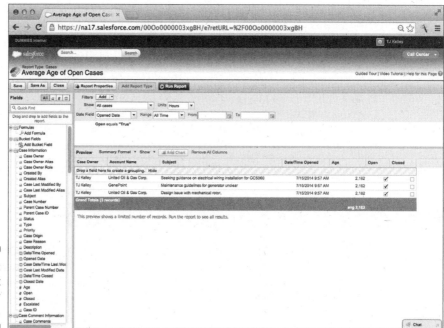

Figure 17-1:
The Report
Builder
window.

- *Preview pane:* Displays in the center of the page beneath the Filters pane and covers the vast majority of page real estate. Use the Preview pane to assess any changes you're making to the report before saving. The Preview pane changes dynamically as you add new columns, change your filters, edit the timeframe, and so on.

4. **In the Preview pane, choose a format for your report.**

   You can select from the following formats:

   - *Tabular:* Provides a basic, tabular view of your data, similar to a spreadsheet.

   - *Summary:* Enables you to expand from a tabular report by adding row groups, subtotals, and charts.

   - *Matrix:* Enables both vertical and horizontal groupings. Use matrix reports if you're trying to compare related totals, particularly if you have a large amount of data.

   - *Joined:* Groups different report types together, as long as they can be linked by a common field.

   If you choose to use Summary or Matrix reports, you can create your horizontal and vertical groupings by dragging and dropping the fields you want to group the report by from the Fields pane on the left side of the page.

5. **Add a chart to your report.**

   If you've selected a Summary or Matrix report, you can add a chart to your report. Click the Add Chart button if you want to add one and choose a chart type. Use the Chart Data tab to select how you want to display your data. Use the Formatting tab to add chart titles and change the appearance or positioning of your chart.

   For more information on the types of charts you can leverage, refer to Chapter 18. You can dig deeper into report customization in *Salesforce.com For Dummies,* 5th Edition, by Tom Wong, Liz Kao, and Matt Kaufman (Wiley).

6. **Summarize fields.**

   To summarize a field, follow these steps:

   1. Hover over the column header of your reports until you see a downward-facing arrow appear.

   2. Click the arrow to access a drop-down menu.

   3. Click Summarize This Field.

   4. Select how you would like to summarize the field.

      You can choose any combination of Sum, Average, Max, or Min.

   5. Click Apply.

7. **Sort information by a column in your report.**

   To sort your report by specific columns, follow these steps:

   1. Hover over the column header until you see a downward-facing arrow.

   2. Click the arrow to access a drop-down menu.

   3. Click Sort Ascending or Sort Descending according to your preference.

8. **Click Save.**

   A window appears to save the report. Choose a name and folder for your report.

   In the Description field, we recommend that you enter a question or additional detail about the report to help you remember the purpose of the report.

9. **Click Save and Run Report.**

   The report saves, runs, and displays on the page.

Modifying Existing Reports

The quickest way to get started with reports is to find a report that you already like using and customize it to fit your needs. For example, if you have a Support Cases by Type report, and you want to see the open cases by week, you can work off the existing report to save time.

To customize an existing report, navigate to the Reports tab, find the report you want to build off of, click the report name, and follow these steps:

1. **Click the Customize button.**

   The report opens in the Report Builder.

2. **Use the Filters pane, the Fields pane, and the Preview pane to make your desired adjustments to the report.**

   You can drag and drop new rows or columns into your report, add or edit filters, and adjust the timeframe of your report.

3. **Select a new format for your report if that is your desired change.**

4. **Optionally, add a chart if you've selected a Summary or Matrix report.**

5. **Click Save As when you're finished making adjustments.**

   A new window pops up to save the report.

6. **Select a name and folder for your report and click Save and Run Report.**

   The report saves and displays.

Sifting through Reports

Remember that slideshow of childhood pictures your mom shows to family friends? Do you find yourself wishing you could filter yourself out of it at a moment's notice and leave your siblings up on the screen without ruining your mom's hard work? No problem — for Salesforce reports anyway. With a number of different ways to quickly adjust data without creating new reports, Salesforce provides you with the flexibility you need to make changes on the fly.

Using the Drill Down feature

While viewing an existing report, you can filter selected rows by a particular field. For example, if you're viewing a Total Open Cases by Agent report, you could select an individual agent, or multiple agents, and filter their cases by another field (for example, status). To select rows, you need to click the check box on the left side of the page. In this example, shown in Figure 17-2, scroll down to the end of the report until you see the Check Rows to Filter, Then Drill Down By picklist. Choose an option that you want to further group your findings by, and click the Drill Down button.

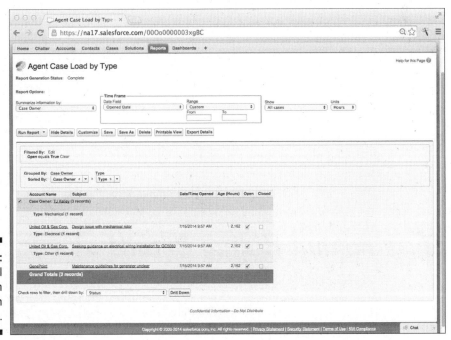

Figure 17-2:
The Drill Down feature on reports.

Setting your report options

You can also quickly change the report options while viewing a report and run the report to display the new results. This will not overwrite your existing report.

At the top of every report, you can change the following report options:

- ✔ **Summarize Information By:** Change the summary rows of the report on the fly. For example, if you're viewing a report by case owner, you can quickly change it to view by case opened date without overwriting the report.

- ✔ **Time Frame:** Change the time frame to view a specific subset of the records you're viewing.

- ✔ **Show:** Change the view to show a subset of the data type you're viewing or show all.

After you change the Report Options, you must click Run Report to refresh the results.

Clearing filters

Another immediately responsive feature of Salesforce reports are the filters. If you've applied a filter to a report and saved it, you can remove the filter while viewing your report to view a larger set of data. For example, if you had created an open support case report for a specific product, you could quickly clear that filter to view all products instead without saving over your original report. This enables you to work off of a single report and analyze multiple datasets without searching through to find three or four different reports. When you're finished, you only need to refresh the page to go back to your original report.

To clear a filter, find the Filtered By section of the report to view your filters and simply click the Clear link (refer to Figure 17-2) next to the filter you want to get rid of and the report results will automatically refresh.

Showing and Hiding Details

When working in a fast-paced environment with large amounts of data, it can be hard to get a quick, easy view of the data that you need in order to make decisions and drive business outcomes. Salesforce reports allow you to hide the details of a report so that you can see the necessary information at a glance when you're in a rush. If you have a more analytical mind, or finally have the time to sit down and dig through the details, you can easily choose to expose those details on the page and dig in.

To show or hide details on a report, click the Show Details or Hide Details button. You can find this button below the Report Options section of the report.

You can choose to show or hide details in the Report Builder at the top of the Preview pane. This will allow you to save a report with the details showing or hidden depending on the target audience of the report.

Chapter 18

Building Contact Center Dashboards

In This Chapter

▶ Diving into dashboards

▶ Understanding the underlying data

▶ Getting familiar with component types

▶ Planning a purposeful and outcome-driven dashboard

▶ Creating and modifying your dashboards

▶ Saving and accessing analytics

*S*alesforce dashboards empower your organization with fully customizable visualizations and analytics. With a simple and intuitive construction platform that is available to all users, your organization can build dashboards to view key performance indicators across the business.

With the ability to view real-time information, spot trends, and drill down into the details, Salesforce dashboards enable every level of your organization to see warning signs, identify causal factors, and make important decisions quickly to adjust and guide the business in the right direction.

In this chapter, we help you understand what exactly a dashboard is and how you can construct one. We walk you through the various types of information that you can display on dashboards and explain how to use each component. Finally, we show you how you can organize and file your dashboards to ensure that the intended users can access them.

Planning for Dashboards

Salesforce dashboards are a collection of reports that have been set up to populate various charts, tables, and metrics in order to enable quick analysis of performance and improve response times to trends and warnings in the business.

Each dashboard is made up of a maximum of 20 components. A component of a Salesforce dashboard is exactly what it sounds like: a piece of the overall puzzle. A dashboard must have a reason for existing, and each component is a small contributing factor to that. For example, if you create a dashboard for a customer support manager to monitor his or her team, there should not be a single component that does not aid the manager in evaluating the team's performance or current workload.

When you create a dashboard, whether you're an administrator, a manager, or a front-line agent, make sure that you have an end goal in mind for the eventual use of the dashboard. For example, you may want to create a simple dashboard for an individual agent to monitor his caseload. Making this decision upfront will help guide the reports and components you choose to create.

Understanding how source reports feed components

Recall that components are each an individual piece of a dashboard (for example, a chart or a table). Dashboard components have a one-to-one relationship with reports in Salesforce. In other words, each component has a single related report that supplies the underlying data for the visualization created on the dashboard. The data found in the underlying report is the only set of data that will be available to feed or display in the component that it relates to.

We go over some specific reports in Chapter 16, and we review how to create reports in Chapter 17.

Discovering the component options

Salesforce dashboards allow you to create the following component types:

✔ **Chart:** Chart components are best leveraged when you need to display your reports in a graph to enable more efficient analysis. The following chart types are available for dashboards:

- *Bar:* Uses horizontal bars to display data and can be particularly useful when comparing time. For example, you could look at the average case time by case type to understand which types of support cases require more or less work.

- *Column:* Similar to a bar chart, but uses vertical columns to display data. Use column charts to compare single groups of data. For example, You could display the number of support cases by issue type to view your most common support issues.

- *Line:* Best for viewing changes in values over a series of important points. For example, day-to-day or even hour-to-hour comparisons of the number of support cases created may help you determine your busiest and most important hours or days of the week.

- *Pie:* Select a pie chart to show the proportional value of a grouped set of data. This would be another great way to view cases by issue type in order to gain a view of the proportion of certain issues as compared to the total volume of cases.

- *Donut:* Choose donut charts if you want to show proportional values for each group of a dataset, as well as the total amount of the grouping. Using the example of cases by issue type, a donut chart would show you the proportion of each issue type, as well as the total number of cases.

- *Funnel:* Use funnel charts if you have groupings of data that progress in a particular order. For example, you could display the total number of cases by status (for example, New, Working, Escalated, Closed, and so on). This would show you the proportional value of each status in your support process.

- *Scatter:* Leverage scatter charts to compare two sets of data and draw your own conclusions. For example, you could use a scatter chart to see the correlation between first call resolutions and days of the week to see if your team is more productive at certain times of the week — or if they're just slacking on Fridays!

✓ **Gauge:** Gauge components should be used to display a range of values against a single, selected value. A gauge component is very useful to show progress towards a predetermined goal. If your support agents are expected to close a certain number of cases per week or month, you could set up a dashboard component to display each agent's progress toward the goal. For example, you could set a minimum of 0, breakpoints at 5 and 15, and a Maximum at 30. This gauge would quickly show you if an agent has fewer than five cases closed, is on her way to ten cases closed, or has more than ten (see Figure 18-1).

✓ **Metric:** Leverage metric components when you have a single, key value that you want to view. For example, if you want to have a simple snapshot of the total number of open support cases, you can use a metric component to display the value on your dashboard.

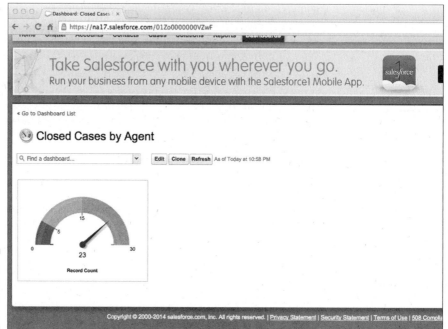

Figure 18-1:
An example
of a gauge
component.

✔ **Table:** Choose table components when you need to view your data in columns. For example, you could view a table with a ranking of support agents or teams with columns for total cases open, total cases closed, and total cases escalated. The values available as columns are the fields used as groupings and report summary fields in the underlying report that feeds the component.

✔ **Visualforce Page:** Only use a Visualforce page if you want to create a custom component. A good use case for a Visualforce component would be if you want to display information from an external system on your dashboard.

Planning a purpose for each component

As you plan and create dashboards in your organization, keep in mind the one cardinal rule: Every component needs to have a specific purpose. Each and every chart, table, gauge, or metric that you choose to place on a dashboard should have intent behind it.

For example, if a customer support agent is looking at a table of his open cases, do you just want him to look at it and be aware that he has six open cases? No, of course not. You want the component to drive a specific action. In this case, you want the support agent to follow up on each of his open cases and resolve them.

If you create a component without a desired outcome or behavior that you want to drive in mind, the component may as well be deleted. Think through your components carefully and make sure you know why they're taking up real estate on the page. Train users of the dashboard to drive the behavior or action you desire.

Creating a Dashboard for Your Contact Center

Dashboards are essential tools in any Salesforce environment to help your organization monitor and manage the business from top to bottom. Whether you're creating your first dashboard or coming back for seconds, you can use this section to get started.

To kick off the process to create a dashboard, follow these steps:

1. **Navigate to the Reports tab.**

   The Reports home page, shown in Figure 18-2, appears.

2. **Click the New Dashboard button located next to the New Report button (refer to Figure 18-2).**

   A dashboard page displays in edit mode (see Figure 18-3). Note that there are three columns displaying. Dashboards always begin with three columns, which you can use to organize your components, but more on that later.

   You can optionally delete columns by clicking the X at the top of each column. You can also add those columns back using the plus signs in between columns.

   You can adjust the width of each column by clicking the drop-down menu where you see the word *Medium* at the top of each column.

You may want to adjust the width of your columns depending on the components you create. For example, if you create a table component with four columns, it may make sense to set the Dashboard column width to Wide to accommodate the large table.

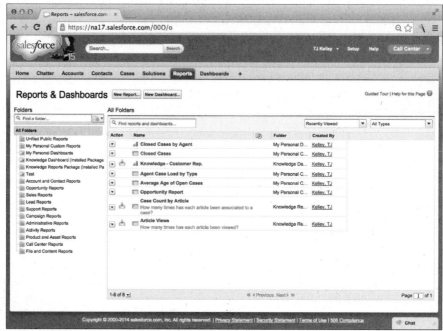

Figure 18-2:
The Reports
home page.

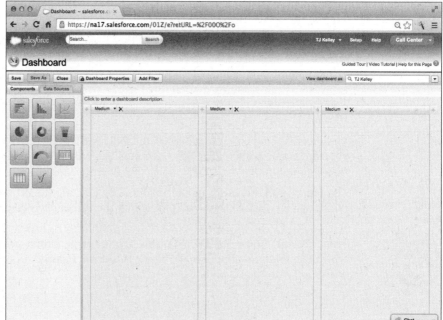

Figure 18-3:
The
dashboard
edit page.

3. **Optionally, enter a dashboard description in the text box at the top of the page just beneath the Dashboard Properties button.**

   Dashboard descriptions can help you remember what purpose your dashboard serves and inform other users of that purpose.

4. **In the top-right corner of the edit page, click the View Dashboard As drop-down that displays your name initially.**

   A small pop-up window appears (see Figure 18-4).

   You have two options to select for what is known as the Dashboard's Running User. The Running User, as explained in the pop-up window, determines the point of view from which users will see the data when they visit this dashboard.

   Here are your options:

   • **Run As Specified User:** This option dictates that you must select a specific user as the running user. Choose this option if you want any user who accesses the dashboard to see the exact same view or set of data.

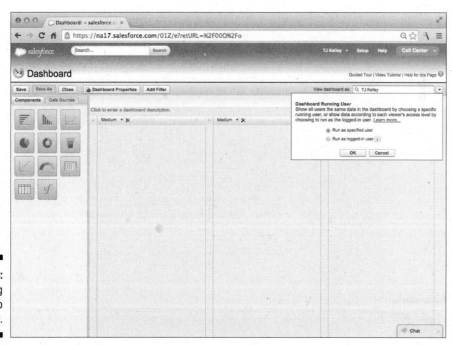

• **Run As Logged-In User:** This option means that the dashboard will display data to the visiting user based on his individual security rights in the system. Choose this option if you want the dashboard to display data dynamically or various sets of users with differing security rights.

This is a great option if you have a dashboard set up for a group of managers, because it can allow each user to view his or her own team's data.

Now that you have the basics down on the edit page for dashboards, read through the following sections to understand how to set the dashboard properties, add helpful components, and format the layout to meet your needs.

Editing dashboard properties

To edit the dashboard properties, follow these steps:

1. **From the edit page shown in Figure 18-3, click the Dashboard Properties button at the top of the page.**

    The Dashboard Properties window, shown in Figure 18-5, appears.

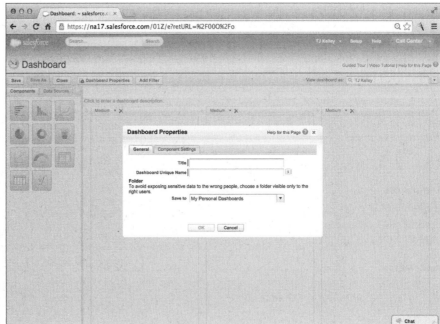

Figure 18-5:
The
Dashboard
Properties
window.

2. **On the displayed tab, titled General, select a title and unique name for your dashboard.**

3. **Select a dashboard folder to save this dashboard in.**

   Read on for information on how to create dashboard folders and how to leverage them to organize your dashboards.

4. **Optionally, click the Component Settings tab to make aesthetic changes to your dashboard.**

   The Component Settings will apply to every single component on your dashboard. You have the following options:

   - Title Color
   - Title Size
   - Text Color
   - Background Fade Direction
   - Starting Color
   - Ending Color

5. **Click OK.**

   The Dashboard Properties window closes and you remain on the dashboard edit page.

Next, you need to fill in the blanks by turning the underlying data into useful and purposeful visualizations to display on your dashboard.

Creating a component

Now, it's time for the critical component of every dashboard: the components!

To create a dashboard component, follow these steps:

1. **On the dashboard edit page, shown in Figure 18-3, locate the Components tab in the column on the left side of the page.**

   The Components tab displays by default.

2. **Choose the Component Type that you want to build, and drag it into one of the three columns of the edit page.**

   After you drag and drop a component type into one of your dashboard columns, the new component will display with the component type listed at the top.

   We review all the available component type options earlier in this chapter.

   Figure 18-6 displays this view with three components added.

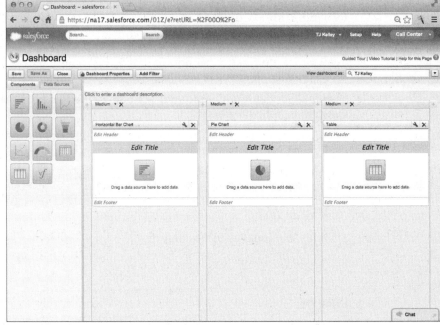

Figure 18-6:
The dashboard with three new component types added.

3. **Click the Edit Header box to add a header for your component.**

   In addition to the text entered in this box, headers also display a horizontal bar across the dashboard column and can serve to create segments or sections within a dashboard column. For example, if you add a header to the first component in a column and display a number of related components without headers beneath that, the header will seem to create a section within the column.

4. **Click in the gray segment that says Edit Title to choose a title for your component.**

   Choose a title that informs users of the purpose of the component. For example, instead of choosing a generic title like Cases, make the title more specific. Examples of more specific titles include Open Cases, Closed Cases, and Escalated Cases.

5. **Click in the box at the bottom of the component that says Edit Footer to add footer text to the component.**

   The footer is an excellent place for supplemental information. You can leverage the footer to ask a hypothetical question that the component answers (for example, "How many cases did my team close this week?"). You can also use the footer to further describe what the Chart, Gauge, Metric, or Table displays. For example, if you have a particularly complex bar chart with values being tracked on the *x*- and *y*-axes, you could add detail about each in the footer to ensure visitors to the dashboard understand what they're seeing.

6. **Select a Data Source for the component.**

In the column on the left side of the page, click the Data Sources tab. This brings up a search section for reports, which you use as the data source or underlying report for your component, as described earlier in this chapter.

The search section, shown in Figure 18-7, allows you to easily find the reports you're looking for.

You can use the tabs at the top of the section to filter the displayed results to your most recently viewed reports, reports that you personally created, or all reports in the system that you have security access to view.

When you select a filter option, you can search for reports in two ways:

- *Quickfind:* You can use the search bar at the top of the section to dynamically search for reports by name.

- *Manual Search:* You can expand and collapse the sections to search through report folders and the contained reports to find the one you're looking for.

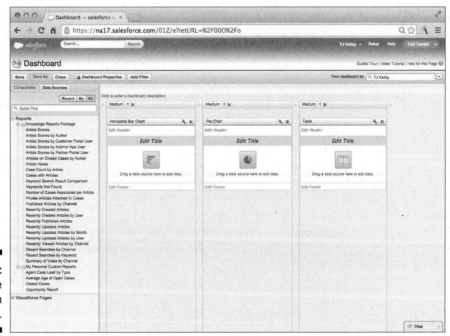

Figure 18-7:
Data source
search in
the sidebar.

You can't save a dashboard if you have an existing component on the page without a data source. As a best practice for creating dashboards, plan to create all the reports you want to leverage and display prior to creating the dashboard. You can create all the reports in advance and save them in the same folder to ensure that you're ready to create each and every component of your dashboard.

Modifying the layout

When you have your components in place, it's important to consider the layout and structure of those components. From the dashboard edit page, you can drag and drop components between columns or up and down columns as you wish.

Place components that share related information or metrics that are likely to be used in conjunction with one another close together on your dashboard. This makes it easy for users to navigate the page and allows their eyes to move intuitively from one piece of information to the next.

As with anything in life, users will have differing opinions on how to create the most efficient layout for a multitude of metrics and charts. Here are a few additional tips for how you might choose to organize a dashboard layout:

- ✔ **Place the most important and most commonly used components at the top of the dashboard.** This saves users time scrolling down the page for the components they want to view most frequently.

- ✔ **If your components tell a story or build off of each other, select a left-to-right or top-to-bottom orientation for the components and keep it consistent as you create additional dashboards.** This allows other users of the dashboards to get used to reading the components in a particular order.

- ✔ **Create sections on your dashboard by leveraging the component headers.** When you enter a component header, a red horizontal bar will appear above the component and can function as a visual separator on the page, creating a section of components within a column.

- ✔ **Always be sure that each component has a relevant purpose on the dashboard.** For example, it may not make sense to place a marketing campaign return on investment (ROI) component on a customer support dashboard.

Organizing Your Dashboards

If you've ever had the experience of painstakingly searching for a file on your computer — let's face it, you have — then you understand the need for a clean, clear system of organization for your files. The same holds true for Salesforce dashboards.

This may seem like a very simple concept, but it's also easy to neglect and find yourself scrolling through a list of thousands of dashboards trying to remember what you named that one dashboard about the things and the important metrics. You know, it was called . . . what was it again?

Fortunately, Salesforce has a native organizational system in place. Dashboard folders work similarly to any folder system you may have used on a personal computer. You can create folders and define access to those folders, in order to ensure only specific teams or roles have access to view the information.

Building dashboard folders

Dashboard folders afford you the flexibility to create containers for dashboards specific to particular groups by using naming conventions to drive users to the correct folders (for example, Executive Dashboards, Management Dashboards, Regional Dashboards, and so on).

To create a dashboard folder, follow these steps:

1. **Navigate to the Reports tab.**
2. **Locate the Find a Folder search bar and click the drop-down menu marked by an image of a folder to the right of the search bar.**
3. **Click New Dashboard Folder.**

   New Dashboard Folder edit page appears.
4. **Select a folder label and a unique name for your folder and click Save.**

   The Reports home page displays.

Defining dashboard access

Selecting a specific level of access for dashboard folders can be immensely useful. Narrowing the number of users who have access to a particular folder can help you be more selective with sensitive or private information.

Additionally, hiding folders for users if they contain irrelevant information for a specific role or group can ensure that searching for dashboards does not become a cumbersome process.

To define a specific level of access for your dashboard folders, follow these steps:

1. **Navigate to the Reports tab.**

2. **Locate the Find a Folder search bar, and search for the folder you want to share.**

3. **Hover over the folder name until you see an image of a pin appear to the right of the name. Click the pin drop-down and select Share.**

   As shown in Figure 18-8, a new window pops up with sharing options.

4. **Choose from among the Share With links at the top of the pop-up window to determine how you want to share the folder.**

   In our examples, we will assume you clicked the Roles link.

   A search bar appears and results are dynamically filtered as you type.

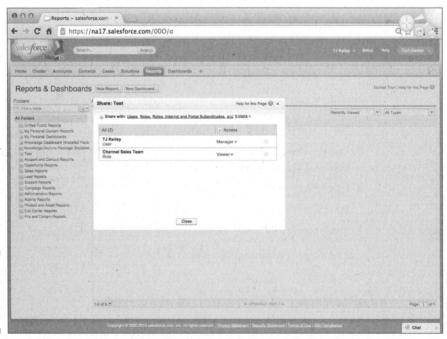

Figure 18-8:
Dashboard
sharing
options.

5. **Search for the roles that you want to share the folder with and click the Share button next to them.**

6. **Click Done when you're finished sharing with all desired roles.**

   The main sharing page on the pop-up window reappears.

7. **In the Access column, click the drop-down and select the level of access each role should have.**

   You can choose from the following access levels:

   - *Viewer:* Can View, Refresh, and Run the dashboards saved in the folder.

   - *Editor:* Same rights as viewer and can also move, edit, save, or delete the dashboards in the folder or the folder itself.

   - *Manager:* Same rights as Editor and can also rename the dashboard folder and manage sharing of the folder.

8. **When you're done, click Close.**

   Changes are saved and the popup window closes.

Part VII

Designing Your Service Solution with Force.com

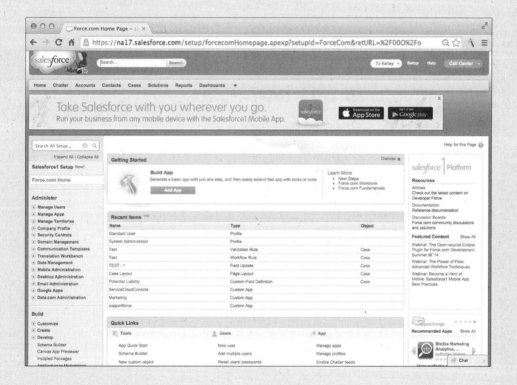

In this part . . .

✔ Get to know the administrative setup menu and configuration for your organization.

✔ Make sense of the configuration menu, its limitations, and how to plan for your organization's security structure.

✔ Discover the various elements and layers of Salesforce security, permissions, and sharing model.

✔ Get to know the foundational elements of Service Cloud configuration.

✔ Extend the power of Service Cloud with the AppExchange.

Chapter 19

Understanding the Configuration for Your Business

In This Chapter

▶ Navigating the Configuration menu

▶ Planning for configuration

▶ Verifying your corporate profile

▶ Defining the role hierarchy

▶ Developing your sharing model

▶ Setting up users and profiles

▶ Leveraging security controls

*W*hat is configuration anyway? In tech speak, *configuration* covers a range of activities, but generally refers to the arrangement of components in a system. It includes setting up certain features, customizing them, and defining parameters and values. The goal is twofold:

✔ To successfully customize a system that aligns with its users' needs while keeping ease-of-use (adoption) and scalability in mind

✔ To establish and maintain the integrity of the system and the data within it

Thankfully, Salesforce Service Cloud makes configuration simple and intuitive. Salesforce uses "clicks not code" to expedite development time and give administrators and business owners the flexibility they need to succeed. It's important to leverage as much out-of the-box configuration as possible. You can get a lot more out of Service Cloud (and save tons of money) if you resist the temptation to overbuild your system by developing and customizing everything.

In this chapter, we show you various steps to take in order to configure Service Cloud, including navigating and modifying your configuration in the system. We discuss configuration best practices and other tips for administrators to keep in mind when configuring Salesforce. We also look at a variety of security features in Salesforce that you can use together to fine-tune and control the access and visibility to your data.

Looking at Administration Setup

As mentioned earlier, configuration in Service Cloud is a way to quickly and easily toggle switches and settings to change features, permissions, setup, and your data model. All this can be easily accessed in one centralized place called the Setup menu.

If you're an administrator and you want to get to the Setup configuration menu, follow these steps:

1. **Choose Setup ⇨ Administer.**

   The Administer menu appears with your edition of Salesforce and a host of sections and links that indicate what you can accomplish from here.

2. **Toggle the arrow buttons to the left of Manage Users, Company Profile, and Security Controls under the Administer menu in the sidebar.**

   These three categories expand to show their subcategories.

These are the set of administrative configuration settings that you should review first when configuring Salesforce. For example, you can give users Service Cloud licenses under Manage Users or configure your call center's business hours.

Planning configuration for success

It's not enough to know where and how configuration is done in Salesforce. First, let's take a step back to think about some useful strategies to keep in mind in order to ensure you're as successful as possible.

As an administrator, your job is to know how Service Cloud should be configured. That means that it's not enough to know how to configure Service Cloud, technically speaking. Salesforce technical knowledge is important, especially to know its limitations to determine what is possible natively versus what requires custom code. However, another important element of the job is understanding your company's culture, size, and business processes to successfully align the technology to it.

There are many questions you need to have answered in order to plan and configure successfully. For example, a major question in any implementation revolves around sharing data. Who should see or do what? This is especially important if you're implementing Service Cloud in an organization already running Sales Cloud.

Service teams have more customer data and knowledge than any other department. Should your sales team have visibility into their account's open cases? Will this help prevent over-communication with your customers? What are other implications of that scenario for your business? Conversely, what sales data does your support team need to access in order to send customers back to sales for a renewal at the end of a support contract? Do multiple people or teams typically work on the same account or case? What should managers be able to do or see that agents shouldn't?

These are only a few examples of questions to ask before configuring Service Cloud for your business.

Viewing Your Company Profile

The Company Profile category houses basic company information settings and is the first (and perhaps easiest) step before jumping into everything else. This category allows administrators to update company information and default settings such as time zone, language, currency business hours, and holiday schedules.

Updating your company information

To update your company information, go to the Setup menu and follow these steps:

1. **Choose Administer ➪ Company Profile ➪ Company Information.**

   The Company Information page appears.

2. **Click the Edit button.**

   The Company Information page appears in edit mode, as shown in Figure 19-1. Review the fields and update as needed. Make sure the required fields are accurate:

   - *Organization Name:* Enter the name of your organization.

   - *Default Locale:* Use this picklist to select the default country or geographic region selected for new users in the organization.

The Default Locale field determines the format for date and time fields, such as 31/12/2014 versus 12/31/2014.

- *Default Language:* Use this picklist to select the default language used for text, help, and new users in the organization.

- *Default Time Zone:* Use this picklist to select the primary time zone where the organization is located, such as Headquarters.

- *Currency Locale:* Use this picklist to select the country or geographic region where the organization is located. (You won't see this field if you have the Multi-Currency feature enabled.)

You're setting company defaults, but users can still override this with their personal locale settings.

3. **Make changes as needed, and click Save when you're done.**

The Company Information page reappears and reflects your changes.

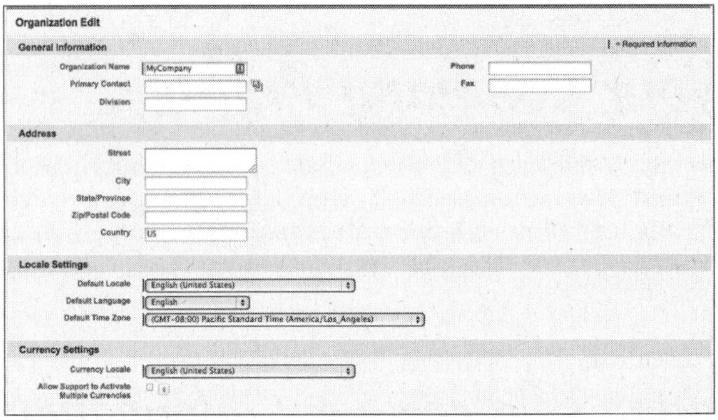

Figure 19-1:
Modifying
company
information.

Setting your organization's business hours and holidays

Under the Company Information page, you can also view the count and status of your user licenses, permission set, and feature licenses.

Two other important settings to cover are Business Hours and Holidays.

Business Hours

Business Hours are a way to specify when your support team is available for service. You can leverage Business Hours in Service Cloud to make case escalations and reporting more accurate and insightful. Business Hours are set by default to 24 hours a day, 7 days a week in your organization's default time zone.

To set Business Hours for your organization, go to the Setup menu and follow these steps:

1. **Choose Administer ⇨ Company Profile ⇨ Business Hours.**

   The Organization Business Hours page appears, with a default created.

2. **Click the New Business Hours button.**

   The Business Hours Edit page appears.

3. **Enter a name for your Business Hours.**

   Include the geographic location, to make it easier to identify later.

4. **Click the Active check box so that users can associate the business hours with cases, escalation rules, milestones, and entitlements.**

5. **Choose a time zone to associate with the hours.**

6. **Unless you're providing 24-hour support, set your Business Hours for each day.**

   Leave all the fields for a day empty (including the 24 Hours check box) to show that support isn't available that day, as shown on Sunday in Figure 19-2.

7. **Click Save when you're done.**

   The Organization Business Hours page reappears, with your newly created Business Hours in the list.

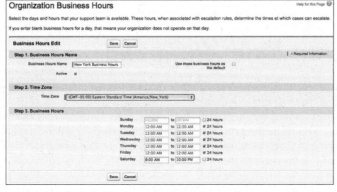

Figure 19-2: Setting your organization's Business Hours.

Holidays

Holidays work with business hours to indicate dates and times at which business hours are suspended. They're exceptions to your business hours. To set up Holidays for your organization, go to the Setup menu and follow these steps:

1. **Choose Administer ⇨ Company Profile ⇨ Holidays.**

   The Holidays page appears.

2. **Click the New button.**

   The Holidays detail page appears in edit mode.

3. **Enter a name and date for your new Holiday.**

4. **Optionally, fill out the other fields and when you're done, click Save.**

   The Holiday Detail page appears with your new holiday information and a Business Hours related list.

5. **Click the Add/Remove button on the Business Hours related to associate the Holiday to your organization's Business Hours; then click Save.**

   The Holiday detail page reappears and your Holiday is associated with your Business Hours, as shown in Figure 19-3.

Figure 19-3: Associating a Holiday to your Business Hours in Salesforce.

Building the Role Hierarchy

The first way to share access to records and reports is by defining a role hierarchy. Roles generally dictate what records and reports a user can *see* that are not owned by the user. The easiest way to think of a *role hierarchy* in Salesforce is a pared-down org chart, representing a hierarchical structure of data access that trickles down the chart. So, if you're assigned to the role at the top of the hierarchy, you have access to everyone's data.

The reason we call it a "pared-down" org chart is because the role hierarchy is not an opportunity to rebuild your org chart in Salesforce; it should be simplified. Because each level in the hierarchy represents a level of data access, plan to only build levels that require distinction. For example, just because the CEO sits above the CIO and CFO in your org chart doesn't mean you have to build a rung for each if they all tend to need access to the same types of records. Just assign them all to the CEO role in your role hierarchy.

Using the role hierarchy, a manager always has the same record access as the record owners of those he manages. For example, if you set up the hierarchy with a Support Rep role subordinate to a Support Manager role, users assigned to Support Manager have read and edit access to records owned by or shared with users in the Support Rep role.

 The Grant Access Using Hierarchies option, in the Organization-Wide Defaults related list, can be deselected for custom objects only, nullifying the significance of the role hierarchy in record access on records of that object.

To build your company's role hierarchy, go to the Setup menu and follow these steps:

1. **Choose Administer ➪ Manage Users ➪ Roles.**

   The Understanding Roles page appears with a picklist for sample hierarchies.

2. **Click the Set Up Roles button.**

   The Creating the Role Hierarchy page appears. You can use the drop-down on the right of the page to view the hierarchy in a number of ways. We use the default tree view in our steps and explanations.

3. **Click the Expand All link to expand the entire hierarchy.**

   Salesforce provides an existing sample hierarchy upon which you can add or remove roles, depending on your needs.

4. **To add a subordinate role, click the Add Role link under an existing role.**

   The New Role page appears in edit mode.

5. **Name your role in the Label field and press Tab.**

   Salesforce automatically brings the name down to the Role Name field.

6. **This Role Reports To field should be populated with the role above the role you're creating, but click the lookup icon and choose a different one if necessary; then click Save.**

   The Role Detail page appears with your new role and a related list of users assigned to it. You can click the Assign Users to Role button to do this or click the New User button to create a new user assigned to this role.

Defining Your Sharing Model

The *sharing model* in Salesforce defines the general access users have to each other's data. In contrast to the role hierarchy, the sharing model refers to a more horizontal sharing of data access. It's composed of three key configurable elements that we will discuss:

- ✔ Organization-wide defaults
- ✔ Public groups
- ✔ Sharing rules

Setting organization-wide defaults

Organization-wide defaults are the baseline of any organization's sharing model. They're used to *restrict* access and dictate the overarching, organization-wide default level of access to objects and their records. They always respect the role hierarchy; instead, they determine how those on the same level of the hierarchy see your data.

This is where you set the most restrictive model for your organization as a foundation of multiple layers of Salesforce security that work together to open up data access. In other words, even if just one individual in your organization should not see case-related data, you must set organization-wide defaults to Private on Cases and grant access back to everyone else but that single user through other means we discuss shortly.

For example, if you want your internal users to have Public Read/Write access on the Account object, but you want to set it to Private for external users, you have to go with the most restrictive option, or Private, at the organization-wide level. When it's locked down for everyone, you can then open up access to internal users by using sharing rules.

Sharing rules can only be used to grant additional access to records; they can't be used to restrict access further than what is set at the organization-wide default level.

Organization-wide defaults can be set to one of the following options:

- ✔ **Private:** This is the most restrictive option. The records are only visible to record owners and those above them in the role hierarchy.
- ✔ **Public Read Only:** The records are theoretically visible to everyone in the organization (although this may vary based on the role and profile) but are not editable by anyone but the record owner.

✔ **Public Read/Write:** The records are visible and editable organization-wide.

To set the organization-wide defaults, go to the Setup menu and follow these steps:

1. **Choose Administer ⇨ Security Controls ⇨ Sharing Settings.**

   The Sharing Settings page appears.

2. **Click the Edit button on the Organization Wide Defaults list.**

   The Organization-Wide Sharing Defaults Edit page appears.

3. **Select your desired settings for each object.**

   When in doubt, leave access generally open at first, to start with a more collaborative system and lock specific objects down as legitimate business needs surface and require it.

4. **Click Save when you're done.**

   The Sharing Settings page reappears. *Note:* It may take a while to update all records in the system with your new selections.

Creating groups

A *group* is simply a set of users. Groups can contain individual users, other groups, or roles.

There are two types of groups in Salesforce:

✔ **Public groups:** These are public sets of users that can be used by anyone in the organization, but only administrators can create them.

✔ **Personal groups:** Anyone can create a personal group for their personal use.

Here, we discuss the public group. You can use public groups with sharing rules to create exceptions to a private sharing model. Use public groups to share records with certain sets of users or groups that you specify.

To create a new public group, go to the Setup menu and follow these steps:

1. **Choose Administer ⇨ Manage Users ⇨ Public Groups.**

   The Public Groups page appears, showing you a list of your public groups.

2. **Click the New button.**

   A New Group edit page appears with empty fields.

3. **Name the group in the required Label field (and press Tab to bring it down to the Group Name field).**

   Use an intuitive name so that you and the other users in your group easily understand it.

4. **From the Search drop-down list, select users, roles, or other groups you want to search for to add to your group.**

   As you click your choice, the Available Members column will populate with a list corresponding to it.

5. **Click the user or group of users you want to add, and click the Add arrow so it moves from the Available Members column to the Selected Members column.**

   Keep doing this until you have everyone you want in your public group, as shown in Figure 19-4.

6. **Click Save when you're finished.**

   The Public Groups page reappears, and your new group now appears in the list.

Allowing further access with sharing rules

Now you can use the public groups you create with sharing rules to open up access to the users within them. You can also use sharing rules with roles, or roles and subordinates.

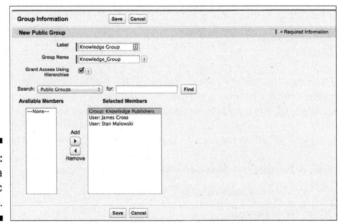

Figure 19-4:
Creating a
new public
group.

For example, if your organization-wide defaults are set to Public Read Only on Accounts, but you want to grant edit access to your call center team to update customer information, create a sharing rule to open up access to the team.

To create a sharing rule, go to the Setup menu and follow these steps:

1. **Choose Administer ⇨ Security Controls ⇨ Sharing Settings.**

   The Sharing Settings page appears.

2. **Scroll down and click the New button on any of the objects' Sharing Rules related list sections.**

   The Sharing Rule Setup page appears related to the object you chose.

   If the New button is grayed out on the lists, the system is probably recalculating sharing settings based on a recent update to organization-wide defaults.

3. **Fill in the rule information, and then use the drop-down lists to select which records you want to share and with whom.**

   In our example, grant your specific public group Read/Write privileges to all account records owned by members of the highest role and its subordinates (for example, CEO) to give edit access to all account records.

4. **When you're done, click Save.**

   The Sharing Settings page reappears with your new sharing rule in the appropriate list.

Creating and Managing Profiles

Generally speaking, where the role hierarchy determines what users *see*, profiles indicate what a user can *do*. Profiles also determine what a user can see within a certain object, as opposed to which objects. For example, profiles control a user's ability to edit an object record or a field, transfer case ownership, view the Setup menu, access the Service Cloud Console, or delete a public list view.

Reviewing standard Service Cloud profiles

If you're on Professional Edition, you won't be able to create custom profiles, so you should be familiar with the standard profiles in Salesforce. Standard profiles can't be edited (with the exception of app and tab settings). In this section, we briefly explain the standard profiles and how they're applied.

These six standard profiles are not Service Cloud–specific. They're the same as the standard profiles in Sales Cloud and may not always be relevant, but they're good to know, especially if you can't create custom profiles.

 ✔ **System Administrator:** We like to call this profile "God mode." System administrator is the most important profile because it comes with full permissions and access across all Salesforce functionality (that doesn't require a feature license). Administrators and users who play a big role in configuring the system should be assigned to this profile.

 ✔ **Standard User:** This profile can run reports, create and edit most records, and view Setup (but can't modify or configure anything).

 ✔ **Read Only:** This profile allows users to run and export reports while viewing, but not editing, most records.

 ✔ **Marketing User:** This profile comes with all the permissions of the Standard User profile, plus a variety of marketing-related permissions, such as managing campaigns and email templates, as well as importing leads.

 ✔ **Solution Manager:** This profile comes with all the permissions of the Standard User profile, plus the ability to review and publish solutions.

 ✔ **Contract Manager:** This profile can't edit anything, but it can create, edit, activate, and approve contracts. They can also delete contracts that aren't activated.

Creating custom profiles

Although standard profiles can't be modified, they can be cloned. To create custom profiles, clone existing standard profiles and modify them to align with your requirements.

To create a custom profile, go to the Setup menu and follow these steps:

 1. **Choose Administer ➪ Manage Users ➪ Profiles.**

    The User Profiles page appears with a list of them.

 2. **Click the name of a standard or existing profile that is most similar to the new profile you want to create.**

 3. **Click the Clone button.**

    The Clone Profile page appears.

 4. **Type in a name for your custom profile and click Save.**

    The Profile page for your custom profile appears.

5. **Click the Edit button to start customizing the permissions on the profile.**

   The Profile Edit page appears.

6. **Modify the apps under the Custom App Settings section to select the apps that are visible for the profile and the default app upon login.**

   These control what the users see in the blue app picker on the top right of the screen.

7. **Under Tab Settings, select which standard and custom tabs are visible for the profile.**

   You can choose Default On, defaulting the tab to display; Default Off, giving the profile access but not defaulting the tab to appear; or Tab Hidden, hiding the tab without giving the user the option to turn it back on.

   Depending on your edition, you may have a tab limit, so go ahead and remove the tabs your company isn't using.

8. **Check or uncheck the check boxes under the Administrative Permissions section to give or revoke administrative tools from the profile.**

   Most of the permissions are named intuitively, but if you don't know what they do, click Help for this Page at the top right of the page to view Salesforce help. These permissions are typically reserved for administrators, but you may want to give some permissions to managers, such as Manage Public List Views so that they can create list views for their team.

9. **Check or uncheck the check boxes under the General Permissions section to give or revoke common user permissions from the profile.**

   For example, if you want support agents to be able to transfer ownership of cases to others, give them the Transfer Cases permission.

10. **Under the Standard Object Permissions and Custom Object Permissions sections, check or uncheck the check boxes to give or revoke standard or custom object permissions from the profile.**

    For example, if you don't want your support agents modifying lead records, select only the Read check box in the row for leads on their custom profile.

11. **If you're using Salesforce Knowledge, give the profile access to article types in the Article Type Permissions section.**

    This works like standard and custom object permissions, but depending on what access the profile needs, the article type permissions may not be enough. See Chapter 11 for more on Knowledge setup and access.

12. Click Save when you're done.

The Profile page reappears for your new profile.

13. Click the View Users button to assign users to your new profile.

Setting Up Users in Your Organization

After updating your company profile, building your role hierarchy, setting your organization-wide defaults, and creating some profiles, you're now ready to add users to your organization.

You need to have available Service Cloud licenses to add users to the Service Cloud before being able to add them. If you don't have them yet, contact Salesforce support.

To add users, go to the Setup menu and follow these steps:

1. Choose Administer ➪ Manage Users ➪ Users.

The Users page appears with a list of your users.

2. Click the New User button to add one user.

The New User edit page appears.

3. Complete the fields.

Make sure you select the appropriate Role and Profile for the user. If you don't see the complete list of profiles, check to see if you selected the correct value from the User License drop-down. Click Generate New Password and Notify User Immediately at the bottom of the page if you want the user to immediately receive an email with his or her username and temporary password upon saving the record.

Note: Click the Service Cloud User check box to enable Service Cloud for the user. Otherwise, the user will only have basic access to cases in the Service Cloud. Make sure you have enough Service Cloud licenses.

The Username field can be a fabricated email address and will serve as the user's login. The Email field should contain the user's real email address where he or she will receive system emails, including reset passwords.

4. Click Save when you're done.

The User detail page appears.

Reviewing Other Security Controls

If you go back to Setup ➪ Administer ➪ Security Controls, you'll see that as an administrator, you have other settings for managing security within Salesforce besides roles, profiles, and the sharing model. You can define parameters for session settings so that Salesforce doesn't lock you out each time you take a coffee break, and you can view your organization's audit trail that details every single change made in the system. We suggest playing around and investigating all your options as an administrator.

One particularly important element of security is the subcategory titled Field Accessibility, which is also called *field-level security* in Salesforce. Field-level security gives administrators much more granular control over profile visibility at the field level.

Defining field-level security

If you're using an Enterprise, Unlimited, Performance, or Developer edition of Salesforce, read on. Otherwise, you may want to upgrade if field-level security is something that interests you.

A main benefit of field-level security is that it allows you to maintain fewer page layouts. You shouldn't have to create a separate page layout just to hide one or two fields. A page layout's primary objective is to organize fields, buttons, related lists, and other data on a page. Field-level security is intended to make field access more restrictive than the page layout, so you can use one page layout with a required field, but make it read-only to some profiles using field-level security.

An additional benefit of field-level security is that it restricts all means of access to a field. Just because a field isn't on a page layout, users can still access those fields elsewhere, like reports, search results, and list views.

Administer field-level security through permission sets or profiles. To view and administer field-level security, go to the Setup menu and follow these steps:

1. **Choose Administer ➪ Security Controls ➪ Field Accessibility, under Administration Setup.**

   The Field Accessibility page appears with a list of objects in your organization whose field access you want to modify.

2. **Select a type of record for which you want to view and manage field access, such as Case.**

   The Field Accessibility page specific to the type of record appears.

3. **Under Choose Your View, select how you want to view field access for that particular type of record.**

   You can define field-level security for a single field on all profiles (select View by Fields) or for multiple fields on a single profile (View by Profile).

4. **Select a field or a profile from the picklist, depending on how you chose to view field access in Step 3.**

   The page reappears with a field accessibility table, displaying field-level security.

5. **In the Field Access column in the table, click a link to edit field access.**

   An Access Settings page appears, showing field access for the particular field and profile you chose, as shown in Figure 19-5.

6. **Define field access in the Field-Level Security section.**

   You have three choices for field access:

   - *Visible:* Check this box to make the field readable and editable.

   - *Read-Only:* Check this box (and visible will be auto-checked) to make the field readable but not editable.

   - *None:* Leave both boxes unchecked to hide the field.

7. **Click Save when you're done.**

   The Field Accessibility page reappears.

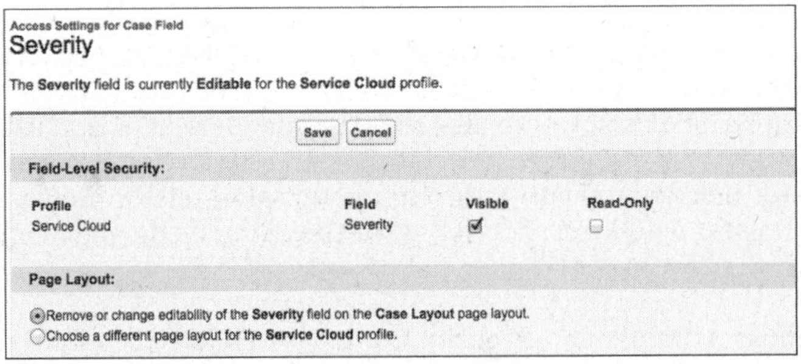

Figure 19-5:
Modifying
field-level
security.

Access Settings for Case Field
Severity

The **Severity** field is currently **Editable** for the **Service Cloud** profile.

Save   Cancel

Field-Level Security:

Profile	Field	Visible	Read-Only
Service Cloud	Severity	☑	☐

Page Layout:

⦿ Remove or change editability of the **Severity** field on the **Case Layout** page layout.
◯ Choose a different page layout for the **Service Cloud** profile.

Chapter 20

Customizing Service Cloud with Force.com

. . . .

In This Chapter

▶ Customizing standard business objects

▶ Modifying page layouts

▶ Managing multiple support processes

▶ Managing record types

▶ Working with workflow

▶ Validating data entry

. . . .

Salesforce provides a standard set of objects to operate your business with, and these objects include their own standard fields and page layouts natively (or "out of the box," as they say in the business). Although the standard setup provides an immense amount of business value right off the bat, Salesforce knows that any successful tool needs to be flexible in order to respond rapidly to changing markets and business focus, or values.

If you're an administrator for your organization or you have permission to customize the configuration, you have the power to help guide and aid your organization by executing system changes to meet the needs of the business.

In this chapter, we unveil the wealth of customization tools and capabilities available on the Force.com platform. *Force.com* is the term used in the Salesforce community to refer to anything and everything that resides under the Setup link in the top-right corner of your browser.

To access the Force.com menu, click the Setup link and you arrive at the Force.com home page, shown in Figure 20-1. From here, you can view recent items if you've visited the Force.com menu before, and you can access the menu directly in the left sidebar.

Figure 20-1:
The
Force.com
home page.

Building and Editing Fields

Creating additional, custom fields or editing existing fields in Salesforce is the simplest way to add value for your organization. The key to creating new fields is to ensure you're capturing information the business needs. Verify that the field is important to key business processes before creating it.

If a record is filled with unimportant or useless fields, it's very unlikely that users will have a good experience entering or referencing the information. On the other hand, if users populate relevant information and can access the record and view all this information in one place, they're more likely to adopt the system and continue entering the information.

Be sure to always update existing fields and create new ones to stay relevant and current with the business. This will create a give/get cycle with the users, who will continue to enter quality information if the system meets their needs.

Creating new fields

Although Salesforce comes with standard fields that will cover many business scenarios, the ability to add your own custom fields allows you to capture information more specific to your business.

In order to add a new field to an existing object in Salesforce, click the Setup link in the top-right corner and follow these steps:

1. **Scroll down to the Build section in the left sidebar of the Force.com home page and click the Customize heading.**

   The available options under the Customize section display.

2. **Click an object heading to expand the menu for that individual object (for example, Accounts, Contacts, Cases).**

   The available options for the heading you choose appear.

3. **Click Fields.**

   The Fields page for the object you select appears and displays a list of standard fields at the top and a list of custom fields and relationships at the bottom.

   Not all tabs under the Customize heading have a link available for fields. The fields link is available for standard objects, such as Accounts, Contacts, and Cases, but not available for other standard features, such as the Agent Console.

4. **At the top of the custom fields and relationships list, click the New button.**

   Step 1 of the New Custom Field wizard displays, and you must select a data type for your new field.

5. **Review the data types and their purposes and select a radio button for the type you want to create. Then click Next.**

   For more information on the data types available to you and when to use each, refer to *Salesforce.com For Dummies,* 5th Edition, by Tom Wong, Liz Kao, and Matt Kaufman (Wiley).

   Step 2 of the New Custom Field wizard appears and requires that you enter certain details about your field. The field label and field name are required details. Field labels are seen by end-users on reports and page layouts throughout the system — for example, "Case Age." Field names require that any spaces be replaced with underscores. Field names are used as unique identifiers in Salesforce and are particularly important for integrations and data loads — for example, "Case_Age."

6. **Enter details and click Next.**

In Enterprise, Unlimited, Performance, and Developer editions, Step 3 of the wizard appears and you need to enter the field-level security settings for each profile.

7. **Set the field-level security settings and click Next.**

Step 4 of the wizard displays.

8. **Choose which page layouts you want to add the field to. Click Save and New or Save.**

If you click Save and New, you're immediately taken back to Step 1 of the wizard to begin creating a new field. If you click Save, the fields page reappears with your new field saved.

Updating existing fields

To make changes to existing custom fields, follow Steps 1–3 in the preceding section in order to arrive at the fields page for the object of your choice. From the fields page, you can make the following updates and changes to existing fields:

✔ **Updating field details:** Click Edit next to any field to update the field details (for example, Field Label, Field Name, and so on).

You can also change the field type of your field by clicking Edit next to a custom field and clicking the Change Field Type button. Step 1 of the Custom Field wizard appears and you can follow the steps to change your field's data type. For example, you could change a picklist field to a free text field.

✔ **Deleting a custom field:** Click the Del link next to any custom field to delete it.

✔ **Adding, removing, or reordering picklist values:** Click the field label of a picklist field from the fields page. Scroll to the bottom to find the list titled, "Picklist Values."

Click New to add an additional value to the list or click the Del link next to an existing value to delete it.

Click Reorder and use the Values box to reorder the picklist values. You can also click the check box to sort the values alphabetically and select a default value for the picklist if you choose to.

✔ **Replacing existing picklist values:** On the fields page, click the Replace Link next to any picklist field to replace an existing value with a different one. This feature can be especially useful if you have outdated records in your system and want to update a particular value to a new one.

✔ **Changing field-level security:** Click the field label of any field from the fields page; then click the Set Field-Level Security button to make adjustments to the security settings by profile.

Customizing Page Layouts

When a sales rep and a customer support agent look at the same record in Salesforce, they're very likely to want different information. Fortunately, in Salesforce, you can customize and rearrange page layouts as needed.

With the Page Layout Editor, you can add, remove, or modify the position of fields, custom links, and related lists, among other page layout attributes. Plus, you can choose to make a field required or read-only on a page layout if desired.

Modifying a page layout

If you have administrative permissions, you can modify page layouts to rearrange fields or sections as needed.

In order to modify a page layout for an object in Salesforce, click the Setup link in the top-right corner and follow these steps:

1. **Scroll down to the Build section in the left sidebar of the Force.com home page and click the Customize heading.**

   The available options under the Customize section display.

2. **Click an object heading to expand the menu for that individual object (for example, Accounts, Contacts, Cases).**

   The available options for the heading you choose appear.

3. **Click Page Layouts.**

   The Page Layout page for the selected object displays.

4. **Click Edit next to the page layout you want to modify.**

   As shown in Figure 20-2, the Page Layout editor displays at the top of the page with a sample of the layout below it.

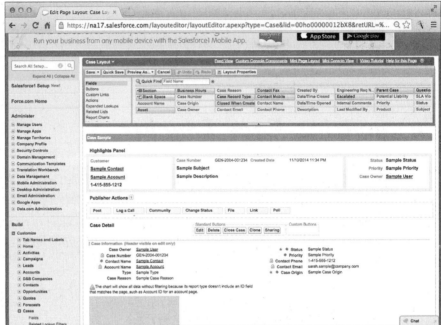

Figure 20-2:
The Page
Layout
editor.

5. Choose from the following actions to modify your page layout:

- *Place fields, buttons, custom links, related lists, or report charts:*
  Choose the category you'd like to arrange on the page layout from
  the left sidebar of the layout editor, and click and drag fields to
  place them on the layout.

  You can also add actions to page layouts from the page layout editor.
  Actions enable users to be more efficient by completing certain
  tasks directly from the Chatter feed of a record. To learn more about
  Actions, go to `https://help.salesforce.com/apex/HTHome`
  and search for an article titled "Actions Overview."

- *Move existing fields:* Click and drag fields currently on the layout
  to new locations. A green, horizontal bar will show you where the
  field will appear on the page before you drop it.

- *Modify field properties on the layout:* Hover over fields on the layout
  and click the wrench icon that appears on the right side. Use the
  check boxes in the pop-up window to decide on required and read-
  only settings, and click OK.

- *Add a section to the page layout:* Click fields in the left sidebar of
  the layout editor and click and drag the Section box onto the page

layout to create a new section. A pop-up window appears, allowing you to choose the Section Properties. Choose a name and edit the properties of your new section, and click OK. You can also edit properties of an existing section by hovering over it on the sample layout and clicking the wrench icon.

- *Add report charts to the layout:* You can add existing report charts to your layout by selecting Report Charts in the left sidebar of the layout editor and dragging an existing report onto the layout. You must have first created the report and added a chart to the report to display it on the layout.

6. **Click Preview As at the top of the layout editor and select a profile to view the layout from a specific type of user's point of view.**

   Close the new window when you're finished previewing the layout.

7. **Click Save at the top of the page when you're finished modifying your layout.**

   The Page Layout page for the object displays.

Assigning layouts to profiles

When you've created page layouts, you can assign layouts by profile, which allows users with specific profiles to have different views of detail pages. This can help your organization work efficiently by showing only relevant fields to various job functions.

To assign layouts to specific profiles, click the Setup link in the top-right corner and follow these steps:

1. **Scroll down to the Build section in the left-hand sidebar of the Force. com home page and click the Customize heading.**

   The available options under the Customize section display.

2. **Click an object heading to expand the menu for that individual object (for example, Accounts, Contacts, Cases).**

   The available options for the heading you choose appear.

3. **Click Page Layouts.**

   The Page Layout page for the selected object displays.

4. **Click the Page Layout Assignment button at the top of the page.**

   A Page Layout Assignment page displays current assignments.

5. Click Edit Assignment.

The same page displays in edit mode.

6. Highlight one or more page layout cells.

You can click and drag to highlight multiple cells in a row. You can hold Control and click to highlight individual, nonsequential cells, or you can select a range of cells by clicking the first one and then holding Shift and clicking the final cell in the range.

7. Use the Page Layout to Use drop-down at the top of the page to select the layout that you want to assign to the selected profiles.

Pay attention to the purple Selected and yellow Changed counts to the right of the Page Layout to Use drop-down to keep track of the changes you're making.

8. When you've made all necessary changes, click Save.

The Page Layout Assignment page reappears.

Managing Multiple Case-Management Processes

Configuring multiple support processes can be very helpful if you have multiple groups of users working on the Cases object in your system. Multiple support processes allow each group to follow their own process instead of trying to squeeze into a one-size-fits-all process.

To set up a new support process to manage your case lifecycle, follow these steps:

1. From Setup, go to the Build section and choose Customize ⇨ Cases⇨ Fields.

The Case Fields page displays.

2. In the Standard Fields section, click the Status field label.

The Status Fields detail page displays.

3. Review the existing values and click New if you want to add any Status values.

An add picklist values page appears.

4. Add one or multiple picklist values and click Save.

If you add multiple values, each value should be on its own line.

5. **Verify that the Case Status values represent every possible stage for a case in any case-management process for your organization.**

6. **Click the Reorder button if you need to adjust the order of case status values.**

   Reorder values as needed and click Save.

7. **In the left sidebar, go to the Build section and choose Customize ⇨ Cases ⇨ Support Processes.**

   The Support Processes page displays.

8. **Click New to create a new case-management process.**

   The New Support Process page displays.

   If Master is selected as the Existing Process, you can choose from all existing Case Status picklist values when creating your case-management process.

9. **Choose a name for the support process (for example, "RMA Process") and click Save.**

   A page appears with a box for Available Values and Selected Values.

10. **Select values and use the arrow buttons to place your desired values in the Selected Values box.**

11. **Choose a default value for new cases in this support process and click Save.**

    The Support Processes page displays with your new process listed.

Leveraging Record Types

Record types in Salesforce allow your organization to create distinct records for subsets of users. You can create record types to allow sets of users to leverage different business processes. For example, if you have a support team split up by the type of cases that they work, and they need to use different case status values in their individual processes, you could create a case record type for each group to leverage their own case-management process. Additionally, you can use the same picklist fields on multiple record types, but choose to display only a subset of values on each type.

You can create record types to support all major objects in Salesforce, including Accounts, Contacts, and Cases. To empower your users with multiple record types, you need to create the record types first and assign them to profiles.

You can create multiple case management processes by choosing Setup ➪ Customize ➪ Cases ➪ Support Processes.

Creating record types

Record types allow you to support multiple business processes and make applicable picklist choices available to the correct users. Plus, record types can be a useful differentiator when running reports on an object. For example, you may want to create different case record types for customer support issues and internal issues. Creating different record types allows you to easily filter out any internal issue cases when evaluating your business.

To create a new record type, click the Setup link in the top-right corner and follow these steps:

1. **Scroll down to the Build section in the left sidebar of the Force.com home page and click the Customize heading.**

   The available options under the Customize section display.

2. **Click on an object heading to expand the menu for that individual object (for example, Accounts, Contacts, Cases).**

   The available options for the tab you choose appear.

3. **Click the Record Types link.**

   The Record Types page for the selected object displays.

4. **Click New at the top of the page.**

   Step 1 of the New Record Type Wizard appears and prompts you to enter the following details for the new record type:

   • *Existing record type:* Choosing Master includes all available picklist values.

   • *Record type label:* Choose a unique label within a given object.

   • *Record type name:* Enter a unique name in your Salesforce organization.

   • *Support process:* Select a case management process to use for this record type.

   • *Description:* Enter a description of what this record type should be used for.

   • *Active checkbox:* Check active to activate the record type.

- *Enable for profile and default settings:* Select the Enable for Profile box to make the record type available for that profile and select Make Default to make the record type the default for users with that profile.

5. **Enter the details and click Next.**

   Step 2 of the wizard, Assign Page Layouts, appears. You may choose to assign one layout to all profiles or apply a different layout for each profile.

6. **Assign page layouts and click Save to finish or Save and New to create another record type.**

Viewing and editing record types

Record types are not set in stone after you create them. Your business may change over time, and you need to adjust existing record types to respond to those changes.

To view or edit an existing record type, click the Setup link in the top-right corner and follow these steps:

1. **Scroll down to the Build section in the left-hand sidebar of the Force. com home page and click the Customize heading.**

   The available options under the Customize section display.

2. **Click an object heading to expand the menu for that individual object (for example, Accounts, Contacts, Cases).**

   The available options for the section you choose appear.

3. **Click Record Types.**

   The Record Types page for the selected object displays.

4. **Click Record Type Label for the type you want to modify.**

   The Record Type detail page displays.

5. **Click the Edit button to change one of the following:**

   - *Record type label*
   - *Record type name*
   - *Support process*

6. **Click Save when you're finished.**

   The Record Type detail page reappears.

7. **Make changes to picklists by clicking the Edit link next to any of the fields listed in the Picklists Available for Editing section.**

   An edit page appears with a box for Available and Selected Values.

8. **Use the arrows to move the values you want available on this record type into the Selected Values box, optionally select a Default value, and click Save.**

   The Record Type detail page reappears.

Defining record-type access

You can define record type access when you initially create record types, but you can also make adjustments if you ever need to change the access for various profiles.

To define record type access for specific profiles, from Setup, find the Administer section and choose Manage Users ➪ Profiles. Then follow these steps:

1. **Click the Profile name that you want to modify record type access for.**

   The Profile page appears.

2. **Scroll down to the Record Type Settings section of the page.**

   If your organization has multiple record types for any objects, those objects will have an Edit link in this section.

3. **Click the Edit link.**

   Edit Record Type settings page appears.

4. **Use the arrows to add or remove record type access for this profile.**

5. **Optionally select a default record type for this profile.**

   The default record type is selected by default when creating a new record.

6. **Click Save.**

Choosing a record type when creating New records

When profiles have been granted access to more than one record type for a single object, users with that profile will have the ability to select which record type they want to create. As shown in Figure 20-3, let's say you have two case record types: Customer Support Issue and Internal Bug/Defect. When users click the New button from the Case home page, a Record Type selection page appears. From the Record Type selection page, users can use the drop-down list to choose which type they'd like to create.

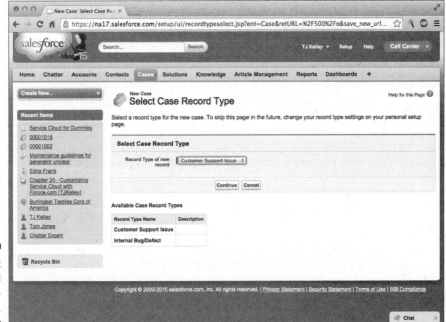

Figure 20-3:
The Record
Type selec-
tion page.

Workflow and Validation Rules

Workflow and validation rules are two simple tools available in Salesforce to make everyone's lives easier. The daily grind in a call center makes it difficult to remember even the simplest of tasks. Did you follow up with a customer to let him know his issue has been resolved or his package has been shipped? Did you remember to send an email to your manager to let her know you esca-lated a case you were having trouble resolving? Do you need to constantly bug your team to remind them to fill in certain case details? These are only a few small examples of the countless tasks, emails, and data entry updates that your business likely needs to make on a daily, or even hourly, basis.

With workflow and validation rules you can take human error and memory out of the equation and ensure that all necessary steps in your business process are functioning properly.

Understanding when to use workflow and validation rules

Workflow and validation rules have a wide array of applications, but generally speaking, you can use workflow rules to automate standard processes and validation rules to ensure business processes are followed and consistent, quality data is captured in your system.

You can build workflow rules to send automatic email alerts, update fields, or assign tasks to different users. For example, you could create a workflow rule to notify your customers when an agent resolves one of their open support cases. Additionally, you could set up an email alert to notify managers of escalations, or field updates to capture date/time stamps when a case changes status.

Validation rules can help you ensure that specific data points are captured in your business process and additionally validate the format of that data. For example, you could create a validation rule to ensure information such as customer contact information, issue type, and issue resolution are always captured on cases.

Creating a workflow rule

Workflow rules will help you automate steps in your business processes. Here are a few key workflow concepts you should review prior to trying to build any rules:

- ✔ **Workflow rules:** Conditions you set that tell Salesforce to execute workflow actions when met.

- ✔ **Workflow actions:** Actions that Salesforce automates whenever the criteria of the associated workflow rule are met. Actions are created separately from workflow rules and exist independently of rules, but they must be associated to one or multiple rules in order to impact the system. Multiple actions can be associated to one rule, and single actions can be associated to multiple rules.

To begin creating a workflow rule, follow these steps:

1. **From Setup, go to the Build section and choose Create ⇨ Workflow & Approvals ⇨ Workflow Rules.**

   If this is your first time accessing the Workflow Rules link, the Understanding Workflow page appears. Read through the information and click Continue when you're ready. The All Workflow Rules page displays.

2. **Click the New Rule button at the top of the page.**

   Step 1 of the New Workflow Rule Wizard displays and prompts you to select an object for your new rule.

3. **Select an object and click Next.**

   Step 2 of the wizard appears.

4. **Choose a Rule Name and optionally enter a description of your rule.**

   At this point you're ready to define your rule and choose the actions that it will trigger in the system. Proceed through the following sections to finish creating your rule and learn more about workflow.

Selecting the evaluation criteria

Evaluation criteria determine when Salesforce will choose to check whether a rule's criteria have been met.

You can have the system evaluate this rule when a record meets one of the following three criteria:

- ✔ **Created:** Salesforce will evaluate the rule only upon record creation and execute the workflow actions only at this time.

- ✔ **Created, and every time it's edited:** Salesforce will evaluate the rule upon record creation and every time the record is edited, regardless of the edits made.

- ✔ **Created, and any time it's edited to subsequently meet criteria:** Salesforce will evaluate the rule upon record creation and again only when the record is edited to meet specific criteria. For example, you may want to use this option when sending email alerts to ensure that the alerts are sent only at certain times (for example, Case Status changed to Closed or Resolved).

Defining the rule criteria

Workflow rule criteria are the specific set of conditions that you define that, when met, will trigger any associated workflow actions (tasks, email alerts, field updates).

You have two setup options for defining when the system should run a rule and execute any associated actions. You can select to run the rule if

- ✔ **The following criteria are met:** Use this option when you have simple rule criteria. For example, if you want the actions to take place when a field or multiple fields equal specific values, you could select this option and enter the rule criteria using the drop-downs displayed at the bottom of the page in Step 2 of the wizard.

✔ **The following formula evaluates to true:** Use this option when you have more complex criteria that you'd like to set to trigger workflow actions. For example, if you want to use more complex functions to evaluate a field's prior value or evaluate only a specific string of characters in a text field, you should select this option. You can use the formula editor to create your criteria. Use the Check Syntax button to check if your formula is properly formatted before clicking save.

Choosing immediate or time-dependent actions

Actions represent the end result of a workflow rule. Workflow actions allow you to automate simple tasks, messages, and updates that otherwise may be forgotten or are too time consuming for day-to-day business.

There are four different types of actions you can create to add to your workflow rules:

✔ **New task:** Create a task for a user.

✔ **New email alert:** Send an email.

✔ **New outbound message:** Send information to an endpoint URL.

Endpoint URLs rely on the configuration of a web service. Work with a developer at your organization if you want to configure an outbound message workflow action.

✔ **New field update:** Update the value of a field.

You can also select existing actions that you've previously created to add to your workflow rule. To add an existing action from Step 3 of the wizard, click Add Workflow Action and choose Select Existing Action.

There are two ways you can choose to execute workflow actions:

✔ **Immediate actions:** Trigger immediately after the rule is evaluated and meets defined criteria.

✔ **Time-dependent actions:** Trigger at a point in time that you specify after the rule is evaluated and meets the defined criteria.

To create a time-dependent action, click Add Time Trigger. You must first associate an action to your workflow rule before you can add a time trigger.

Understanding workflow limitations

Workflow rules are an excellent tool for automating your business process and small administrative tasks, but they do have their limitations. Here are some workflow limitations to be aware of:

- ✔ **Professional Edition:** Workflow rules are available only at an additional cost in Professional Edition.

- ✔ **Created, and every time it's edited:** Selecting this option as the evaluation criteria of your workflow rule means that you'll be unable to add time-dependent actions to the rule. The reason for this limitation is that any time-dependent action would continuously start over whenever the record is edited. For example, if you created a workflow email alert to send 14 days after a case record is created, the 14-day "clock" would reset each time the record is edited.

- ✔ **Email alerts:** You can't create email alert actions for workflow rules with Activities as the selected object.

- ✔ **Picklist and multi-select picklist fields:** When writing your rule criteria, keep in mind that picklist fields can only be used in certain functions. To learn more about working with picklist fields, go to `https://help.salesforce.com/apex/HTHome` and search for an article titled, "Tips for Working with Picklist and Multi-Select Picklist Formula Fields."

Activating your workflow rules

After creating a workflow rule, you must activate the rule in order to ensure that the desired action takes place in the system. To activate a workflow rule, click the Activate button from the workflow detail page. The detail page displays immediately after you finish creating a rule. You can also find the rule from the Setup menu by going to the Build section and choosing Create ➪ Workflow & Approvals ➪ Workflow Rules.

Creating a validation rule

Validation rules can help you ensure certain data points are captured in your business process. For example, you can prevent agents from changing a case status to specific values if they haven't yet entered information that they should've captured from the current status. For example, you may want to capture an escalation reason if they try to move a case into an Escalated status. You can also use validation rules to verify that data gets entered correctly. For example, you could enforce the format of a phone number field for case contacts.

To create a validation rule, click the Setup link in the top-right corner and follow these steps:

1. **Scroll down to the Build section in the left sidebar of the Force.com home page and click the Customize heading.**

   The available options under the Customize section display.

2. **Click an object heading to expand the menu for that individual object (for example, Accounts, Contacts, Cases).**

   The available options for the tab you choose appear.

3. **Click the Validation Rules link.**

   The Validation Rules page for the selected object displays.

4. **Click New at the top of the page.**

   The Validation Rule edit page displays.

5. **Choose a Rule Name for your validation rule and optionally enter a description.**

At this point, you're ready to define your rule. The following sections show you how to finish creating and activating validation rules.

Defining the properties of your validation rule

Similar to workflow rules, validation rules trigger based on a defined set of criteria, but instead of *resulting* in action in the system, they *require* action in the system. Validation rules display error messages for users to inform them of missing or improperly formatted data.

You must define the following properties for your validation rule:

- ✔ **Error Condition Formula:** If the condition formula evaluates to true, the validation rule will apply and the error message you define for users will display.

- ✔ **Error Message:** The error message displays anytime a user tries to save a record and the condition formula evaluates to true.

- ✔ **Error Location:** You can choose to display the error message at the top of the edit page for users or directly next to a field. You should display the message at the top of the page if your rule validates multiple fields. If it only evaluates one field, you should place the error message next to that field.

Activating your validation rule

Unlike a workflow rule, a validation rule defaults to active upon creation. The Active check box is checked by default when you're creating a new rule. You may choose to uncheck or check the box in order to deactivate or activate the validation rule at any point in time. All you need to do is open the edit page for the validation rule. Keep this in mind in case a particular rule becomes troublesome. For example, if support agents are unable to open cases due to a validation rule that requires information they don't have when opening the cases, you may want to deactivate the rule and reevaluate the error condition formula.

Chapter 21

Extending beyond Service Cloud

In This Chapter

▶ Understanding the AppExchange platform

▶ Deploying AppExchange apps for your organization

*I*f you've read all the chapters leading up to this one, you probably can't imagine how Salesforce could possibly offer more than everything Service Cloud already provides. We're happy to tell you that you're wrong! (Not in a mean way, of course.) On top of everything that comes out of the box, Salesforce extends its power and reach beyond Service Cloud with offerings in its business app store, called the AppExchange.

Before we talk about the AppExchange and what it is, it's important to get a little background on the Force.com platform at a high level. Force.com is the platform that makes Salesforce what it is today: an easy-to-use cloud-based business database that allows administrators to create and customize apps with clicks, not code.

It's easy to overlook the power and significance of this. Where once it took IT teams months or even years to build applications, the Force.com platform enables nontechnical users to develop Salesforce-compatible apps within hours or days, through pointing and clicking. You can now customize existing apps on Force.com or build entirely new cloud apps for your business in a fraction of the time and at a fragment of the cost.

In this chapter, we discuss what the AppExchange is and why it's valuable. We cover how to get to the AppExchange, as well as how to find apps you didn't even know you needed. Then we give you a glimpse of how to test and deploy applications that suit your business needs, as well as giving you some tips to plan and prepare for it.

Defining the AppExchange Platform

Launched in 2005, the AppExchange is the world's leading cloud marketplace for business applications. It's also the largest. It features thousands of enterprise and small business applications for every department or industry.

With the AppExchange, you can quickly deploy applications created by and for the thousands of developers and enthusiasts in the Salesforce ecosystem. In this way, you increase productivity and enhance the way you run your business.

These apps range from sales apps that allow users to close deals faster with electronic signatures to service apps that give agents access to the data they need while out in the field. Your IT teams can find apps to quickly clean data, recruiting can find HR apps to help find and hire the right candidates, and executives can get analytics apps that provide your organization key insights. What's more, many of these apps are free!

You can read reviews and test apps before downloading them, and then install them with the click of a button. The best part is that because users contribute to the AppExchange, more apps are created and uploaded every day as the Salesforce community continues to grow.

Accessing the AppExchange

Let's take a look at the AppExchange. In your instance of Salesforce, follow these steps:

1. **Navigate to the Setup menu.**

   The Setup sidebar appears on the left side of the page.

2. **Under the Build section, click AppExchange Marketplace.**

   The AppExchange appears in the body of the page, as shown in Figure 21-1.

Alternatively, open your browser and navigate to `http://appexchange.salesforce.com`, shown in Figure 21-2.

Browsing the AppExchange

Once you're in, you can browse hundreds of applications for Service Cloud. Of course, there are also plenty of apps for Sales Cloud that you can check out and recommend for your buddies over on the sales team.

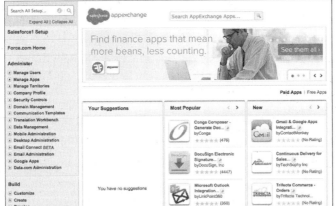

Figure 21-1:
The App-
Exchange in
Salesforce.

Figure 21-2:
The App-
Exchange
website.

Searching the AppExchange

Browse the store and quickly find specific apps that pertain to your business needs. To find apps specific to Service Cloud, you can search for keywords in the search bar at the top. If you're looking at the AppExchange from within Salesforce, searching will open a new browser tab with the AppExchange website.

Sorting and filtering in the AppExchange

When you're looking at the AppExchange directory on the website and not in Salesforce, expand the Categories menu on the left sidebar and click Customer Service, as shown in Figure 21-3. Here, you find a list of featured apps, both free and at a cost, that help enhance everything from agent productivity to automating customer surveys.

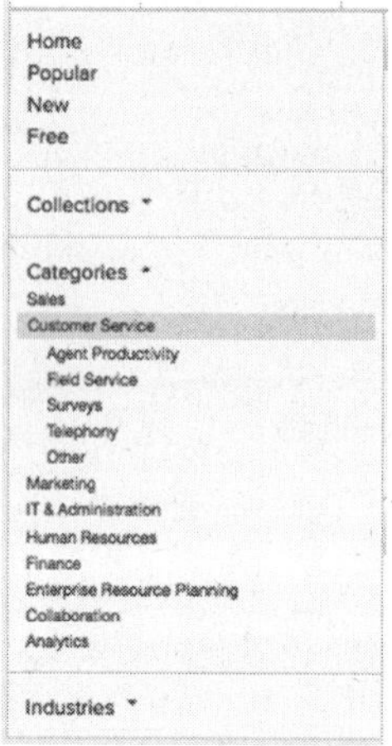

Figure 21-3:
Refining
your search
in App-
Exchange.

You can also apply filter criteria when browsing the directory. Under the
search bar at the top of the screen, there are a series of drop-down filters to
help refine your search. Apply these filters to find exactly what you're looking
for, as shown in Figure 21-4. You can sort by rating, language, price, release
date, and even device compatibility. As soon as you add a filter, the Apply
button turns green. Click the Apply button to see these filters take effect.

Take a minute to click around and see how easy it is to browse the
AppExchange. You can look at apps created specifically for your industry, or
just the most popular apps on the market.

Navigating apps in the AppExchange

Hover over the app to display a description of it. You can click the Save button
to keep the app in mind for later or click More to go to the app's information
page and learn more about it. You can see all kinds of useful information about
the app here, such as its system requirements, individual reviews, provider
information, and other details including screenshots and demos of the app.

Figure 21-4:
Applying
filters in
the App-
Exchange.

Preparing to install AppExchange apps

To install apps from the AppExchange your administrator needs to give you the Download AppExchange Packages permission on your user record. Before installing an app, there are a few best practices you should follow:

✔ **Check your edition compatibility.** Under the Details tabs in the app information, you should see which Salesforce editions the app is compatible with. Make sure you have one of those before preparing an entire install strategy.

✔ **If applicable, make sure you have custom tab and custom object availability.** Depending on the edition, you have a limit to the total number of your organization's custom objects and tabs. Many AppExchange apps include custom objects and tabs. Make sure these align and that installing the app won't cause you to exceed your limit.

✔ **Test, test, test.** Many AppExchange apps have test drives available. You can usually find this under the Overview tab in the app information. Use this feature if it's available to test the functionality and if it suits your business.

✔ **Install the app in a developer org or your sandbox before deploying in your production environment.** As with any deployment, use a testing environment before installing an application or any configuration to a live one.

Deploying Apps for Your Company

Now let's install the app. When you've decided on the app you want installed, follow these steps:

1. **From the search results, hover over the app you want and click More.**

   The app's information page appears.

2. **After reviewing the app information and details, click the green Get It Now button on the right.**

   If you haven't already, the page prompts you to log in to the AppExchange using your Salesforce credentials, as shown in Figure 21-5.

3. **Choose where you want to install the app.**

   If you're installing it in a developer org, choose the production option. Otherwise, use a sandbox.

4. Accept the terms and conditions by clicking the check box.

5. Click Confirm and Install.

The Salesforce login page appears.

6. Enter your login credentials and click Log In to Salesforce.

The Package Installation Details page appears with a list of all the package components you're installing to your target environment.

7. Review the components, make sure they don't conflict with existing configuration or exceed any limitations, and click Continue when you're done.

The Approve Package API Access page appears, telling you that the package has the same level of access as the profile of the user installing it.

8. Review the API access and click Next.

The Choose Security Level page appears.

9. Select who should get access to the package and click Next.

The Install Ready page appears.

10. Click Install to install the package.

The Processing page appears. When the package install is complete, you'll receive an email in your inbox.

Figure 21-5:
Installing
the app.

Congratulations! Your application is now installed in your organization. You're not done yet, though. Now you still have to verify the package made it, test it, and sometimes make it generally available to other users.

This post-installation process usually requires three steps:

1. Verify successful installation.

2. Test the app and run through scenarios in a sandbox or developer org.

3. Configure and give other users access to the app.

Testing your AppExchange apps

A package usually comes with its own app in the blue App menu on the top right of the page. To find your new package and test it, click the App menu and select the name of the app you just installed. If it's not there, make sure it was properly installed in your environment by following these steps:

1. **Go to the Setup menu.**

   The left-hand sidebar menu appears.

2. **Under Build, click Installed Packages.**

   The Installed Packages page appears with your installed app in the Installed Packages related list.

3. **Click the Package Name.**

   The Package Details page appears.

4. **Click the View Components button to see what you've installed.**

   A list of installed package components appears.

Now that you've confirmed that you have the package installed, start giving it a try. Run through typical use cases and scenarios for your company with the new application, and if you're an administrator, you can log in as other users and attempt to try using the app as them. If you can't, the app is not enabled for their profile and you'll have to give them access to those objects and components.

Part VIII

The Part of Tens

Get ten resources to help you master Service Cloud in a free article at www.dummies.com/extras/salesforceservicecloud.

In this part . . .

- ✔ Ask the right questions before implementing Salesforce Knowledge.

- ✔ Ensure that your new system doesn't become a legacy.

Chapter 22

Ten Questions to Ask Before Implementing Knowledge

. . . .

In This Chapter

▶ Identifying or confirming a need for Knowledge

▶ Understanding the benefits of Knowledge

▶ Thinking about an agent's Knowledge needs and use cases

▶ Asking how your Knowledge will be consumed

▶ Considering the implications of committing to Knowledge

. . . .

*N*o matter the breadth or depth of your organization's knowledge, you need to ensure that your employees, customers, partners, and the public can interact with the information they need in the right moment, the right place, and the right format.

Salesforce Knowledge provides the framework for a knowledge base that can enable your organization to quickly create and easily manage information that you want to share with internal or external users.

Regardless of whether your organization has already decided to leverage Salesforce Knowledge, important questions and decisions need to be evaluated prior to embarking on an implantation.

In this chapter, we provide a set of ten basic questions that you should review before implementing Salesforce Knowledge. The answers you discover will help you not only determine whether an organizational need for Knowledge exists, but also identify the features of Knowledge that will be most important for planning and executing the implementation.

How Much Control Does Your Organization Need over the Article Lifecycle?

Maybe you want to empower your support teams to create, edit, review, and publish articles for repurpose to solve customer's issues, but you're worried about giving too much freedom in the publishing process. Salesforce Knowledge provides flexible solutions for managing your organization's articles. You can select article managers and even create an approval process specific for articles. You may require an approval process for specific article types that require legal or management review prior to publication.

Would Your Organization Like to Present Articles to Agents in Various Formats?

There are plenty of options out there to house your organizational support articles, but none can match the power and quality of Salesforce Knowledge or the depth of customization allowed when creating articles. You can create custom article-type templates to render the information to users in various formats. You can also create article-type layouts and various article types to organize your support articles.

Does Your Organization Need to Target Particular Audiences with Certain Types of Articles?

If subsets of your organizational knowledge are only intended for specific groups or audiences, you can leverage Data categories to ensure the right groups have the right information. Data categories are a set of criteria organized into a hierarchy of groups. Articles are categorized according to the groups that you define (for example, product categories, regional categories, and so on). After you've defined data categories and assigned them to articles, they make it easy for users to find the articles they need.

Will Your Organization Need to Access Detailed Reports and Metrics about Support Articles?

If your organization wants to not only supply customer support agents with top-notch knowledge articles, but also run detailed reports about how the support articles are being used in an effort to continually maintain and improve the knowledge base, then Salesforce Knowledge is definitely the tool to use. With Salesforce Knowledge, you can create custom article reports or download and install the Knowledge Base Dashboards and Reports app from the AppExchange. With these tools, you can view article usage, ratings, and search statistics by channel or role to proactively manage your organization's content.

Does Your Organization Leverage Multiple Channels for Support?

If you want to share your support articles with more than just internal support teams, Salesforce Knowledge is an excellent option. You can share your articles through four different channels, in addition to your own website. Internal users can access articles directly in Salesforce, while Customer and Partner users can access articles via Customer and Partner Communities, respectively. Finally, your articles can also be made available to the general public with a Public Knowledge Base by leveraging the Public Knowledge Base for Salesforce Knowledge app from the AppExchange.

Do Your Agents Need to Be Able to Rate Articles?

Salesforce Knowledge comes with an article rating system to ensure that your organization can identify popular, useful articles and continue to maintain them, while weeding out the unhelpful articles. The rating system allows users to rate articles on a scale from 1 to 5; it weights the ratings based on how recently users have submitted their votes. The article rating system, combined with Salesforce Knowledge analytics, empowers your organization to stay ahead of the game when it comes to managing outdated content and understanding what type of information and formats agents or customers find most helpful.

Should Your Agents Be Able to Find, Create, and Send Articles?

Salesforce Knowledge allows your agents to easily find the articles they need with a one-click search feature. Additionally, you can empower your agents to contribute to the knowledge base by enabling them to create a draft article as they're closing out a case. Finally, many tools may leave your agents copying and pasting paragraphs to share with customers, or even typing manually into an email, but with Salesforce Knowledge your agents will be able to send PDFs of support articles to your customers directly from the case records.

Do Your Agents Need to Collaborate on Support Articles Using Chatter?

With Salesforce, collaboration via Chatter is the name of the game. Whether sales reps are collaborating on a deal or agents are collaborating on a case, the speed and ease of Chatter allows for real-time collaboration from anywhere on any device. Salesforce Knowledge doesn't miss a beat — agents can collaborate and share ideas directly on article records in the system to correct or improve content.

Do Your Agents Need Robust Search Functionality to Locate Articles?

In addition to having data categories and article types to leverage as search criteria for an enhanced search experience, Salesforce Knowledge allows users to search for articles by language or status and view results by ratings or views. Your organization can also leverage an auto-complete function when searching to have suggested article titles appear as users type in the search bar. Additionally, the article search functionality incorporates stemming and you can optionally define search synonym groups.

Stemming is the process of reducing a word to its root form. For example, if you ran a search for the word *fix,* stemming would return matches for *fix, fixing,* and *fixed.* Synonym groups allow your organization to define words that you want to be treated as equivalents in article searches.

Do Your Agents Use the Service Console View?

Hopefully your support agents are already leveraging the awe-inspiring power of the Service Console to make their lives efficient and your customers' experience smooth, fast, and convenient. If they are, the Salesforce Knowledge sidebar will appear whenever they select a case record. As agents type in the subject of a case, the sidebar displays suggested articles that have been updated within the last 30 days. From the Knowledge sidebar, agents can filter down or expand article results, attach articles to cases, or remove articles. They can hide the sidebar with one click as soon as they're finished looking for articles. Turn to Chapter 8 to find out more about the Service Console.

Chapter 23

Ten Bad Habits to Leave with Your Legacy System

- -

In This Chapter

▶ Thinking differently about Service Cloud

▶ Letting go of email

▶ Determining necessity

▶ Maximizing value

▶ Understanding constant evolution

▶ Embracing change

- -

*I*f you're trading in an old beat-up 1986 Honda for a brand-new Beamer, chances are, you're not going to be trying to replace some new car parts with the old Honda parts. Same goes here. If you're replacing your old system with Service Cloud, read on!

As creatures of habit, we sometimes have trouble letting go of the old way of doing things. Yes, you've accumulated over two decades of good times and memories in that Honda, but if it's time for an upgrade, go for the upgrade and let the Honda go! Sure, it'll take a little while to adjust to all the new buttons and features, but have faith that it was created with you in mind and that, in a matter of days, it will become second nature and you'll forget what it replaced.

In this chapter, we provide a list of ten bad habits that you should leave behind you when moving onto Service Cloud from another system. Whether you're replacing a legacy system or integrating with it, this list provides some beneficial and practical tips to keep in mind that will help smooth the transition and increase odds for successful adoption.

People form a lot of habits when they're used to one thing or another. Do not take this list personally. This could or could not reflect what you do, but is meant to help you on your journey toward Service Cloud greatness.

Using Microsoft Outlook Folders for Everything

We know Outlook is your life. You've organized everything neatly in Outlook folders and you think that living without them is simply non-negotiable. That's fine. Our advice to you is to leverage what Service Cloud offers. The best way to have high adoption rates and set an example for other users is to have a centralized one-stop shop for your workday. Leverage knowledge articles. Use Chatter. Take advantage of Content. Upload documents to Document folders in Salesforce. Stop using your Outlook folders for everything.

Reopening Cases

Different Salesforce organizations vary in how they treat the reopening of cases. Ultimately, this decision is business-process specific. The options are varied, and the metrics can get complicated to track. If your organization is using Entitlements and Milestones, it can get especially tricky and messy. Either way you look at it, unexpected things happen and sometimes a case is mistakenly closed or just needs to be reopened for one reason or another. What's more, the frequency of reopening cases can be a valuable metric to track. You can report on this and group by user or by team, gaining insight into those individuals who are most efficient and thorough in (truly) closing cases.

Instead of building a complex solution to account for edge cases, perhaps you should evaluate your business process. If you've provided a solution to your customer, should you immediately close the case? Maybe it makes more sense to change the case status to Solution Provided and wait for confirmation before changing that status to Closed. You can even create a time-dependent workflow rule that will auto-close your cases in the Solution Provided status if there are no updates to it within a certain length of time.

Recreating a Legacy System to Relieve Your Separation Anxiety

Why are you renaming cases? Does it really matter if cases are called "service requests" or "tickets" in your system? At the end of the day, it doesn't. If you don't have faith in yourself or your colleagues to handle new terminology, how can you handle a new system? Of course, it won't be the end of the world either way, but the point we're trying to make here is that you're entering the world of Service Cloud. This world has been embraced by countless individuals and businesses around the globe. Consequently, the more you can adopt the new technology and its terms, the more information you'll be able to access and share with experienced users, in related forums, and through support networks that will all be speaking the same language.

Don't re-create Siebel — or any other legacy application, for that matter — in Service Cloud. Salesforce spends millions of dollars researching, testing, and building their products with businesses like yours in mind. This means that you shouldn't have to. Leverage as much out-of-the-box configuration and functionality as possible. Don't spend time and money trying to reconfigure the entire user interface (UI) just to save one or two clicks. This will cost you more now and in the future.

Using Email Too Much

Service Cloud has plenty of functionality that can replace or drastically reduce email traffic. Use Chatter to strengthen internal team communication. Do you need to ask your colleague a question about a specific product line? Why not use Chatter? That way, not only do you save on inbox clutter, but your question can be searched and viewed by many others who potentially want to know the same thing. No longer do answers need to get lost in your inbox, never to be seen again.

Leverage approval processes for Knowledge article publication or any other relevant process. Instead of emailing drafts and comments back and forth, you can use approval processes to ensure a consistent flow of progress. An added bonus is that you can report on its status to see where the bottlenecks are. Be efficient, and join the 21st century: Use email only when you have to.

Data Quality: Do You Really Need All These Fields?

So, you used to capture a lot of data points. We get it. Data is allowing every type of company to wow customers with personalized service. But do you really need to know Jane Smith's eye color? Just because you feel comfortable having all your old fields mapped to your new system doesn't mean it makes sense porting them over if you rarely use the fields. This is especially true if there's bad or irrelevant data captured in them. Your CRM is only as good as the data within it, so think twice before you go to great pains to bring something over that you'll use twice a year.

Think about it this way: You're getting a fresh, clean environment from Salesforce. You want to keep it that way! This is the *best* time to do a little spring cleaning and make some choices. Consolidate where you can and don't be afraid to leave some fields behind. Only bring over what you need to track and use for your analytics.

Users Don't Always Know Best

We have to share some words with you administrators that you probably thought this book could never utter: Your customers are *not* always right. Let us explain.

As an admin, your "customers" are the users of the system you administer. You receive countless requests for enhancements or changes to profiles and security. Don't give Cindy from Customer Care access to Rob's caseload just because she asks for it. Don't immediately create a custom object just because Jerry wants one and points out a benefit or two. Sure, Salesforce makes it easy to meet these demands, but that doesn't mean it's smart to do so. Make sure there is a solid business case for system enhancements and funnel your requests through a prioritization process. Think through the ripple effects within Salesforce. What impact do these changes make? If the stakes are high, remind yourself of the core requirement and see how you can get there in a better way.

Don't Go Chasing Waterfall

The *waterfall approach* is a chronological software development process that progresses through fixed sequential phases. It's usually associated with older software, heavy documentation, and development that makes changes very expensive and time-consuming. In the world of on-premises applications, each new release (which is infrequent anyway) requires lots of work and release management.

Welcome to enterprise cloud software. Salesforce Service Cloud attributes much of its success to its agile approach to software development. To those of us accustomed to large, bureaucratic companies with a waterfall mentality, moving to Salesforce and developing in it may seem nerve-wracking. The sheer speed, flexibility, and evolutionary nature of agile development stands in stark contrast to the approaches of the old guard.

Fear not! Agile methodology and Salesforce go hand in hand, and this is crucial not to overlook. Don't be afraid to fail early and often (well, not too often), as agile methodology emphasizes early delivery, continuous improvement, and swift response to change.

It Doesn't End at Go-Live

Don't fall into the trap of believing that all requirements must be met before go-live. Identify the highest-priority items that, if not completed, are go-live show-stoppers. Ensure the progress and success of those items while keeping track of a backlog of lower-priority ones. We understand the uncontainable excitement that comes with building your dream customer service platform, but it's important to recognize that you aren't unveiling a finished product. Service Cloud will change and evolve whether you like it or not, to meet the changing demands of your business as well as through Salesforce's three releases a year. Things will only get better. Don't be nervous if you can't fit everything into your aggressive go-live deadline. Trust us, some things can wait. And the good news is, they no longer have to wait very long.

Not Leveraging a Certified Administrator

This one is obvious. Your system is constantly evolving and you need a certified administrator to manage this change. Someone should inevitably own the responsibility for Salesforce administration at your company, and incentivizing that individual to get certified, or hiring one who is, is a worthy investment. This is true especially if you're relying on Salesforce for a huge piece of your business.

A good administrator is not just a "doer." A really valuable admin is someone who can understand the needs of your business, while providing sound analysis followed by options and strategic direction to meet them.

Embracing the Change

You have a new system, and you should embrace it. The same goes for new features in Service Cloud. Salesforce as a company tends to push its weight and its customers behind new functionality, slowly phasing out dated predecessor functionality. Although Salesforce often continues to support these outdated features, it makes sense to get behind the new ones as new development and new releases improve upon them.

Index

• *Symbols* •

(hashtag symbol), 108

• *A* •

access
  allowing with sharing rules, 298–299
  to articles, 159–161, 171–172
  for case teams, 96
  to dashboards, 283–285
  opening up to users and public groups for
      Salesforce Knowledge, 173–176
  record type, 316
accessing
  AppExchange, 326
  metrics, 337
  Reports, 337
  Setup configuration menu as
      administrator, 290
Account Name, as standard case field, 54
Activate Validation Status field setting, 173
activating
  validation rules, 323
  workflow rules, 321
adding
  apps for Service Cloud Console, 142–144
  article types in Salesforce Knowledge,
      156–158
  Live Agent skills, 124
  Live Agent users, 122
  members to Communities, 222–225
  tabs to Communities, 226–229
  team members to case teams, 99–100
  users in organizations, 302
  users to Live Agent Chat feature,
      122
administration, in Communities, 210
Administrative permissions (Live Agent
      Chat feature), 123

administrator, accessing Setup
      configuration menu as, 290
Agent Case Load by Type report, 257–258
agent hierarchy, Service Cloud Console
      and, 149
agent interactions, improving quality of, 13
all profiles, searching, 222
Allow users to add external multimedia
      content to HTML setting, 173
Allow users to create and edit articles from
      the Articles tab setting, 173
analytics
  Community, 244–246
  visualizing with dashboard snapshots,
      27–28
Answers Settings, 173
Apex customization, 178
Apex pages, in Communities, 211
Apex triggers, in Communities, 211
AppExchange
  about, 325–326
  accessing, 326
  browsing, 326–328
  filtering in, 327–328
  navigating apps in, 328
  preparing to install apps, 329
  searching, 327
  sorting in, 327–328
  testing apps, 331
  website, 155, 261, 326
approval process
  for Salesforce Knowledge, 159
  setting up for article review and
      publication, 200–202
apps
  adding for Service Cloud Console,
      142–144
  building customized, 142–144
  defined, 19
  deploying, 329–331

apps *(continued)*
installing, 329–330
navigating in AppExchange, 328
preparing to install AppExchange, 329
testing AppExchange, 331
Archived status, for articles,
155, 182
archiving articles, 190–193
article actions, in Salesforce Service Cloud,
175
article management, automating, 199–202
Article Management tab, searching for
articles using, 189
Article Managers
about, 156
restricting, 182–183
Article Summaries Settings, 173
Article Type field, 166
article types
adding in Salesforce Knowledge, 156–158
building, 165
categorizing in Salesforce Knowledge,
156–158
creating custom fields for,
167–168
customizing layouts for, 169
defined, 154
identifying properties and fields, 166–168
segmenting knowledge with, 164–172
articles
about, 181
Archived status for, 155, 182
archiving, 190–193
assigning, 186–187
attaching to cases, 179–180
categorizing, 181–202
categorizing into data categories, 193–199
Category Group for, 156, 193
collaborating on, 338
creating, 338
Data Category for, 155–156, 193
defined, 154
designating access, 159–161, 171–172
designating permissions, 159–161
displaying, 158–159
enabling submission upon case closure,
178–179

finding, 338
formats of, 336
lifecycle of, 336
managing, 181–202
publishing, 187–188
rating, 337–338
searching for, 188–190, 338–339
sending, 186–187, 338
sending for approval, 186–187
suggesting, 177
updating, 190–193
article-type layout
defined, 154
modifying, 168–171
article-type templates
assigning, 169–170
changing, 170–171
defined, 154
assigning
articles, 186–187
article-type templates, 169–170
cases, 80
interaction logs, 145–147
layouts to profiles in Force.com, 311–312
Live Agent configurations, 124–125
users to permission sets, 225
assignment rules, creating, 80–82
attaching articles to cases,
179–180
audiences, targeting, 336
authenticating, 18–19
authorizing customers, 57
automating
article management, 199–202
case escalation, 102–103
using, 79–84
auto-response rules, defining, 83–84
Average Age of Open Cases report, 258–260
Average Case Age by Agent report, 260

• *B* •

Back to List link, 32
bar chart, 272
brand loyalists, as a reason for using
Salesforce Service Cloud, 11–14
branding and customization

Communities, 231–239
as feature of Salesforce Communities, 208
browsing AppExchange, 326–328
building
  Agent Case Load by Type report, 257–258
  article types, 165
  articles, 338
  assignment rules, 80–82
  auto-response rules, 83–84
  Average Age of Open Cases report, 259–260
  Average Case Age by Agent report, 260
  case queues, 78–79
  cases, 52–53
  Chatter groups, 107–108
  communities, 215–230, 218–221
  components for dashboards, 279–383
  custom fields for article types, 167–168
  custom profiles, 300–302
  customer users, 225
  customized apps, 142–144
  dashboard folders, 283
  dashboards for contact centers, 275–282
  draft articles, 184–185
  email templates, 62–64
  escalation rules by criteria, 102–103
  fields in Force.com, 306–309, 307–308
  groups, 297–298
  interaction logs, 144–147
  Live Agent Chat feature buttons and deployments, 125–127
  partner users, 225
  personal groups, 39–40
  Popular Knowledge Articles report, 261
  predefined case teams, 98–99
  profiles, 299–302
  public groups, 77–78
  record types in Force.com, 314–315
  records, 21, 28–30
  reports from scratch, 263–266
  role hierarchy, 294–295
  sharing rules, 299
  skills, 124
  Top Articles Associated with Cases report, 262
  validation rules, 321–323

  views, 70–75
  workflow rules, 202, 318–321
business health, measuring, as a reason for using Salesforce Service Cloud, 9
business hours, setting up, 292–294
business integration, as feature of Salesforce Communities, 208
buttons, as Live Agent Chat feature, 125–127

• **C** •

Calendar
  managing, 26–27
  sharing, 43–44
Calendar & Reminders section (My Settings page), 44–45
capturing case details, 57–59
Case Comments feature, 60
case fields, customizing, 54–55
case management
  about, 51, 69, 113
  assigning cases, 80
  automation, 79–84
  capturing case details, 57–59
  closing cases, 65–67
  communicating solutions, 60–61
  Computer Telephony Integration (CTI), 120–121
  creating assignment rules, 80–82
  creating case queues, 78–79
  creating views, 70–75
  defining auto-response rules, 83–84
  email templates, 61–65
  implementing Email-to-Case feature, 117–120
  implementing Live Agent Chat feature, 121–130
  investigating content, 85–88
  managing multiple processes in Force.com, 312–313
  managing views, 75–78
  offering multiple service channels, 114
  opening cases, 52–57

case management *(continued)*
researching issues, 59–60, 84–94
resolving issues, 59–60
setting up automatic responses, 82–83
setting up Web-to-Case feature, 114–117
social channels, 130
solving with Salesforce Knowledge, 91–94
solving with suggested solutions, 89–91
Case Number, as standard case field, 54
Case Origin, as standard case field, 54
case queues, creating, 78–79
Case Reason, as standard case field, 54
case records
about, 53–56
searching for articles using, 189–190
Case Settings, 173
case teams
about, 96
access for, 96
adding team members to, 99–100
predefined, 98–99
roles for, 96
setting up, 97–98
case volume, Service Cloud Console
and, 149
cases
assigning, 80
attaching articles to, 179–180
collaborating on, 95–109
enabling in Communities, 229
enabling submission upon closure of,
178–179
escalating, 100–105
leveraging Chatter on, 105–109
reassigning, 101–102
reopening, 342
solving, 69–94, 89–91
solving with Suggested Solutions, 89–91
transferring ownership of,
101–102
using with Salesforce Knowledge,
177–180
Cases tab, as a landing tab, 228
categorizing
article types in Salesforce Knowledge,
156–158

articles, 181–202
articles into data categories, 193–199
Category Group
for articles, 156, 193
planning, 194
centralization, as a reason for using
Salesforce Service Cloud, 10
Certified Administrator, 345
change, embracing, 346
changing
article-type layouts and templates,
168–171
article-type templates, 170–171
case fields, 54–55
Chatter preferences, 46–47
dashboard layouts, 282
display, 40–42
footer in Communities, 232–233
header in Communities,
232–233
page layouts in Force.com, 309–311
password, 38
reports, 266
user records, 38
channels
defined, 155
for support, 337
Chart components (dashboard), 272–273
Chatter
changing preferences, 46–47
collaborating on articles using, 338
communicating with customers and
partners, 109
enabling, 105, 108
leveraging on cases, 105–109
searching profiles, 222
tracking in, 108–109
Chatter Answers, using in communities,
250–251
Chatter feed, 24–25
Chatter section (My Settings page), 46–47
Chatter tab, as a landing tab, 228
Cheat Sheet (website), 3
checking
edition compatibility, 329
Salesforce Knowledge users, 164

choosing
  color schemes in Communities, 233–234
  Community Manager,
      241–242
  community moderators, 247
  domain names for
      Communities, 217
  email templates/settings for communities,
      238–239
  evaluation criteria, 319
  intermediate actions, 320
  landing tabs for community members,
      227–228
  list displays, 147–148
  public groups, 76–77
  record types, 316–317
  roles, 76–77
  time-dependent actions, 320
  users, 76–77
  users for Service Cloud
      Console, 149
clearing filters in reports, 268
closing cases, 65–67
collaboration
  about, 95
  on articles, 338
  case teams, 96–100
  Chatter on cases, 105–109
  with coworkers, as a reason for using
      Salesforce Service Cloud, 10–11
  escalating cases, 100–105
collapsing sidebars, 21
color schemes, choosing in Communities,
      233–234
column chart, 273
communicating
  with customers, 109
  with partners, 109
  solutions, 60–61
Communities
  about, 205, 215, 231
  adding members to, 222–225
  adding tabs to, 226–229
  administration in, 210
  branding, 231–239
  comparing, 209–212

  creating, 215–230, 218–221
  customer, 206–214
  customer community for new members,
      212–214
  customizing, 231–239
  disabling, 217
  displaying Salesforce Knowledge in, 251
  enabling, 216–217
  enabling cases, 229
  enabling Global Header for, 219–221, 223
  features of, 208
  governing, 240–251
  integrating, 249–251
  migrating from Portals to, 209–210
  moderating, 246–247
  navigating to, 248
  optimizing, 231–251
  partner, 206, 208
  planning, 215–216
  previewing, 229–230
  publishing, 240–251
  searching in, 211, 249
  selecting domain names
      for, 217
  setting up, 216–217
  statuses, 221
  use types and, 205–208
  using Chatter Answers in, 250–251
  utilizing analytics, 244–246
  what's new in, 210–212
Community Engagement Console, 242–244
Community Manager, selecting, 241–242
community moderators, selecting, 247
company information, updating, 291–292
Company Profile, viewing, 291–294
comparing communities, 209–212
components
  creating for dashboards, 279–383
  of dashboards, 272–275
Computer Telephony Integration (CTI),
      120–121
configuration
  about, 289–290
  administration setup, 290–291
  assigning in Live Agent Chat feature,
      124–125

configuration *(continued)*
building role hierarchy, 294–295
planning, 290–291
profiles, 299–302
security controls, 303–304
setting up users in organizations, 302
sharing model, 296–299
viewing Company Profile,
291–294
contact centers, creating dashboards for,
275–282
Contact Name, as standard case field, 54
content, investigating, 85–88
content libraries, 85
content pack, 85
Contract Manager profile, 300
coworkers, collaboration with, as a
reason for using Salesforce Service
Cloud, 10–11
Create and Customize Communities
permission, 232
Created Date field, 166
creating
Agent Case Load by Type report, 257–258
article types, 165
articles, 338
assignment rules, 80–82
auto-response rules, 83–84
Average Age of Open Cases report,
259–260
Average Case Age by Agent report, 260
case queues, 78–79
cases, 52–53
Chatter groups, 107–108
communities, 215–230, 218–221
components for dashboards, 279–383
custom fields for article types, 167–168
custom profiles, 300–302
customer users, 225
customized apps, 142–144
dashboard folders, 283
dashboards for contact centers, 275–282
draft articles, 184–185
email templates, 62–64
escalation rules by criteria, 102–103
fields in Force.com, 306–309, 307–308

groups, 297–298
interaction logs, 144–147
Live Agent Chat feature buttons and
deployments, 125–127
partner users, 225
personal groups, 39–40
Popular Knowledge Articles
report, 261
predefined case teams, 98–99
profiles, 299–302
public groups, 77–78
record types in Force.com, 314–315
records, 21, 28–30
reports from scratch, 263–266
role hierarchy, 294–295
sharing rules, 299
skills, 124
Top Articles Associated with Cases
report, 262
validation rules, 321–323
views, 70–75
workflow rules, 202, 318–321
criteria, creating escalation rules by,
102–103
CTI (Computer Telephony Integration),
120–121
Custom help settings, 211
custom HTML email templates, 61
custom links, using, 20–24
custom objects, in Communities, 211
Customer channel, 184
customer communities
about, 207–208
for new members, 212–214
uses cases and, 206
customer frustration, reducing, 12
Customer Portal users, 160
customer satisfaction
as benefit of offering multiple service
channels, 114
as a reason for using Salesforce
Service Cloud, 8
customer users, creating, 225
customers
authorizing, 57
communicating with, 109

creating connections with, 12
defined, 155
giving options to, 12
identifying, 56–57
qualifying, 56–57
customizing. *See also* branding and
    customization; modifying
case fields, 54–55
color schemes in Community, 234
Communities, 231–239
email settings, 45
with Force.com, 305–323
interaction logs, 145–147
layouts for article types, 169
page layouts, 55–56, 309–312
page layouts in Force.com,
    309–312
pages, 42
Reports, 263–269
tabs, 40–41

• *D* •

dashboards
about, 271
access to, 283–285
building folders, 283
components of, 272–275
creating components for, 279–383
creating for contact centers, 275–282
editing properties, 278–279
enabling, 245–246
modifying layouts, 282
organizing, 283–285
planning for, 271–275
saving, 282
visualizing analytics with snapshots,
    27–28
data access
quality of, 343–344
as a reason for using Salesforce
    Service Cloud, 11
Data Category
for articles, 155–156, 193
categorizing articles into,
    193–199

setting up, 194–197
deactivating external users, 225
defining
auto-response rules, 83–84
criteria for list views, 72–73
record-type access
    in Force.com, 316
rule criteria, 319–320
deleting records, 30–32
deploying apps, 329–331
deployments, as Live Agent Chat
    feature, 125–127
Description, as standard case field, 54
designating
article access, 159–161, 171–172
article access and permissions, 159–161
visibility, 75
Detail page, 32–33
details, showing/hiding in reports,
    268–269
determining community types, 207
Developer Edition
about, 16
Salesforce Knowledge in, 153
disabling
On-Demand Email-to-Case, 118
Salesforce Communities, 217
display, changing, 40–42
Display & Layout section (My Settings
    page), 42
displaying
articles, 158–159
layouts, 158–159
lists, 147
Salesforce Knowledge in Communities,
    251
tabs in Communities, 226–227
Documents tab, 211
domain names, selecting
    for Communities, 217
donut chart, 273
draft articles, creating, 184–185
Draft status, for articles, 155, 182
Draft translation, 156
Drill Down feature, 267
Dummies.com (website), 3

• E •

ease of use, 16
editing
  dashboard properties, 278–279
  default data category visibility settings, 197–199
  fields in Force.com, 306–309
  record types in Force.com, 315–316
  records, 30–32
editions
  about, 15–16
  checking compatibility of, 329
email
  in Communities, 210–211
  settings, selecting for communities, 238–239
  templates, selecting for communities, 238–239
  using, 343
Email section (My Settings page), 45
Email-to-Case feature, implementing, 117–120
embracing change, 346
employee communities, uses cases and, 206–207
enabling
  article submission upon case closure, 178–179
  cases in Communities, 229
  Chatter, 105, 108
  Chatter feed, 24
  dashboards, 245–246
  Global Header for Communities, 219–221, 223
  Highlights panel, 141–142
  interaction logs, 144–145
  keyboard shortcuts, 135
  Knowledge sidebar, 148
  Live Agent Chat feature, 121
  Reputation levels, 243–244
  Salesforce Communities, 216–217
  Salesforce Knowledge, 148, 172–176
  Web-to-Case feature, 116–117

enhancing login page for communities, 235–238
Enterprise Edition
  about, 16
  article access in, 160
  Salesforce Knowledge in, 153
entitlement management, 57
Error Condition Formula, 322
Error Location, 322
Error Message, 322
escalating cases, 100–105
escalation actions, setting up, 103–105
escalation rules, creating by criteria, 102–103
evaluation criteria, selecting, 319
executing workflow actions, 320
exposing relevant data, 73–74
external users
  about, 248
  Communities and, 225, 229
  resetting passwords for, 248–249
  setting up self-registration for, 236–238

F

field-level security, 303–304
fields
  article type, 166–168
  building in Force.com, 306–309
  editing in Force.com, 306–309
filtering, in AppExchange, 327–328
filters, clearing in reports, 268
finding articles, 338. *See also* searching
First Published Date field, 166
Flag Content feature (Community), 246–247
flagging items in Communities, 246–247
folders
  dashboard, 283
  Microsoft Outlook, 342
footer, changing in Communities, 232–233
Force.com
  about, 305–306
  building fields, 306–309
  customizing page layouts, 309–312

customizing with, 305–323
editing fields, 306–309
home, 34
leveraging record types, 313–317
managing multiple
case-management processes, 312–313
validation rules, 317–323
workflow rules, 317–323
Force.com Connect Offline application, 46
formats, of articles, 336
funnel chart, 273

• G •

Gauge components (dashboard), 273, 274
general settings (Salesforce Knowledge),
173
Global Header, enabling for Communities,
219–221, 223
global search bar, searching for articles
using, 190
"going live," 345
governing Communities,
240–251
Grant Access Using Hierarchies option, 295
granting
Live Agent users permissions, 122–123
login access, 42–43
groups
Chatter, 106–108
creating, 297–298
defined, 39

• H •

hashtag symbol (#), 108
header, changing in communities, 232–233
Header Background option (Community),
233
Help menu, 33–34
hiding details in reports, 268–269
hierarchy, planning, 194
Highlights Panel (Service Cloud Console)
about, 136
enabling, 141–142
holidays, setting up, 292–294

Home page
navigating, 19–28
Reports, 255–256
searching from, 21–23
Home tab, as a landing tab, 228
hover links, 32
HTML email templates, 61

• I •

icons, explained, 2–3
identifying
article type properties and fields,
166–168
customers, 56–57
implementing
Email-to-Case feature,
117–120
Live Agent Chat feature,
121–130
Salesforce Knowledge,
335–339
Service Cloud Console, 139–149
installing apps, 329–330
integrating Communities, 249–251
Interaction Log (Service Cloud Console)
about, 136
assigning, 145–147
building, 144–147
customizing, 145–147
enabling, 144–145
interface, 15
intermediate actions, choosing, 320
internal app, 155
Internal app channel, 184
internal knowledge, 106–108
internal profiles, searching, 222
internal users, 160, 248
investigating content, 85–88
Is Latest Version field, 166
issues, researching, 84–94

• K •

keyboard shortcuts (Service Cloud
Console), 134–136

Knowledge
  about, 91–94, 153, 163–164
  adding article types, 156–158
  approval process, 159
  categorizing articles types, 156–158
  designating article access and
    permissions, 159–161
  displaying articles and layouts, 158–159
  displaying in communities, 251
  enabling, 172–176
  enabling sidebar, 148
  implementing, 335–339
  opening up access to users and public
    groups, 173–176
  segmenting knowledge with article types,
    164–172
  setting up, 163–180
  terminology in, 154–156
  using cases with, 177–180
  verifying users, 164
Knowledge Agent, 156
Knowledge articles, reading, 171
Knowledge One Settings, 173
Knowledge Tab, searching for articles
  using, 188–189
Knowledge tool, 59–60

• *L* •

landing tabs, choosing for community
  members, 227–228
Language Settings, 173
Last Published Date field, 167
layouts
  article-type, 154, 168–171
  assigning to profiles in Force.com,
    311–312
  customizing for article types, 169
  dashboard, 282
  displaying, 158–159
  page, 55–56, 309–312
legacy system, 341–346
leveraging
  Chatter on cases, 105–109
  record types in Force.com, 313–317
licenses, reassigning, 210

lifecycle, of articles, 336
limitations
  of Web-to-Case feature, 115
  to workflow, 321
line chart, 273
links, custom, using, 20–24
list displays, choosing, 147–148
list views, 70–71, 72–73
lists, displaying, 147
"live, going," 345
Live Agent Chat feature
  adding skills, 124
  adding users, 122
  assigning configurations, 124–125
  creating feature buttons and
    deployments, 125–127
  enabling, 121
  granting users permissions, 122–123
  implementing, 121–130
  reporting on sessions, 129–130
  setting up transcripts and visitors,
    127–129
login
  in Communities, 211
  granting access, 42–43
  Salesforce Service Cloud, 16–19
login page, enhancing for communities,
  235–238
logos, uploading, 235–236
Logout page settings, 211

• *M* •

Manage Articles permission, 161
Manage Data Categories permission, 161
Manage Public List Views permission, 75
Manager Salesforce Knowledge permission,
  161
managing
  articles, 181–202
  Calendar, 26–27
  multiple case-management processes in
    Force.com, 312–313
  My Tasks, 25–26
  profiles, 299–302
managing cases

about, 51, 69, 113
assigning cases, 80
automation, 79–84
capturing case details, 57–59
closing cases, 65–67
communicating solutions, 60–61
Computer Telephony Integration (CTI), 120–121
creating assignment rules, 80–82
creating case queues, 78–79
creating views, 70–75
defining auto-response rules, 83–84
email templates, 61–65
implementing Email-to-Case feature, 117–120
implementing Live Agent Chat feature, 121–130
investigating content, 85–88
managing multiple processes in Force.com, 312–313
managing views, 75–78
offering multiple service channels, 114
opening cases, 52–57
researching issues, 59–60, 84–94
resolving issues, 59–60
setting up automatic responses, 82–83
setting up Web-to-Case feature, 114–117
social channels, 130
solving with Salesforce Knowledge, 91–94
solving with suggested solutions, 89–91
Marketing User profile, 300
Matrix report, 265
measuring business health, 9
members
  adding to Communities, 222–225
  welcoming to Communities, 240–241
membership, in Communities, 210
Metric components (dashboard), 273
metrics, accessing, 337
Microsoft Outlook folders, 342
migrating from Portals to Communities, 209–210
mobility, as feature of Salesforce Communities, 208
moderating Communities, 246–247
modifying

article-type layouts and templates, 168–171
article-type templates, 170–171
case fields, 54–55
Chatter preferences, 46–47
dashboard layouts, 282
display, 40–42
footer in Communities, 232–233
header in Communities, 232–233
page layouts in Force.com, 309–311
password, 38
reports, 266
user records, 38
My Settings page
about, 35–37
Calendar & Reminders section, 44–45
Chatter section, 46–47
Display & Layout section, 42
Email section, 45
Personal section, 37–45
My Tasks, managing, 25–26

• N •

navigating
apps in AppExchange, 328
to Communities, 248
Home page, 19–28
Reports home page, 255–256
Salesforce Service Cloud, 15–34
through reports, 267–268
Navigation tab (Service Cloud Console), 136, 140
notifications, in Communities, 210–211

• O •

offline, working, 46
Offline status (Communities), 221
Old Questions tab, 211
On-Demand Email-to-Case, setting up, 118–119
opening
cases, 52–57
Salesforce Knowledge access to users and public groups, 173–176

operational cost, decreased, as benefit of offering multiple service channels, 114
Opportunities tab, as a landing tab, 228
optimizing Communities, 231–251
options
dashboard, 272–275
Report, 268
organizations
setting up automatic responses for, 82–83
views, 75–78
organization-wide defaults, setting, 296–297
organizing dashboards, 283–285
ownership, case, 101–102

• *P* •

Page Background option (Community), 233
page layouts
customizing, 55–56, 309–312
customizing in Force.com, 309–312
pages, customizing, 42
"pared-down" org chart, 294–295
Partner channel, 184
partner communities
about, 208
uses cases and, 206
Partner Portal users, 160
partner users, creating, 225
partners
communicating with, 109
defined, 155
passwords
changing, 38
resetting, 17–18, 248–249
resetting for external users, 248–249
setting up, 16–17
Performance Edition
article access in, 160
Salesforce Knowledge in, 153
permission sets
adding members to Communities with, 223–225
assigning permissions via, 247

assigning users Manage Communities permission
via, 242
granting user permissions
via, 171
in Live Agent Chat feature, 122–123
permissions
Administrative (Live Agent Chat feature), 123
for articles, 159–161
Live Agent Chat feature, 122–123
for Salesforce Knowledge, 161
Standard object (Live Agent Chat feature), 123
Personal Groups
about, 297
creating, 39–40
personal information, updating, 37–45
Personal section (My Settings page), 37–45
personalizing Salesforce Service Cloud, 35–47
pie chart, 273
Pinned lists (Service Cloud Console), 136
planning
category groups, 194
Communities, 215–216
configuration, 290–291
for dashboards, 271–275
hierarchy, 194
pre-chat forms, 129
purposes for components, 274–275
Popular Knowledge Articles report, 261
Portal profiles, searching, 222
Portals, migrating to Communities from, 209–210
pre-chat forms, planning, 129
predefined case teams, 98–99
preferences, Chatter, 46–47
preparing
to enable Web-to-Case feature, 116
to install AppExchange apps, 329
Preview status (Communities), 221, 229–230
previewing Communities, 229–230
Primary option (Community), 233

Primary tab (Service Cloud Console), 136, 140
Printable View, 32
Priority, as standard case field, 54
Private access, for case teams, 96
Private option, for sharing, 296
Professional Edition, 15–16
profiles
  adding members to Communities using, 222–223
  assigning layouts to in Force.com, 311–312
  assigning permissions via, 247
  assigning users Manage Communities permission via, 242
  creating, 299–302
  granting user permissions via, 171
  in Live Agent Chat feature, 122
  managing, 299–302
  searching, 222
  standard, 299–300
properties
  article type, 166–168
  editing for dashboards, 278–279
  of validation rules, 322
Public Groups
  about, 39, 297
  creating, 77–78
  opening up Salesforce Knowledge access for, 173–176
  selecting, 76–77
Public Knowledge Base
  channel, 184
  defined, 155
  users, 160
Public Read Only option, for sharing, 296
Public Read/Write option, for sharing, 297
Publication Status field, 167
Published status
  for articles, 155, 182
  Communities, 221
Published translation, 156
publishing

articles, 187–188
Communities, 240–251

• Q •

qualifying customers, 56–57
quality, of agent interaction, 13
quality, of data, 343–344
queues, managing cases with, 69–79
Quick Create feature, 21

R

rating articles, 337–338
Read, Create, Edit, and Delete permissions, 161
Read Only access, for case teams, 96
Read Only profile, 300
reading Salesforce Knowledge articles, 171
Read/Write access, for case teams, 96
reassigning
  cases, 101–102
  licenses, 210
Recent Items list, reviewing, 23
record types
  choosing, 316–317
  creating in Force.com, 314–315
  defining access in Force.com, 316
  editing in Force.com, 315–316
  leveraging in Force.com, 313–317
  viewing in Force.com, 315–316
records
  about, 28
  creating, 21, 28–30
  deleting, 30–32
  editing, 30–32
  sharing, 32
re-creating legacy systems, 342–343
Recycle Bin
  about, 24
  removing records from, 31
Related list, 32

Remember icon, 3
remote access, 46
removing records from Recycle Bin, 31
reopening cases, 342
reporting
  on Communities usage, 244–245
  on Live Agent sessions, 129–130
Reports
  about, 255
  accessing, 337
  Agent Case Load by Type report, 257–258
  Average Age of Open Cases report, 258–260
  Average Case Age by Agent report, 260
  building reports from scratch, 263–266
  clearing filters, 268
  customizing reports, 263–269
  Drill Down feature, 267
  hiding details, 268–269
  modifying existing reports, 266
  navigating home page, 255–256
  navigating through reports, 267–268
  Popular Knowledge Articles report, 261
  setting options, 268
  showing details, 268–269
  Top Articles Associated with Cases report, 261–262
Reputation levels, enabling, 243–244
researching issues, 59–60, 84–94
Reset My Security Token option, 38
resetting
  external users' passwords, 248–249
  password, 17–18, 248–249
resolving issues, 59–60
restricting Article Managers, 182–183
reviewing Recent Items list, 23
role hierarchy, building, 294–295
roles
  for case teams, 96
  selecting, 76–77
rule criteria, defining, 319–320

rules
  assignment, 80–82
  auto-response, 83–84
  escalation, 102–103
  validation, 317–318, 321–323
  workflow, 317–321

• S •

Salesforce Communities
  about, 205, 215, 231
  adding members to, 222–225
  adding tabs to, 226–229
  administration in, 210
  branding, 231–239
  comparing, 209–212
  creating, 215–230, 218–221
  customer, 206–214
  customer community for new members, 212–214
  customizing, 231–239
  disabling, 217
  displaying Salesforce Knowledge in, 251
  enabling, 216–217
  enabling cases, 229
  enabling Global Header for, 219–221, 223
  features of, 208
  governing, 240–251
  integrating, 249–251
  migrating from Portals to, 209–210
  moderating, 246–247
  navigating to, 248
  optimizing, 231–251
  partner, 206, 208
  planning, 215–216
  previewing, 229–230
  publishing, 240–251
  searching in, 211, 249
  selecting domain names for, 217
  setting up, 216–217
  statuses, 221
  use types and, 205–208
  using Chatter Answers in, 250–251

utilizing analytics, 244–246

what's new in, 210–212

Salesforce Console Integration Toolkit (Service Cloud Console), 136

Salesforce Knowledge

about, 91–94, 153, 163–164

adding article types, 156–158

approval process, 159

categorizing articles types, 156–158

designating article access and permissions, 159–161

displaying articles and layouts, 158–159

displaying in communities, 251

enabling, 172–176

enabling sidebar, 148

implementing, 335–339

opening up access to users and public groups, 173–176

segmenting knowledge with article types, 164–172

setting up, 163–180

terminology in, 154–156

using cases with, 177–180

verifying users, 164

Salesforce Service Cloud. *See also specific topics*

article actions in, 175

logging in, 16–19

navigating, 15–34

personalizing, 35–47

solving business challenges with, 7–14

saving dashboards, 282

scatter chart, 273

searching

AppExchange, 327

for articles, 188–190, 338–339

Chatter profiles, 222

in Communities, 211, 249

from Home page, 21–23

Secondary option (Community), 234

security and scalability, as feature of Salesforce Communities, 208

security controls, 303–304

segmenting knowledge with article types, 164–172

selecting

color schemes in Communities, 233–234

Community Manager, 241–242

community moderators, 247

domain names for Communities, 217

email templates/settings for communities, 238–239

evaluation criteria, 319

intermediate actions, 320

landing tabs for community members, 227–228

list displays, 147–148

public groups, 76–77

record types, 316–317

roles, 76–77

time-dependent actions, 320

users, 76–77

users for Service Cloud Console, 149

self-registration

setting up for external users, 236–238

settings for, 212

self-service, as feature of Salesforce Communities, 208

Send Notification Email to Contact check box, 60

sending

articles, 186–187, 338

articles for approval, 186–187

emails from cases, 64–65

Salesforce Service Cloud. *See also specific topics*

article actions in, 175

logging in, 16–19

navigating, 15–34

personalizing, 35–47

solving business challenges with, 7–14

Service Cloud Console

about, 131, 139

adding apps for, 142–144

agent hierarchy and, 149

building interaction logs, 144–147

case volume and, 149

choosing list displays, 147–148

components of, 140

defined, 136

Service Cloud Console *(continued)*
  enabling Highlights Panel,
    141–142
  implementing, 139–149
  keyboard shortcuts, 134–136
  selecting users, 149
  strategy for, 137–138
  terms, 136–137
  using, 132–134
Service Console View, 339
service process, expediting, 13–14
service-level agreement (SLA), 72
sessions, Live Agent Chat feature,
    129–130
settings
  Activate Validation Status
    field, 173
  Allow users to add external multimedia
    content to HTML, 173
  Allow users to create and edit articles
    from the Articles tab, 173
  Article Summaries Settings, 173
  Case Settings, 173
  Custom help, 211
  general (Salesforce Knowledge), 173
  Language Settings, 173
  Logout page, 211
  organization-wide defaults, 296–297
  report options, 268
  for self-registration, 212
setup
  approval process for article review and
    publication, 200–202
  automatic responses for organizations,
    82–83
  business hours, 292–294
  case teams, 97–98
  Communities, 216–217
  data categories, 194–197
  escalation actions, 103–105
  Highlights Panel (Service Cloud Console),
    141–142
  holidays, 292–294
  live chat transcripts and visitors,
    127–129
  On-Demand Email-to-Case, 118–119

  passwords, 16–17
  Salesforce Knowledge, 163–180
  self-registration for external users,
    236–238
  support processes, 312–313
  users in organizations, 302
  Web-to-Case feature, 114–117
Setup configuration menu, accessing as
    administrator, 290
Setup menu, 33–34
sharing
  Calendar, 43–44
  records, 32
sharing model, 296–299
shortcuts, keyboard, 134–136
Show option (Reports), 268
showing details in reports,
    268–269
sidebar
  about, 18
  collapsing, 21
  using, 20–24
Siebel, 343
skills, adding in Live Agent Chat feature,
    124
SLA (service-level agreement), 72
social channels, 130
Social Customer Service feature, 130
social feed, as feature of Salesforce
    Communities, 208
Social Hub licenses, 130
social intelligence, as feature of Salesforce
    Communities, 208
softphone, 120
Solution Manager profile, 300
solutions, communicating, 60–61
Solutions tool, 59–60
solving
  cases, 69–94, 89–91
  cases with Suggested Solutions, 89–91
sorting, in AppExchange, 327–328
source reports, dashboards and, 272
standard case fields, 53–54
Standard object permissions (Live Agent
    Chat feature), 123
Standard User profile, 300

Status, as standard case field, 54
statuses
  Archived, 155, 182
  Communities, 221
strategy, for Service Cloud Console,
    137–138
Subject, as standard case field, 54
Subtabs (Service Cloud Console), 136, 140
Suggested Solutions, solving cases with,
    89–91
suggesting articles, 177
Summarize Information By option
    (Reports), 268
Summary field, 167
Summary report, 265
System Administrator profile, 300

• *T* •

Tab template
  about, 169
  defined, 154
  Salesforce Knowledge, 159
Table components (dashboard), 274
Table of Contents template,
    154, 169
tabs
  adding to Communities, 226–229
  customizing, 40–41
  defined, 19
  displaying in Communities, 226–227
taking action, on articles, 171
targeting audiences, 336
tasks, in Communities, 211
team members, adding to case teams,
    99–100
Technical Stuff icon, 3
templates
  article-type, 154, 169–171
  in Communities, 210–211
  email, 61–65
  modifying, 168–171
terminology, in Salesforce Knowledge,
    154–156
terms, Service Cloud Console, 136–137
Tertiary option (Community), 234

testing AppExchange apps, 331
text-only email templates, 61
"a 360-degree view of the customer," 9
Time Frame option (Reports), 268
time-dependent actions, choosing, 320
Tip icon, 3
Title field, 167
Top Articles Associated with Cases
    report, 261–262
top-level solution category, 212
tracking, in Chatter, 108–109
training users on communities,
    247–249
transcripts, as Live Agent Chat
    feature, 127–129
transferring case ownership, 101–102
turning on. *See* enabling
Type, as standard case field, 54

U

Unlimited Edition
  about, 16
  article access in, 160
  Salesforce Knowledge in, 153
updating
  articles, 190–193
  company information, 291–292
  fields in Force.com, 308–309
  personal information, 37–45
uploading logos, 235–236
URL Name field, 167
user management, in Communities, 210
user record, modifying, 38
users
  about, 344
  adding in organizations, 302
  adding to Live Agent Chat feature, 122
  assigning to permission sets, 225
  Customer Portal, 160
  granting permissions in Live Agent Chat
    feature, 122–123
  internal, 160, 248
  opening up Salesforce Knowledge access
    for, 173–176
  partner, 225

users *(continued)*
  Partner Portal, 160
  selecting, 76–77, 149, 242
  selecting as Community Manager, 242
  selecting for Service Cloud Console, 149
  setting up in organizations, 302
  training on communities, 247–249
  verifying in Salesforce Knowledge, 164

V

validation rules, 317–318, 321–323
verifying
  edition compatibility, 329
  Salesforce Knowledge users, 164
Version Number field, 166
viewing
  Company Profile, 291–294
  record types in Force.com, 315–316
views
  creating, 70–75
  managing cases with, 69–79
  organization, 75–78
visibility
  designating, 75
  editing settings for default data
    categories, 197–199
Visible in Public Knowledge Base field, 167
Visible to Customer field, 167

Visible to Partner field, 167
visitors, as Live Agent Chat feature,
    127–129
Visualforce Page
  in Communities, 211
  components (dashboard), 274
  email templates, 61
visualizing analytics with dashboard
    snapshots, 27–28

W

Warning! icon, 3
waterfall approach, 344–345
websites. *See also* Force.com
  AppExchange, 155, 261, 326
  Cheat Sheet, 3
  Dummies.com, 3
Web-to-Case feature
  enabling, 116–117
  limitations of, 115
  preparing to enable, 116
  setting up, 114–117
welcoming members to Communities,
    240–241
workflow actions, 318
workflow limitations, 321
workflow rules, 202, 317–321
working offline, 46

About the Authors

Jon Paz: A Salesforce consultant, Jon has worked with enterprise clients to deliver world-class solutions to perplexing business challenges. Previously, he worked as an editor for a major international organization. After working with various clients and industries to implement Service Cloud, Jon has witnessed the transformative value of the product. He is an avid globetrotter, can talk to you about your business in five different languages, and is a staunch advocate for the legalization of unpasteurized cheeses!

TJ Kelley: TJ is a consultant at Bluewolf, a Global Strategic consulting partner of Salesforce. He is a certified Service Cloud consultant and has worked with Fortune 500 clients to analyze and solve their individual business challenges, leveraging the Force.com platform. Prior to diving into the Salesforce ecosystem, TJ earned a degree in both economics and Spanish, completing his studies at Amherst College and the University of Granada. A staunch Salesforce advocate, TJ lives in the San Francisco Bay Area and enjoys traveling near and far to explore the outdoors and experience new cultures. He also hopes that the Force may always be with you.

Dedication

To my family, my friends, and those who blur the negligible line between the two. Thank you for putting up with me all the way to the finish line.

—Jon Paz

To Alie, Tom, Kathy, and all my wonderful family and friends. Thank you for always supporting me and encouraging me along the journey. Your love has made all the difference in this glorious world.

—TJ Kelley

Authors' Acknowledgments

Our most sincere and heartfelt thanks go out to all those who supported and contributed to this endeavor. There are countless friends, family, and coworkers whose tireless work and vast knowledge helped make this not-so-insignificant undertaking a reality. We'd also like to send gratitude to our project team at Wiley and the talented employees at Salesforce.com who fostered an environment of collaboration, flexibility, and education from beginning to end.

We would like to express our profound gratitude to Liz Kao who has been a friend, a colleague, a mentor, and a believer in both of us. Thank you for your dedication to the cause and your unfailing sense of humor at all twists and turns.

A special thanks goes out also to Amy Fandrei and Elizabeth Kuball. Thank you for guiding us through the process, and for your tireless support and flexibility.

A final thanks goes out to past and present pack members and friends at Bluewolf, a truly special collection of individuals without whom we would never have been able to realize this venture.

Publisher's Acknowledgments

Acquisitions Editor: Amy Fandrei

Project Editor: Elizabeth Kuball

Copy Editor: Elizabeth Kuball

Technical Editor: Liz Kao

Editorial Assistant: Claire Johnson

Sr. Editorial Assistant: Cherie Case

Project Coordinator: Melissa Cossell

Cover Image: © iStock.com/triloks

Apple & Mac

iPad For Dummies,
6th Edition
978-1-118-72306-7

iPhone For Dummies,
7th Edition
978-1-118-69083-3

Macs All-in-One
For Dummies, 4th Edition
978-1-118-82210-4

OS X Mavericks
For Dummies
978-1-118-69188-5

Blogging & Social Media

Facebook For Dummies,
5th Edition
978-1-118-63312-0

Social Media Engagement
For Dummies
978-1-118-53019-1

WordPress For Dummies,
6th Edition
978-1-118-79161-5

Business

Stock Investing
For Dummies, 4th Edition
978-1-118-37678-2

Investing For Dummies,
6th Edition
978-0-470-90545-6

Personal Finance
For Dummies, 7th Edition
978-1-118-11785-9

QuickBooks 2014
For Dummies
978-1-118-72005-9

Small Business Marketing
Kit For Dummies,
3rd Edition
978-1-118-31183-7

Careers

Job Interviews
For Dummies, 4th Edition
978-1-118-11290-8

Job Searching with Social
Media For Dummies,
2nd Edition
978-1-118-67856-5

Personal Branding
For Dummies
978-1-118-11792-7

Resumes For Dummies,
6th Edition
978-0-470-87361-8

Starting an Etsy Business
For Dummies, 2nd Edition
978-1-118-59024-9

Diet & Nutrition

Belly Fat Diet For Dummies
978-1-118-34585-6

Mediterranean Diet
For Dummies
978-1-118-71525-3

Nutrition For Dummies,
5th Edition
978-0-470-93231-5

Digital Photography

Digital SLR Photography
All-in-One For Dummies,
2nd Edition
978-1-118-59082-9

Digital SLR Video &
Filmmaking For Dummies
978-1-118-36598-4

Photoshop Elements 12
For Dummies
978-1-118-72714-0

Gardening

Herb Gardening
For Dummies, 2nd Edition
978-0-470-61778-6

Gardening with Free-Range
Chickens For Dummies
978-1-118-54754-0

Health

Boosting Your Immunity
For Dummies
978-1-118-40200-9

Diabetes For Dummies,
4th Edition
978-1-118-29447-5

Living Paleo For Dummies
978-1-118-29405-5

Big Data

Big Data For Dummies
978-1-118-50422-2

Data Visualization
For Dummies
978-1-118-50289-1

Hadoop For Dummies
978-1-118-60755-8

Language &
Foreign Language

500 Spanish Verbs
For Dummies
978-1-118-02382-2

English Grammar
For Dummies, 2nd Edition
978-0-470-54664-2

French All-in-One
For Dummies
978-1-118-22815-9

German Essentials
For Dummies
978-1-118-18422-6

Italian For Dummies,
2nd Edition
978-1-118-00465-4

 **Available in print and e-book formats.**

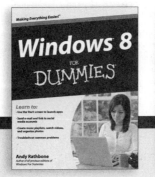

Available wherever books are sold. For more information or to order direct visit www.dummies.com

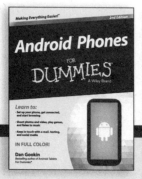

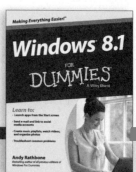

Take Dummies with you everywhere you go!

Whether you are excited about e-books, want more from the web, must have your mobile apps, or are swept up in social media, Dummies makes everything easier.

For Dummies is the global leader in the reference category and one of the most trusted and highly regarded brands in the world. No longer just focused on books, customers now have access to the For Dummies content they need in the format they want. Let us help you develop a solution that will fit your brand and help you connect with your customers.

Advertising & Sponsorships

Connect with an engaged audience on a powerful multimedia site, and position your message alongside expert how-to content.

Targeted ads • Video • Email marketing • Microsites • Sweepstakes sponsorship

Custom Publishing

Reach a global audience in any language by creating a solution that will differentiate you from competitors, amplify your message, and encourage customers to make a buying decision.

Apps • Books • eBooks • Video • Audio • Webinars

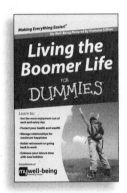   

Brand Licensing & Content

Leverage the strength of the world's most popular reference brand to reach new audiences and channels of distribution.

For more information, visit www.Dummies.com/biz

A Wiley Brand